OCEAN BOULEVARD

An epic and exhilarating voyage all the way…
from a boy to a man.

DAVID BABOULENE

This edition published in 2007 by
DreamEngine Media Ltd.
Email: publishing@dreamengine.co.uk
www.dreamengine.co.uk

In collaboration with:
Summersdale Publishers Ltd
46 West Street, Chichester
West Sussex, PO19 1RP
www.summersdale.com

Previously published in 2002 by Summersdale
as 'The Blue Road' by Windy Baboulene.

Unspeakably good cover illustration by Steve Byass:
email: sbyass@dreams2realityart.com

Printed and bound in Great Britain.

ISBN 978-1-84024-590-5

"Once a man comes to like a sea life,
He is no longer fit to live on dry land."

Dr. Samuel Johnson (1708–1784)

To my gorgeous mum, without whom...

Author's Mitigation

Some things in life are flexible and friendly. They realise that a brittle nature does nothing for their popularity, and so adopt an admirable willingness to change. Thus our lives are enriched as we coax these considerate allies into wonderful new forms without disturbing their fundamental chemistry.

Take, for example, The Truth.

Estate agents and solicitors build highly successful careers on the malleable nature of The Truth, and I suppose all of us must admit that at some time or another, in the collar-tugging sweat of an uncomfortable predicament, we have found The Truth to be so wholly unsatisfactory in one form that we have set about it with vigour and come up with a far more pleasing Truth; one which has proven a great deal more palatable to the authorities than the original.

So, in this context, let me answer the most common question asked of me regarding this weighty tome:

'Did the tales in this book really happen? Is this book The Truth?'

And the answer is a resounding, 'Yes!'

This book represents a genuine journey, real people, places and events. I admit I have polished a little here, and pummelled a touch there, and drawn an attractive veil over unseemly detail where decorum requires. And just in case you are a libel lawyer (or are maybe thinking of calling one) it might also be worth noting that the events and characters in this book have been drawn from four years' worth of shipboard life. Additionally, within all stories depicting events involving ex-colleagues, I have changed the ranks of the individuals concerned as well as their names, so you can't get me that way either.

So liberties have been taken for the sakes of the author's marriage, vanity and bank balance, but let there be no doubt about it, this book is The Truth. As Jerome K. Jerome so (much more) succinctly put it:

'I have merely added colour, for which no extra charge is made.'

David Baboulene
Brighton, Sussex
2007

www.baboulene.com

DreamEngine.co.uk

DreamEngine Media

In association with:

Summersdale Publishers

Summersdale.com

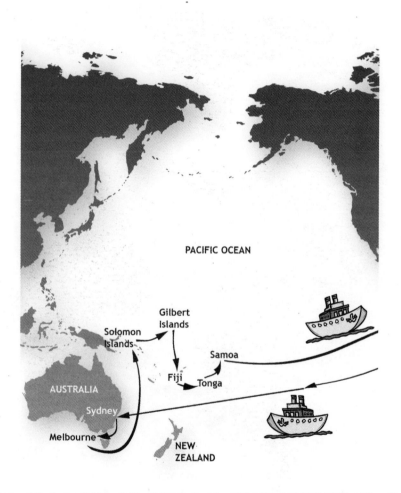

PACIFIC OCEAN

Gilbert
Islands

Solomon
Islands

Samoa

Fiji   Tonga

AUSTRALIA

Sydney

Melbourne

NEW
ZEALAND

Contents

Global Wanderer – Personnel and Rank Chart

Captain Benchmerson, aka 'The Old Man'

Navigators
Chief Officer (The Mate/First Mate) 'Harry Tate'
Second Officer (Second Mate) 'Cranners'
Third Officer (Third Mate) 'The Famous Dick Wrigley'

Radio Officer 'Sparky'

Navigating Cadets (Apprentices)
Blom
Giewy
NotNorman
Windy (That's me)

Engineers
Chief Engineer (The Chief) 'Chiefy'
Second Engineer (The Second) 'Jinx'
Third Engineer (The Third) 'Skippy'
Fourth Engineer (The Fourth) 'Benny the Dog'
Fifth Engineer (Fiver) 'SmallParcel'
Sixth Engineer (Sixth) 'Crate'

Engineering Cadet 'Cookie Short'

Electrician 'MegaWatt'
Second Electrician 'KiloWatt'

Chapter 1

MOTHERSHIP

A battle for supremacy. School loses out. Windy goes toe-to-toe with the Global Wanderer. Who gets the top bunk? The chief officer seems upset. Work begins. The coconuts make too much of themselves.

I WAS SWEET sixteen and my examinations were approaching like mortar-boarded vultures over the horizon. The received wisdom amongst the academic alumni up and down the country was that I was going to fail everything, and, to cap it all, Miss Fitch was clambering along behind the tennis courts, about to find us in our hiding place in the bushes. Things did not look good.

Actually, Miss Fitch looked good. Miss Fitch was a young teacher. She wore short skirts and her hair dropped over one eye when she turned from the blackboard just like the girl in the Silvikrin advert. I would have done anything to please her, and I desperately hoped she might be harbouring a deep admiration for my revolutionary spirit; a passion that was agony for her to hold inside, but which would now reveal itself at this critical junction in my life. There were two ways she could go: she could exclaim her love for me in an emotional outpouring, we could run away together and she could take my political coup in a new and full-breasted direction; or she could act like a teacher and hand us over to the authorities. In my dreams it had somehow seemed plausible that the former might just be possible. Indeed, in my dreams, it had worked every time. Now, in the cold light of a late winter's day, I got a sinking feeling that it might not be as likely as I had led myself to believe.

However, as she arrived at our hidey-hole it became evident that we would not find out her views immediately, because she was wheezing hard, having chased us a long way. I felt this was a Good Thing, as our punishment would be at least partially hampered by her exhaustion. She parted the bushes and lit up the dark of our camp with her fiery eyes. I tried to look cool for my fellow political activists, a difficult trick when you are, after all, cowering in the bushes behind the school tennis courts.

'You boys – huerr, huerr – you huerr, are all – huerr, all – huerr, all – huerr!'

She gave it up, withdrew her face from our camp and flopped against the wire fence of the tennis courts to indulge in the asthmatic rattles of an unfit person. Her whole body pumped and pulsated like a stranded heart. Beyond her, across the fields and over at the main school, two fire engines arrived. The firemen leaped out and set about rescuing the chemistry lab that we student activists had liberated as a first move towards overthrowing the government.

We had been watching a black-and-white programme about student activists on television – in Paris, I think it was. Not only were they very cool – the clothes, the posing, the attitude – they were also thoroughly applauded the world over, didn't appear to have to attend lessons, and were allowed out very late indeed. So why wasn't it working for us?

A couple of policemen were jogging our way. I gulped and looked at my fellow gang members. Paton, Carter, Wilson, Anderson, Curtis (R), Curtis (P), Cauty, Craggs and Tuckerman. Nine pairs of scared, round eyes, like baby owls in a nest. I felt reassured by the presence of Tuckerman. He took the edge off my fear. I looked around and saw others feeling calmed by the lad in the same way. In an instant our collective conscience came to a solid and unspoken agreement in those bushes: We would all blame Tuckerman.

The policemen were nearly upon us when a vision formed in the corner of my mind, and I heard the haunting tones of my Uncle Joe, reminding me of the philosophy he took into many interviews with policemen (and into each of his five marriages): 'No Problem is so Big That it Cannot be Run Away From,' he whispered.

I knew what I had to do. As my Freedom Party was ushered out of the bushes I stayed at the back. I dug myself into the darkest corner of those bushes, covered myself in leaves and simply did not emerge. The other lads were marched off and – miracle of miracles – I was left alone.

I knew the authorities would not be long establishing my presence at the scene of the crime, or my absence from the captured gang, so it was at that very moment, there and then, as I dug my way under the perimeter fence and legged it across the gardens behind the school, that I followed in the footsteps of thousands of desperados before me... and ran away to sea.

I didn't stop running until I found a careers office, established the joining procedure, filled in some forms for a merchant shipping line, and begged the lady to make it all happen quickly. She found a company that was recruiting for an imminent intake, and asked me to sign here, here and here. I ticked the box marked 'Yes please – I would like to avoid sticky interviews with policemen' and sauntered off to find a game of football, full of the joys of that stuff that fills a man's thingy when he's slain the savage something-or-other.

And a mere fortnight later – a fortnight brim-full of teachers 'You've-done-what?'-ing, fathers bouncing off walls, and stricken mothers passing out clutching their bosoms – I had left school and was on a train to Tyneside for my induction course. It was as simple as that.

The induction course was something of an eye-opener, but they always over-egg that stuff about alcohol, ladies of the night, fighting in foreign ports, venereal disease, fires, narcotics, sharks and the rest of it, don't they? I couldn't admit it, of course, but it sounded to me like a good, long list of all the things that were missing in my life.

As the planet revolved slowly beneath the aircraft, and America manoeuvred itself into position below, I stared down at the tiny ships and miniature towns that moved with it. I was dumbfounded. Barely a month had passed since I was a mere caterpillar of a schoolboy, living a schoolboy life with schoolboy routines. Now I was a beautiful Officer Cadet Butterfly in Her Majesty's Merchant Navy, heading for New Orleans to join my first ship. My head swam. Planes? New Orleans? Ships? These were the trappings of an exciting, cosmopolitan lifestyle, not a schoolboy's lot. But it was real. A new life with a big, rusty boat in all the places I used to keep a mother.

So it was that on the 10th of August 1977, I could be found on a quayside in New Orleans, my bags dropped to the floor on either side, gorping up at the steep metal sides of the mighty vessel *Global Wanderer*. They were rusty and overworked. They certainly did not appear to be in tune with the company information I had read in open-mouthed wonder. The literature had spoken of a magnificent 12,000-ton starship, with pictures of her enhancing the famous landmarks of the world. Under the Golden Gate Bridge, in front of the Manhattan skyline, passing in front of the

Sydney Opera House, the ship schmoozing at a party with Brad Pitt and Julia Roberts. One of the pictures was an aerial shot of the *Global Wanderer* cutting a swathe through a turquoise sea close to a tropical island. Another depicted the scene on the bridge as masterful, square-jawed officers in smart white uniforms guided her around the world.

I loved the literature. It was romantic and global, adventurous and exciting. I wanted to be on that bridge and to look that important. I wanted to control a ship in turquoise waters. That would be me, setting my jaw manfully to the breeze and thinking profound thoughts about stars and navigation.

Now I had arrived, however, the real *Global Wanderer* – in close up and with no soft focus or spectacular backdrop – was somewhat different. The romance of the literature was reflected by the reality, in the same sense that romance is surely present in an ageing prostitute – if the paint job is good enough and the photographs taken from far enough away.

While some of my peers on newer ships were enjoying computers, electronics and a swimming pool on the boat-deck, the *Global Wanderer* featured Morse code as its primary means of communication, and a sextant as its hi-tech positioning equipment. Satellite navigation was spoken of in suspicious whispers as a mysterious form of black magic. This was raw Merchant Navy from a bygone era. A tramp steamer, somehow still running thirty years after its sell-by date. I felt cheated. Even the Mississippi failed to be turquoise, but there was no turning back now. Like a child facing his first hypodermic, I had no escape – just a grim notion that what was to follow might involve pain.

I struggled aboard my new home, anxious to meet some reassuring signs – a friendly face to greet me; a hand with all my luggage; perhaps an offer to phone home and tell my family I had arrived safely - but my expectations were punctured on the sharpness of reality. Any people with whom I coincided looked down their noses at me as if I was a poo on the carpet, and my cabin, when I eventually slumped through the door, gave off the still, haunted aura of a room in which there had recently been a dead body.

Suddenly I was alone. Very alone. It was the first time I had been without company for some time and I didn't like it. As I sat in the cabin I felt strange. I was thousands of miles from my life. The porthole. The bunk-bed. The desk. The wardrobe. They all seemed to belong to someone else.

'Is this all such a great idea?' I asked them. They knew, they'd seen it all before, but they were saying nothing.

I didn't have much time to contemplate my situation – or my solitude – because the significance of the bunk bed hit me at the same time as the door did – when my room-mate crashed in with his luggage. I had been led to believe that I would be sharing with one Norman Smith, so, when he arrived, I shook him politely by the hand.

'You must be Norman,' I smiled.

'And you must be Mistaken,' he said, smiling back with a certain edge. 'If you start calling me Norman, I shall set fire to you.'

'Ah. Fire, you say? Er... I guess that means you're not Norman?'

'Correct! And if you insist on calling me NotNorman, I will have to invent an equally excellent title for you. Judging by the smell in this room, I guess you must be Windy.'

In that short moment of misunderstanding our nicknames were set in stone for the rest of time. NotNorman became NotNorman. I became Windy.

NotNorman was an impressive presence for a first tripper. He was large and sported a full beard already. At seventeen, he was only a year older than me, but already had the deportment of a sea-captain. He came with a ready smile, a sharp eye for mischief and bags of misplaced confidence, a bit like a cross between Captain Birds-Eye and a Labrador puppy. He was from the Lake District, and had extensive sailing experience on small boats. As he seemed to have all the answers, I stuck to him. What he did not have, however, were the *right* answers, but it's surprising how far people can get in life with the wrong answers provided that they believe in them strongly enough.

'OK, Windy, which do you want,' he shouted (I don't know why he shouted), 'top or bottom bunk?' I was about to reply in the uppermost tense when he added, 'Because whichever you choose, you're having the other one.'

I eyed the man narrowly. Did he think I would fall for the old double bluff? Maybe it was a treble... quadruple? You know the thing, 'Now he's thinking that I'm thinking that he's thinking that...'

I was way ahead of him.

'Bottom,' I said, smiling knowingly.

'OK,' he said, shrugging his shoulders. 'But don't say I didn't offer.' And he clambered on to the top bunk.

'HA! You fell for it!' I yelled, assuming the bottom bunk with gritted teeth. I could see I was going to have to stay tough with young NotNorman if I wasn't going to lose the upper hand in our relationship.

We had been lying on our bunks for only a matter of seconds when the cabin door crashed open again. NotNorman and I sat bolt upright in our beds (but only I banged my head).

'RRRRight then, you SCUM!' screamed a nine-headed whirling dervish occupying the airspace. 'Let's getchooo basta... WHAT IN THE NAME OF SWEET JESUS ARE YOU DOING IN BED? You've not been on board three minutes and you're IN BED?' The red-faced blur roared a spine-curdling laugh and from somewhere a boiler suit flew into each of our faces. 'Get in to those boilies and out on deck NOW! And don't let me ever – EVER – catch you in bed at any time of the day or night EVER AGAIN or your lives will NOT be worth living. I PROMISE. UNDERSTAND?!'

We meekly expressed our understanding, but the door had slammed behind the hurricane long before our words reached open air.

We sat stunned for a moment as papers and dust floated down into the silence that followed the storm. We must have looked like a couple of Aborigines transplanted from the parched outback of central Australia, given a twenty-second icy blast at the North Pole, then put back where we came from. It all seemed so unreal. NotNorman was first to find words.

'Did that really just happen – or have I had too many wine gums?'

I was in the middle of confirming that I had shared his hideous visitation when the door flew open once again. We both let out involuntary screams and drew the bedcovers up to our chins, but this time it was someone else. Someone already dressed in a boiler suit and work boots. Someone we recognised. This was Blom, the senior cadet, and no, I don't know where his nickname came from. Mostly, it seemed, the rule was to call him something close to Blom, but not actually Blom, such as 'Officer Blom', 'Blomstein', 'The Blomster' or my personal favourite, 'Blim-Blom'. Apparently, the word Blom becomes extremely funny if you focus on it for long enough when drunk enough, which was why his name was given extraordinary focus and concentration for at least twenty minutes every night in the bar. I had chatted with him for a while on the flight over, so I knew that this was Blom's fourth trip, and that he was in charge of us cadets. He shook his head at our flushed features and his round Irish tones filled the room. 'Well, come on then, girls!' he laughed. 'If he has to come back for you, you may not survive the experience!'

'Who the hell WAS that?' I asked. 'He frightened the crap out of us!'

Blom's chubby cheeks wobbled. 'That,' he said, 'was the chief officer of this fine vessel. Also known as 'First Mate', also known affectionately – if men like him are ever known affectionately – as 'the Mate' or for the cockneys among you, 'Harry Tate'. Also known as 'Your Boss'.'

'Also known as Total Bastard,' added NotNorman, searching through his trunk for some working boots. 'I can see he's gonna be a barrel of laughs.'

'Harry Tate is one of the busiest blokes on board, so if you get in his way, you'll get trampled on,' Blom continued cheerfully. 'Rule one: do not upset him. Rule two: if you DO upset him, hide under the spare propeller on the poop deck. He is responsible for EVERYTHING: the loading, organisation and care of all cargo; ship stability; maintenance of the entire ship; the four-to-eight watch at both ends of the day; and anything else that is going spare or wrong. He has an Asian crew of around twenty-five work-shy individuals to hinder his progress, and of course, he is lucky enough to be in loco parentis for US! We are his punch-bags!'

Blom began to leave the cabin, but threw in one last gem as NotNorman and I remained rooted to the spot. 'And if you're not out on deck in under ten seconds, I think you'll be in for another fairly one-sided and motivational conversation delivered from close range at high volume, with generous helpings of saliva and a headache to follow. See you out there!'

Oh Miss Fitch, Miss Fitch. Whatever have I done?

Nine seconds later NotNorman and I appeared on deck. Nobody had said which deck, or where, but we were out there. OK, so we looked like Laurel and Hardy with our boots on the wrong feet and both legs down one leg-hole of our respective boiler suits, but we were there, ready to set about our first constructive undertaking, or, to use Blom's technical terminology, 'gutty job'.

We followed Blom out of the accommodation and on to the foredeck. He walked purposefully, instructing us on something or other as NotNorman and I leaped to avoid being clattered by pulleys and got shouted at by men working the cargo as we got in the way, banged our heads on cargo hooks and tripped over all the odd looking stuff that filled our new world. Everything we walked by instantly jumped into life and threw itself at us. Pipes, capstans, shackles, chains, cargo, machinery, hooks, tools, planks, derricks, bollardy things – it was gloriously chaotic. Hell knows what it was all for, but as a working environment, the place was lethal. Ropes and wires ran in all directions from the deck to high into the masts and rigging above our heads, and everything seemed to move. It was as if a family of giant spiders had been given plenty of drugs, then set free to express themselves on deck.

As we made our way up the foredeck, various crew members stopped what they were doing to look at us. The ship was crewed by around fifty Asians working the accommodation, the engine room and the deck. Ours was a Bangladeshi crew. Blom said something confident in Hindi and they nodded back beaming white smiles, and said 'Sa'ab'. They wore ragged clothes and their boots had holes. Blom told us they stayed at sea for two years at a stretch. He then stopped to introduce us to one of them. The serang – the Asian equivalent of the bosun - was in charge of the deck crew and was a vastly experienced seaman. He had the beard and belly of a man in charge and would prove to be a very handy man to have onside through the trip. Other crewmen of status came to meet us; the chippy - or handyman – not only had great craft but also decent English, and the 'tindal' who was the man in charge of the stores. They all bowed their heads and smiled and called me 'Sa'ab'. I had already met Ahmed in the accommodation who, for a few quid a month, was to do my 'Dhobi' (laundry), wake me with tea, organise my meals and breaks when I was working and generally look after me. He was about seventy years old, and had called me 'Sir'. I felt embarrassed that these men – who knew more about the sea than I ever would – had to treat me with any sort of respect. Blom said I would get used to it. I wasn't so sure.

Blom introduced us to what is known as a 'deep-tank' – a special hold for carrying valuable liquids. The tank had just been emptied, having been full of coconut oil. The oil is transported and pipelined at a high temperature because it solidifies as it cools. Having discharged the oil, the heating had been turned off to allow us to enter and clean the tank. Of course, the tank was now relatively cool (although still very hot), so every inch of the inside of the tank was covered with a two-inch layer of sweaty coconut gunk, with the consistency of an alcoholic's stools and a smell that could drop a buffalo at 200 yards.

We lowered a light into the tank and, with our faces screwed up like a convention of bulldogs in a perfume factory, climbed in through the only access, a small manhole in the floor, sorry – 'deck'. Beneath this manhole was a ladder welded to the deep-tank side and we began our descent of twenty-five feet to the dank, eerie bottom. Apart from the stench – which made me gag – the clingy, humid atmosphere began rotting away at my bones before I'd got halfway down. By the time I had reached the bottom of the ladder I was already soaked through and highly uncomfortable. As a working environment it was impossible. Everything was slippery and every rusty nook and cranny was full of thick, unforgiving crap; the bilges, the ladder, the cross-girders, every footfall and handhold – everything was coated in an inch of this disgusting warm sludge. Blom had seen it all before.

'This,' he said, and the echo in the tank was dulled by the serrated atmosphere, 'is the worst job on earth. It is gross, unpleasant and quite staggeringly dangerous. It's hard enough just standing up, but when we are up there,' he pointed through the steamy fug to a girder running all around the tank some fifteen feet above us, 'trying to wield a hose when the ship is rolling and it's as slippery as a duck on a plate of snot, we'll be breaking every safety rule in the book and have every chance of a serious accident.' His cheerful face had become disturbingly sincere. 'Add to that our tiredness and boredom towards the end of a sixteen-hour day, and I think you can see the dangers. This job has to be finished before we refill the tanks in Houston in seven days' time.'

'Not too bad, is it?' I said, trying to strike the

optimistic chord. 'There are four of us. If we get stuck in...'

'You don't get a choice, my son,' continued Blom, pointedly giving Optimism the red card. 'You get stuck in all right. And as far as "not too bad" goes, if you think seven sixteen-hour days of this crap is "not too bad", then I dread to think what you'd consider to be a tough one. There are SIX of these tanks, Spanner-brain, and the inspectors in Houston will want to see their faces in five of 'em. One speck of dust and we'll have to clean the bastards all over again. By the end of this week, your "not too bad" will be "I wish I was dead." You're going to wish you'd never been born.'

He took the words right out of my mouth.

Initially the four of us worked together to get everything set up and to run through the drill. Then Blom set us into two groups of two, working eight-on eight-off, until five of the six tanks were completely clean behind the ears, under the arms, ties straight, and ready for Grandma. As the nightmare began to unfold, my mind went back to my thoughts on the plane a few hours earlier. I thought we'd have a couple of days (and nights) up the road in New Orleans, especially as it was the weekend. I thought we'd have some time to mooch around and generally get settled into shipboard life. I thought the cruise round the Caribbean to Houston would be spent discussing the finer points of navigation on the bridge under a clear blue sky and over a gently undulating sea.

I thought wrong.

And as if life wasn't grim enough, the cadet with whom I was paired for deep-tank cleaning purposes was a dead loss. I had felt that the team was shaping up nicely, and I have already introduced three-quarters of the squad. But I am sorry to say that there was a weak link. A runt in the litter. A bad egg in the nest. Because apart from NotNorman and me, with the experienced Blom as our leader, there was a fourth specimen making up the 'A' team.

The most striking thing that hit one upon first being

confronted by Giewy was that the English language provided the perfect word to describe him, and that word was 'gormless'. He was a walking definition of 'gormless' and a quite exceptional example of someone entirely without gorm – although, when I say he was a 'walking' definition, I must add that it was nothing short of a credit to his creator that a vehicle so distorted could perambulate in any distinct fashion at all; because the second thing that struck one was that he was a physical impossibility, confounding every rule of nature, balance and mechanical principle. Darwin would have chucked the towel in straight away if he had met Giewy, and I have to admit I had similar urges.

Within twenty minutes of our starting work together it became clear that he had spent his life being bitten by dogs, losing money, walking into lamp-posts and failing miserably to impress the opposite sex. Giewy was humanity's toe stubbed endlessly on the furniture of life, and yet despite all this, he was somehow convinced (and it was this that drove people to despair) that he was God's gift to shipping, mirrors, humanity, womankind and Great Britain.

The third thing to strike one was that, for a chap of only seventeen years, he had achieved an extraordinary degree of physical degradation. He was basically skinny, but sported a paunch that would impress the purists amongst construction workers. Above the paunch was a sunken, bony chest, and atop the alleged chest was... nothing. He had no shoulders, and you had to look elsewhere for his head. His neck emerged horizontally from the space between the places his shoulders weren't and curved immediately downwards. It then took a U-bend back up before you got to the head. The tallest point on his superstructure was, therefore, his hunched lack of shoulders, giving him the overall appearance of life's dopiest vulture. This impression was further enhanced by his big hooked nose, goofy teeth, and his vocabulary, which consisted exclusively of a single call, the depressed expletive

'Giew!' that indicated the delivery of the latest in a lifetime of disappointments and rejection. And this was to be my working partner. Perfect. Just perfect.

Despite the fact that we worked eight hours on and eight off for an eternity or two, the deep-tanks stubbornly refused to get any cleaner. We hosed the bulkheads until we ached, we scrubbed at rusty metal until our fingers bled, we hauled bucket after bucket of sludge up through the manhole, and we did headstands into the bilges to clear the pumps. It was like working in a labour camp. Pretty soon my brain lost track of right and wrong, my eyes began to deceive me, and all co-ordination and strength disappeared. The days and nights melded into one coconut hallucination, and all eight hours off were taken up with sleep, sometimes without even bothering to get out of my boilie and into the shower. Personal hygiene was simply too much effort when I emerged from the deep-tank – manky, upset and too exhausted even to eat – so a clear stretch of boat-deck sufficed for those brief moments when we were not up to our necks in recalcitrant coconut muck.

I cannot possibly put into words just how distressed I was getting with the job. Apart from anything else there was the coconut. My entire life and everything in it was impregnated, flavoured, coloured and possessed by coconut. I was coated in coconut. My hair was matted in coconut. There was coconut mosh between my toes and under my arms. I became convinced that while we were out working someone was nipping in and carefully soaking our cabin carpet, our bedding and our clothes in coconut. Meals (taken, if at all, on the run in the duty engineers' mess) consisted of potato-shaped coconut, with vegetable-shaped coconut, and meat-shaped coconut, all cooked in coconut oil and covered in thick brown coconut gravy. Pudding was always a chunk of coconut (with optional coconut custard) washed down with a delicious cup of hot coconut tea. One day there was actually an item on the menu which was 'delicately augmented with desiccated coconut'. It was several weeks before the chief cook could safely show his face in public again.

As the ship steamed round towards Houston, the interminable drudgery of working until I dropped, sleeping until woken, then working again, continued unabated for a full week. My life consisted of nothing else.

We finished the last deep-tank two hours before our arrival in Houston. I was exhausted. No, no, don't just skip over that. Read it properly – I was EXHAUSTED. Let's have no doubt about it, we're talking shagged out here. I hadn't so much as seen the bridge yet, or even the officers' mess where we were supposed to eat with civility in our uniform whites. I hadn't unpacked my uniform whites yet. I had hardly seen the sun or moon. Just coconuts in the sky.

Despite my exhaustion, I was so very pleased that we had finished that I dragged my aching limbs, screaming and kicking, from the sleep they so desperately craved, into the shower and gave them as good a wash as my drained muscles could muster.

The shower did nothing to alleviate the presence of coconut. It was impossible to gauge where the layers of coconut ended and my skin began, but I did feel better for it nonetheless. It was eight o'clock in the morning, and having worked all night and most of the day before without rest, I was looking forward to the deepest, most deserved sleep any man ever had. My eyes took in the humble bunk. I felt as if I had just been given a general anaesthetic as an uncontrollable desire to sleep washed over me. The bed opened up its loving arms and gathered me in like a long-lost son. I felt the pillow close around my head. My eyes began to quiver shut and – for the first time in a week – a smile drew across my coconut lips and the mists of sleep drew irresistibly into the coconut skies of my mind.

WHUNG! The door flew open. I tried to sit bolt upright (as was becoming the accepted norm on these occasions) but I was face downwards and too tired to spin. Somewhere, my brain was telling me to be startled and alarmed – frightened, even; but I just couldn't be arsed, and just lay there hoping that if I was going to die, whoever it was would just get it over with.

'FOR'D STAND-BY, WINDY! Fifteen minutes. Let's getchoo UP THEEERRRREE. . . OI! I THOUGHT I TOLD YOU NEVER TO GO TO BED! ARE YOU DELIBERATELY DEFYING ME? You cheeky bastard! I'll see you on the fo'c'sle in five minutes. LOOK LIVELEEEEY!'

I dragged my sleepy head up through one hundred fathoms of sleep. What? Get up? ME? I'd only been asleep three minutes! Only the echoes of his screamed commands and the recoil of the slammed door lingered. I could have cried. There must be some mistake. I had to talk to the man. To reason with him. Even at this level of exhaustion, I could not bring myself simply to turn over and go back to sleep – he'd rip my head off – so I decided to go up to the fo'c'sle and explain things to him. Surely the man had some compassion? Maybe he'd got the wrong cabin; he should be pleased with me for the work I'd done!

I blundered around trying to get myself together. I wished my mum were there to go and talk to him for me. She'd sort him out; but she was thousands of miles away, so this was down to me. My first job as an independent grown-up. I would go and have it out with the man.

I only had one pair of boots and they were turgid with cold coconut oil. The thought of squelching into them brought my stomach rising up into my throat. I'd given up with socks days before. They'd all rotted away. I looked through the congealed pile of boilies. They were all brown and gunked up with a heady mix of sweat and coconut oil. So, although I was still glowing from the luxurious shower of all those minutes ago, I had no choice but to ease myself unhappily into a cold, clingy, coconut boilie and a clammy pair of boots without socks. I tramped miserably up the foredeck trying not to come into contact with any of my clothing, but every step sent a cold, phlegmy shiver down my spine.

I took one look at the fire in the mate's eye and, in the absence of my mother, made another grown-up decision. I decided it would be impolite for me to turn down his invitation to participate, and besides, it's not every day one arrives in Houston. The mate just didn't want me to miss it. Might as well enjoy it now I'm here, eh? No point in having a go at him – the man's probably got enough on his plate without me giving him a mouthful. I would give him the benefit of the doubt this time. Maybe I'd have a quiet word with him later so he didn't wake me up unnecessarily again. I sighed and took up my position high on the fo'c'sle head for the forward stand-by.

Chapter 2

COME IN, HOUSTON

Windy meets America and injures a representative. Notes on Ugly Mobs and tobacco spitting. Life under the spare propeller.

A S THE SHIP enters or leaves a port there are three stand-by positions. Down aft with the second mate or on the fo'c'sle with the mate (known respectively as the 'after stand-by' and 'forward stand-by' – both physically demanding posts) or on the bridge with the third mate, the captain and the pilot, a more cerebral and cleaner post with the added benefit of being somewhere other than where the mate is. I had pulled the short straw. In fact, not only was it the short straw, it was the shortest of all short straws. With so little sleep and so sticky a boilie, closer examination revealed my straw to be so short that it was actually taller if it was laid down than stood upright.

OCEAN BOULEVARD

So I am sorry to report that I probably did not appreciate the true wonder of arriving in Houston as much as I otherwise might. By rights I should have been at least awe-inspired and possibly even agog. In fact, I felt wretched and would gladly have skipped the whole ghastly episode in preference to an hour's kip; but as the pace picked up, the general buzz of a stand-by coupled with a few educational thoughts roared in my direction from the mate helped me to find an interest. The pilots arrived on a launch and climbed a rope ladder slung over the side of the ship, ropes and winches were prepared, tugs were connected by huge wires, and the busy life surrounding the Houston Ship Canal bustled by. The walkie-talkies crackled, the sun shone and, in spite of everything, life began to look a little brighter. At least I was doing something more interesting than cleaning deep-tanks.

Soon our berth hove into view. The mate shouted across the two yards at me.

'RRRRIIIGGHHT, BABOULENE! Get that heaving line and, when you reckon you can make the distance, sling the heavy end on to the quay for those shore-wallahs to drag our mooring ropes ashore with. And DON'T FORGET TO KEEP HOLD OF THE OTHER END!'

I picked up the coil of cord-like line. On one end was a heavy ball to allow it to be thrown a goodish distance. I looked around at the crew eyeing me suspiciously. None of them said a word, but it was clear they didn't think I should be given this responsibility. I could see binoculars trained on me from the bridge. On the quay, the wharfies were looking up expectantly for the first line to come ashore. It was up to me to make the distance. This was my moment. Anybody could clean a deep-tank, but this was a chance to make a name for myself. It was like playing for England. Here we were at our first international venue and the pressure was on me to heave that line. I stood proud and high on the fo'c'sle and the eyes of the world bore down their sternest test. Would I respond to the pressure or

COME IN, HOUSTON

capitulate? The Hero or the Chump?

I watched and waited attentively as the ship edged closer and closer. My judgement was fine, my instinct honed… my moment arrived. I took a deep breath, wound myself up for the throw, let out an Olympic roar that made even the mate jump, and gave it everything I had. I put my heart and soul into that heave, and as I recovered and looked out at the line, the world went into slow motion. The balled end was off like a rocket, and the entire ship held its breath as the line ate up the miles, but would it make the quayside? I believed very strongly that it would. The trajectory was perfect, the delivery fine. I had responded to the pressure and pulled out a beauty. I relaxed and prepared to soak up the glory. The thought even crossed my mind that I might receive a round of applause from the crew, the bridge and the wharfies for making their jobs that much easier, and with such style to boot.

Suddenly there was a whipping rip in my right hand, and before I could say 'Yeee-ouch!' my glory was disappearing over the side along with the non-balled end of the heaving line.

The whole rope was now airborne.

I considered this new turn of events and a couple of indisputable facts raised their ugly heads. Not only had I failed to keep hold of the other end as bidden, but it was also becoming evident that I had been a little too vigorous with my throw. Because as the near end of the line left the fo'c'sle head and set off in hot pursuit of the balled end, the wharfies had their backs to us in order to watch the balled end heading off towards Canada. It was prevented in this aim only by the considerable presence of the shoreside bosun. He was oblivious to the approach of incoming enemy fire and was passing from left to right way over by the dockside buildings. He cut a curious figure (as do many Texans) in that, rather like my short straw, he would be taller lying down than he was standing up, this by virtue of the enormity of his stomach. I am able to make this statement with conviction because, after the leaden ball

31

caught him with a sickening thud just under the right ear, he obligingly lay down, thus providing the empirical evidence required to support the theory.

Before lying down, however, he proved that he was not just a man with a stomach. He provided indications of hidden talents. Because as the balled end found its mark, he spat his chewing-tobacco a record-shattering 52 yards across the quay. I did not have time to patent the idea that a sharp and unexpected crack under the right ear is just the tonic a champion tobacco-spitter needs to break world records, because as he assumed the prostrate position with his mouth open and his tongue lolling to one side, his colleagues were turning their attention back to the ship to ascertain the identity of his assailant. Sticking together like true British Bulldogs – united by our proud history and great country – I knew I was safe amongst my compatriots and fellow crew members. As I ducked down to avoid being spotted, each of them to a man dropped what he was doing and pointed at me, crying, 'It was him! It was him!'

Hindered in their joint ambition to interview me by the lack of gangway, a queue of America's Most Ugly – all with large stomachs and mouths grinding angrily on tobacco – lined up along the quay and began hurling abuse. Now we Baboulenes are well prepared for these things, so I was quick with the right response. A newcomer to ugly mobs might get the idea into his head that they are content merely to line up and present their case from a respectful distance. He might stand his ground and listen with a critical ear for inconsistencies in their arguments. He would be wrong. It is my unerring experience that the verbal period of mob behaviour is merely a prelude to the main event. I would bet anybody that these stout chappies were merely filling in time with the fist waving and the choral stuff until they could more positively express themselves with blunt instruments. I made a dash for it.

As the gangway went down and the ugly mob (including one member with an ear like a hammered tomato) came on board rolling up their sleeves and flexing their fingers, I could be found (or hopefully, could not be found) in a reflective mood under the spare propeller on the poop deck.

'Join the Merchant Navy,' I reflected. 'See the world, enjoy the glamour, savour the excitement, meet interesting people and get paid for it.'

Huh.

Chapter 3

BARBADOS

Lessons in how to impress girls with stories of drainage. Great sexual promise in the air for Welsh gardeners. Windy goes for a sex drive.

AS OUR SHIP materialised gracefully into the panorama of Bridgetown, Barbados, things were beginning to settle into some sort of cohesive pattern. I was getting a rough idea of how the ship ran, I had caught up on my sleep, and the Windy brain was back in control of the world. The names and routines of the lads around me were taking shape, all the deep-tanks we had cleaned were safely full of cargo, and I was beginning to feel a lot happier with life. The thought of our impending visits to Barbados and Jamaica helped considerably, and the words of the old sages who had been there before, as they held forth in the bar, had us all champing at the bit to get out there with the red paint.

'Make the most of these ports,' saged Cranners, the posh second officer from Surrey. 'Most of the places you'll visit on ships are not like this. Here you may taste the fine life and mix with the glitterati; excellent restaurants, haute cuisine and splendid company, in some of the world's most glorious settings.'

'What he means,' interrupted Benny the Dog, 'is that instead of getting rat-arsed and fighting in the port, here we can go up the road to dead flash joints, pretend to be rich and pick up some upper-class skirt. They don't expect no yobbos 'ere, so we can get away with murder. Any plans, Jinx?'

The second engineer nodded slowly, his eyes afire with sinful designs. He was known as 'Jinx' because of his uncanny ability to secure the most attractive female companionship out of thin air, and had a highly agreeable habit of coaxing them back to the ship to meet his friends. It was said of Jinx that, were he to find himself wandering aimlessly across the middle of the Kalahari Desert, he would be stopped by a coach-load of nymphomaniac models at a loose end, asking if he could find them anything to do. His reputation preceded him as an organiser of ladies and mischief, so I was not surprised to find he was extremely well spoken and sported a dashing moustache under sparkling blue eyes.

'Barbados,' he said in a slow drawl, like that of a dastardly blackguard outlining his vile plans to a helpless maiden tied to a railway track, 'is indeed ripe for the deflowering of its high society by uncouth sailors, but it is essential that we have a plan and stick to it, or the word will get round and we won't get a look in. With a little well-placed effort in the early stages, we could be set up for a splendid time. Everybody in? Leave now if you are not prepared to stand by your mates, because my scheme involves a little... 'dishonesty'. Any potential squealers should leave now, or expect to lose vital organs. All in? Gooooood. Here's the plan...'

And with much twirling of moustaches, despicable laughter and rubbing of hands, Jinx outlined his devilry to his cackling cronies.

The following evening was warm and still. The moon was full, and the air was full of fragrant promise. Barbados was everything I imagined a paradise might be, and I was beside myself with excitement at the prospects ahead. As it turned out, I had every right to be.

At 9:30p.m., two pairs of eyes carefully followed the mate as he left the ship and headed into Bridgetown with the captain and the chief engineer.

'Thank God for that,' said a relieved NotNorman. 'Let's go to work!'

We nipped round and knocked on half-a-dozen doors, and five minutes later a troop of extremely smart young gentlemen in bow ties and suits gathered on the afterdeck where Cranners, who was on cargo watch, had been unloading rather more than he was supposed to unload.

'This is the last one,' he announced, intimating the whirring cargo-wires, taut under the weight of their heavy load. As they raised slowly upwards and drew together to a hook, their payload swung slowly into view, emerging from the hold like a submarine from the deep. 'The other six are behind those containers.'

We peered out onto the quay and could see the dark hulks of the other six cars loitering like muggers in the shadows of the containers. 'The keys are in them. Get them back by four in the morning or we are in the deep and unpleasant. OK?'

I was beside myself with excitement. The ship was carrying a cargo of Mini-Mokes, and part of Jinx's plan was to unload one each and use them around the island at night. A Mini-Moke is like a small jeep with a Mini engine and frame. Ideal for Caribbean islands, sand-dunes and chicanery. They would be back in the hold before daybreak and nobody need be any the wiser. It was brilliant. We would majestically sweep up to one of the top night spots in seven brand new, identical cars, masquerading as 'International playboys racing each other round the world on our yachts'. Top off a scheme like that with our suits and impeccable good looks, and what girl in her right mind could resist us?

We climbed into our chariots and started them up. I had neglected to mention that I hadn't passed a test and could barely drive, but there was no way I was going to be a passenger with this sort of opportunity around, so while the others popped the clutch and snaked off expertly into the warm night air, I brought up the rear with a hop, a skip, a jump, a backfire, and the death knell of twisting gearbox echoing round the docks. I hoped I would get the hang of it before I had the girl of my dreams in the passenger seat. International playboys are usually racing drivers and pilots. It would be something of a passion-killer to have to attend hospital with whiplash injuries before any romance could get under way. After a while I was knocking along fairly well, and I had to admit that seven clean-cut young men flying through the night in their fashionably understated and identical machines cut an impressive swathe through the island's wide-eyed populace.

By the time we swung in through the grand gateway of 'Alexis', Barbados's premier restaurant and nightclub, we were certainly turning heads. Nobody was looking at the guy emerging from his Ferrari; they had seen all that before. The smoothie who had landed his helicopter on the lawn a couple of minutes before us might as well have been the bin-man for all the effect he was having now. Seven Mini-Mokes arriving in high speed formation through the trees of the long driveway, and sliding alongside one another with skids and roars, drew all the attention. We leapt out over the doors and all eyes were upon us as we horsed around, casually trying to give the impression that we did this sort of thing every night. We looked good. We were the rebels. The anti-fashion. The avant-garde. And, just as Jinx had predicted, everyone – including a large number of society's juiciest young ladies – was impressed.

The doormen opened the double doors with bows and without question. We flung our jackets at the attractive hostesses and breezed into the restaurant like a troop of James Bonds. As we clicked our fingers for menus and dispatched waitresses for drinks we could hear the buzz going round. Who were we? Where were we from? What were we doing here?

The place was packed to the rafters with girls, and I was immediately in love. I wasn't quite sure with whom, as yet, but my eyes met hers across a crowded room with about fifteen girls in as many seconds, and I wasn't fussy. Like every other teenager on earth, I had, of course, had loads of sex. Unfortunately, most of it was with myself. Tonight, however, it was going to be a piece of cake to change all that. Just look around! It was simply a matter of mingling until I found out which lady would be the lucky recipient of tonight's star prize. But my quest was halted by Jinx leaning across and speaking in a quiet but urgent undertone.

'This is the critical time,' he whispered. 'Keep calm now, and we're right in. Don't talk to anybody. If we go to them we've blown it. Wait and see who comes to us.'

I did not see the logic in this. In fact, I could see no redeeming features to such a policy whatsoever. I wanted to strike while the iron was hot. To make hay while the sun shone. To love and be loved. These girls would certainly not remain available all night and I could see that I was not alone in feeling that Jinx had lost his grip. He should be urged to go to his bed and leave us youngsters to do what we do best. I furtively scanned the eyes of those around me, and found the general loathing was unanimous. In fact, it was becoming difficult to remember exactly what it was that we found to commend the man in the first place. The thing to do now was to talk to these fine young ladies who were so encouragingly maintaining eye contact for just that moment too long. Make them laugh. Be erudite, witty and cultured. Be the lunatic, the lover and the poet – and don't mention sailors. I looked around hopefully for a new leader. A champion to lead the mutiny against Jinx, but I was stopped in my tracks by the approach of a tall brunette with Bambi eyes, scarily white teeth and an American accent. She could have stepped straight off the pages of Playboy.

'Hey, guys,' she purred in a deep southern accent, flicking her hair and posing as if she had reached the end of the catwalk. 'Mah frayands and ah are in a little deeyasagreeyament, and we was a-wondrin' if y'all could heyalp us owut heeya?' I considered a comment about heyalping them owut of their payants, but, thankfully, she continued before I could. 'Y'all British, riyut? Wale, Roxanne reckons y'all heeya for the surfin' champeenships and ah reckon y'all moosicians working up the stoodio on the Poyint. Y'all a rock bayand, riyut?'

I hadn't thought of either of these options. 'International playboys racing each other round the world in our yachts' seemed like the gravy to me, but these suggestions were match-winners. I knew the way to handle this one. We would be anything they would like us to be. Anything at all. Say, 'Shucks, you found us out,' and admit to being rock stars. Or surfers. Either would bring home the bacon. Jinx had been rescued by this turn-up, and we all turned expectantly to hear him redeem himself. He could simply tell them they were both right; that we were rock-star surfing champion Bee Gees. Anything! I willed him to answer along these lines, but I'm afraid he wasn't up to it. He had gone to pieces.

'Oh, we're nothing special,' he said, averting his eyes and fiddling bashfully with his drink. 'We're just here to clean out the drains. Barbados has awful sewerage problems you know.'

I was horrified. He had completely lost the plot now. I began looking for something to shove in his mouth to shut him up – the table included a vase of flowers which looked like it might fit him - but, amazingly, the girl did not spin on her heel and carry her spectacular body off to some men who knew what they were doing. Jinx was unbelievably lucky tonight. She patted him affectedly on the forearm and shrieked with laughter.

'Come oooon! You can not expeyact me to bullieve thayat! You are havin' me on! Say, do you mind if me and mah frayands join y'all? We're a-gittin' hayrassed bah those deyad-heyads over theyer and it would be mahty fine of you to lurk after us and git theyem offof our backs.'

She pouted pathetically.

'Of course you may,' said Jinx with chivalry. 'Make some space there, lads, the ladies are going to join us.' And with that, half-a-dozen stunning girls abandoned their Ferrari-driving, helicopter-piloting millionaires, and came curving deliciously over to sit with the sailors.

Half-an-hour later, I was deep in conversation with the most amazing-looking girl I had ever seen without staples in her face and stomach. I never once had to say that we were international playboys racing each other round the world on our yachts; firstly, because Roxanne was nineteen and talkative, and secondly, because I had come up with a brilliant idea. Inspired by Jinx's good fortune, I didn't crow about being a high-flyer; I blushed and insisted I was nothing special. And the more I talked myself down, the grander the belief in my pedigree became. She laughed aloud when I said we were escaped convicts and that our suits were really the property of the band, who could be found naked, bound and gagged in the ballroom downstairs. She wouldn't have it when I said we were private detectives, hired to find Trinidad. It got to the point where I could say, 'Listen. We're a bunch of sailors off a merchant ship and we nicked the cars out of the cargo,' and achieve nothing but the further cementation of the belief that we were making a film on the north beaches. My plan was working like a charm. If Jinx had been a bit slicker he could have claimed to have planned the whole thing from the very start.

Not even Cookie Short – the uncouth Mancunian engineering cadet – could spoil things. A quite superb hostess wafted up to him as a fantasy floats into a dream. She licked her lips, then spoke in husky tones, 'While you await your main course, sir, perhaps you would enjoy whetting your appetite with a fondue on the terrace?' Long fingers indicated the French windows that opened on to an impressive balcony overlooking the gardens.

'You betcha!' enthused Cookie, tongue hanging out. 'Is that like doggy fashion?'

Even the weight of such evidence against us was laughed off. Our lack of finesse, our accents, and the battle the poor hostess was having to disentangle herself from a puckering Cookie – all counted for nothing. The incongruities simply seemed to confirm to onlookers that we were in fact British royal family. We could do no wrong.

During the course of the evening, most of the lads found female companionship of a class and demeanour way above that which humble sailors would usually expect even to meet, let alone grope. I feel sure several of the finest ladies of the cosmopolitan jet set were severely traumatised that night. I would think that even the most cynical gold-digger, having left a club on the arm of a supposed millionaire and arriving at 3:00 a.m. on the biggest yacht she had ever seen, would possibly adjudge that her ship had come in, so to speak. So as I watched three of these sweet young things heading off with their playboys to go back to the 'yacht', I could not help feeling they would be psychologically scarred for life when they awoke in the morning on a merchant ship, having been unceremoniously rogered by three cheapskates called Cookie Short, Crate, and Benny the Dog. It doesn't bear thinking about.

Incidentally, I should mention that Cookie Short was not the man's full nickname. I don't want you running off with the idea that he had something irretrievably cool about him as the name might suggest. I know his nickname made him sound like a jazz musician, but it was actually his supreme readiness to make basic errors of judgement that led to his full title: 'Cookie Short of the Full Biscuit', or Cookie Short, for short, if you see what I mean.

Me? Ah. I was hoping we could move on to Jamaica rather than discuss my evening. I know I was doing pretty well at the last bulletin, and as I danced opposite the heavenly body of the hot-blooded Roxanne, futures in Windy Inc. looked set fair to rise. As the lights flashed and the pulsating music whipped us into a frenzy, she began to really let go. She had a freedom of self-expression, an energetic eroticism to her dancing and that air of carefree abandon that are such potent indications of excellent horizontal prospects. She was physically superb, lithe and fit. I was actually scared of her, and yet drawn irresistibly. I could not have walked away if my life had depended on it. I was spellbound. Her long hair flew hypnotically, her eyes were shut and her full lips were gently parted. I kept finding myself staring at her. It was as much as I could do to force myself to shut my mouth and keep dancing; but as the music beat on, and her tantalising motion bedazzled my feeble male brain, I found myself standing still with my eyes on stalks time and again. Just to kiss a vision like Roxanne, without even having to drug her first, would be the pinnacle of my life. Nothing else would ever live up to the importance of this night. And so far, if I could just control my dribbling, things were going precisely to plan.

Whenever you want a slow dance it never happens. They play upbeat, boogie-and-sweat numbers back-to-back all night. Ogling Roxanne as she writhed provocatively was all well and good but I could not excusably get my hands on her at this pace. As each song drew to its high-kicking finale, I implored the heavens to bequeath to me that soothing saxophone and gentle keyboard intro' that are the green light to leap on top of the girl you've been so carefully shepherding about the dancefloor throughout all the fast ones.

Eventually, my patience was rewarded. Some old slush started up, and I leapt. We moved into an intense clinch, entwined like climbing plants. I felt her fingers on the back of my neck. This was it. My time had come. Every inch of me tingled and shivered. I had to keep cool. Don't do anything stupid. Don't come on too strong. I decided to skip the fancy stuff and just cling on. Incredibly, fate was on my side, and as the dance built to its powerful middle eight, her upturned face appeared longingly in front of mine.

We kissed.

I have no idea how long we remained locked in divine fusion, because, although my lips stuck to their post, my brain left the building through the roof like a firework display. After an aeon or two, Roxanne was first to come up panting for air. She licked her lips and her eyes were ablaze.

'Shall we leave?' she panted hungrily. I tried for the self-assured, 'You wanna go? Sure.' All cool and off-hand, but only a meek whimper emerged into the air. Leave? Together? Just us? This could only mean one thing! This monumentally beautiful girl wanted to be alone with me! She wanted ME! My stomach hit the ceiling, then dropped through the floor. This was My Night. This was IT.

I was convinced she was finding my style and sensual expertise irresistible, and couldn't control herself a moment longer, but I guess, with hindsight, she was probably more keen to leave in order to stop me from humping her leg in public like some kind of demented spaniel. She led the way from the building, and I followed like a hydrogen balloon floating along behind her. If she hadn't been holding my hand I'm sure I would have become lost amongst the chandeliers.

On the way across the grounds to the Mini-Moke we stopped for another desperate grapple. I was insane with passion, and she was matching me all the way. If the owner of the car upon whose bonnet we were performing our acrobatics had not returned, it might have been all over there and then, but we had to move on. We tried again against a tree before we got to the car, but Roxanne was unhappy with all the people watching from the balcony.

'Not here,' she purred. 'I want this to be veeeery special. Let's drive out to the beach.'

So with a hop, a skip, a jump and a hey nonny nonny, and leaving a trail of gearbox cogs in our wake, we headed off into the night towards the beach.

OCEAN BOULEVARD

'This is Sam Lord's castle,' she said as she led me through the grounds of a magnificent castle and down a narrow path lined with palm trees. 'We can be alone down here.'

The path unfolded onto a moonlit tropical beach. The waves tumbled together like playful kittens all along the sandy white shoreline and the scintillating phosphorescence shimmered on their dancing crests as far as the eye could see. The palm trees leant out over the beach like dark old men looking for dropped money, the steel band played infectious, carnival rhythms and the happy sounds of the joyful revellers filled the night air as they danced on the beach and drank exotic cocktails around the open wooden bar. What? Joyful revellers? Steel band? I thought we were going to be alone?

'Oh no!' cried Roxanne as we took in the scene. 'There's a goddam party going on! Let's try further along the beach. There's a waterfall up there.'

I followed her doggedly. Anywhere. I didn't care where. Just anywhere, and the sooner the better. If ninety per cent of my mind was not being ruled by my genitals, I feel sure I would have marvelled at the beauty of the scene, but the only available ten per cent was concerning itself with the basic motor functions engaged in tracking Roxanne, so I was merely frustrated that the scene of my greatest triumph was so overcrowded. Didn't these people have homes to go to?

Further along the beach, we turned inland and walked up a track through the palm trees. The full moon lit our way as only a full moon can, and even my preoccupied grey cells could appreciate the exquisite setting of a tall, dignified waterfall, tumbling into a small lagoon. It was nothing short of breathtaking.

'C'mon!' Roxanne shouted, and ran towards the water, stripping off as she went. The picture of her naked form, reflected gently in the moonlight as she dived into the water, will remain with me until my dying day, but I had a more immediate problem. Girls are lucky. Their state of arousal is not immediately obvious to other swimmers. For men, things are different. Especially for shy young men who are too embarrassed to strip off. There was only one answer. I ran headlong for the lagoon and jumped in fully clothed. Her laughter was challenging and sexy, and I chased her energetically until I finally got hold of her. I wasn't going to let her get away again. This was it. We kissed under the cascading waterfall. She tore at my suit, and I felt her naked body press urgently against mine. I was at the gates of frantic heaven once more, and this time, nothing could stop us from...

'What did you say?' I asked her.

'I didn't say anything, I think it...'

'Last one in's a banana. Wheee!' About twenty of the revellers from the beach party were running towards us, stripping off as they ran.

'I do NOT believe this!' I said as my heart sank. 'This island is like Piccadilly Circus!' The romance faded like a burst balloon.

'Let's go back to my place,' said Roxanne, rushing to cover up. 'My folks will be asleep by now. We'll have the whole place to ourselves.'

On the way to her father's villa, Roxanne teased me the whole time. She wouldn't let me stop driving and get hold of her, but she kept flashing her thighs and touching me, and whispering suggestive things in my ear. She was fascinated that I had maintained a steadfast erection for nearly two hours now, and she was determined to enjoy my frustration. In between teases, she asked sensible questions and tried to put me off, then started on me again, using her sexual expertise to prevent things from wilting. One of the questions she put to me was what I really did for a living. Even with the limited brainpower of a man with an erection, I could see that there was no point in lying. The truth was best. I wanted to see her again, so I might as well be honest – I just came right out with it. I was still explaining as quickly as I could when she lifted her shirt and asked me if I liked her stomach. She took my hand and brushed it over her flat, soft belly. Then she suddenly bent across my midriff and kissed me on the thigh before pulling away once more as I reached for her. Every time I tried to join in, she would back off, insist that I concentrate on driving, and then ask another question. By the time we pulled into her driveway, I was beside myself.

Her father was some sort of businessman, and, judging from the size of his Barbados retreat, I should say he was pretty successful. She opened a side door and I followed her, tip-toeing into an enormous kitchen, then on through a dining room lined with a thousand books. We didn't make a sound. As she reached the door at the far end, she looked back at me with big, hungry eyes and I knew my greatest moment was once more beckoning. The moment when I would finally, at long last...

'Oh! Hello Daddy!'

... meet Roxanne's parents.

'Hey, baby!' came the cheery reply. 'Come on in! We're playing cards with the Robinsons here. Wanna try a hand?'

'Er, no thanks, Pops. This is Windy Baboulene. He's the – what did you just tell me you do for a living? – the British and Commonwealth Surfing Champion. He's here for the tournament at the weekend.'

I sidled sheepishly into the room. I was not looking my best, still damp and in a bedraggled suit with no shirt, I looked like Charlie Chaplin would if they dug him up now, but what could I do? Apologise for having been skinny-dipping with their daughter? The Robinsons looked mildly alarmed, but Roxanne's dad, after a lifetime of dealing with difficult businessmen, was equal to the challenge.

'Ha, ha, ha! Good nickname for a surfer, eh? Windy! And British Champion, eh? That's great! We're all keen surfers here – you could give us some tips! Say, I thought the British Champion was Grahame someone... Grahame Park? That's it! Grahame 'Tube-runner' Park. What's happened to him?'

My mind blanked out. How the hell did I know what

had happened to him? I'd never even heard of him.

'Oh. Ah. My ol' mate Grahame. Yes. Are you sure? Is he still the British Champion?' The company nodded. They had read it just yesterday. He was still the reigning British Champion. 'Because I am actually the, er... WELSH Champion. Roxanne had it a bit wrong there. Welsh Champion. That's it. Out there every day on the river Avon doing my thing!' With a grin and a wink I did a quick impression of how I imagined I spent my days out taming the three-inch swell of the river Avon. The assembly looked a little bemused, but once more Father showed his steel.

'Well now, that's great! Listen. If you're staying the night you could give us a few tips in the morning. We only get the ten-footers over this side of the island, but they're great for learning on. What do you say?'

I gulped. Only one idea came to mind, and it wasn't one of my best. 'What? Oh! Ha, ha! You thought I said Surfing Champion! Ha, ha! No, no, no! You misheard. I'm the Welsh Turfing Champion and one of Britain's premier landscape gardeners. I can turf two acres of fallow spinney in under four hours using nothing more than –' Roxanne came to my rescue.

'Oh, very funny Windy. He's so modest about his surfing. Anyway, sorry Pops, but we can't stop. We just dropped in to get some dry things and now we're off to a party. See ya!' And with that she swept me from the room. Within seconds we were back in the car, Roxanne in tears of laughter.

'Turfing Champion? Turfing Champion!'

'Shut UP, Roxanne.'

'Mmm-mm-mwhahaHAHAHAHAHAHAH-HAAAAA!'

'Where NOW?' I said, curtly. I was exasperated. Something had to give soon or I would do myself a mischief. Roxanne's sexy laughter filled the car.

'Mr Sausage never went down the whole way through!' she giggled. 'All that turfing stuff, and he stood to attention the whole damn time! Mrs Robinson couldn't take her eyes off your groin! She believed you're a surfer all right. She thinks you carry your surfboard down your pants! So how about we go back to your place, and go for a ride on your surfboard?'

'Umm, OK,' I said. 'But you might not like it – my place, that is – not my, er... surfboard. I'm staying on a ship in the harbour.' I crossed my fingers as the news sunk in.

'So you really are a bunch of sailors? HA! That's GREAT! HAHAHAHAHAHAAAAA!'

She was laughing fit to burst, but I didn't feel humiliated. What was important was that she didn't care that I was a sailor! She wasn't after the glamour and prestige of a prize-winning Welsh turfer – she wanted me for myself! Nothing could stop us now. If I could get her back to the ship, they would be dragging me off her exhausted body in three days' time so the ship could leave. I drove back out on to the open road with renewed belief. The rollercoaster was on the way up once more. Tonight seemed destined to be The Night, irrespective of what the world could throw at us.

She began to tease me again as we flew across the island towards the *Global Wanderer*, a ship now transformed in my mind from an atrocious old rustbucket to my sexual utopia. She whispered in my ear the details of what she was going to do to me once we were alone, then she took my hand and placed it under her short skirt. She invited my hand along her bronzed thigh and took a sharp intake of breath as my fingers touched her. She wasn't wearing underwear. She threw back her head and thrust herself hard against my searching fingers. I could not believe this. She refused to let me stop the car, and kept saying, 'Faster, FASTER!' So I drove as best I could, but I wanted to look at her far more than I wanted to look at the road. The only light was that from the moon, and she looked gloriously erotic. I took a couple of bends at ten miles-an-hour in fourth gear, but – despite the complaints from the engine – she didn't notice. As the car built back up to speed, she built up with it. Her pelvic thrusts became wilder and wilder and her moans became screams. The engine's roar grew louder and louder, she was nearly there. The speed of the night air in her hair grew faster. She was nearly there. She squeezed the life out of my hand with her thighs and cried with pleasure. Nearly there. *Nearly there.* She bucked and squealed and bucked again, her rhythm getting stronger and more intense and closer and closer. Her back arched and she lifted herself completely off the seat. She cried through clenched teeth, 'Yyyyyess! Yyyyyeesss! Nooooowaaahhhh!' and her eyes rolled back. She froze as if she had been shot, went into the most phenomenal muscular spasm, and had a volcanic orgasm there and then in the car.

So did I.

The car went into a ditch.

Chapter 4

THAT SINKING FEELING

The return of the deep-tanks. Windy is given a job to himself. Explosive reaction of his colleagues over breakfast. The old man submits his views.

FROM MY POST on the after stand-by I laughed at myself as the sun set on my vibrant paradise. I had adored Barbados, and to this day my mind carries a thousand snapshots of the happy, dancing nights and the rhapsodic tropical ambience - and another thousand of Roxanne's outrageous eroticism. I could see that leaving people and places that had grown on me was going to be one of the hardest things to get used to on my travels. I sighed a happy-sad sigh, and began the wait for the day that I returned to Barbados.

THAT SINKING FEELING

Straight from stand-by, I went to meet the other cadets on the boat-deck as agreed.

'Right lads,' said the Blomster, rubbing his hands, 'we've had our break. Two days to Jamaica and – you've guessed it – deep-tank six has to be done before we get there.' My knees went weak. I'd forgotten about the last deep-tank. 'We'll get a few hours in tonight, then steam in on it all day tomorrow. Windy, NotNorman, you get up the fo'c'sle and get the gear. Giewy, sort out some lights. I'll go and open the hatch.'

So off we went again. Deep-tanks. They didn't mention deep-tanks in the literature. I don't need to tell you how I felt. I just wished I'd known this was coming before we'd left port. I'd have jumped ship in Barbados and lived happily ever after. The choice was, on the one hand, Roxanne. On the other, a deep tank. Roxanne – Deep-Tank. Roxanne – Deep-Tank. It wasn't a tough call. And the reality more than matched my dread. The sixth tank turned out to be the worst of all, having had an extra week or two for the coconut sludge to become crusty and solid. We worked hard throughout the evening until nearly eleven, then dragged ourselves out of the mire, tried to stay awake in the showers, then flopped into bed. No sooner had my head hit the pillow than it was five in the morning (or to use the correct nautical terminology: 'oh-fuck hundred hours') and I was being shaken awake. Before I knew which way was up, I was back cleaning the tank. Time slowed to a snail's pace as we slogged away at the unyielding tank sides, then time raced by as we had breakfast, only to slow up almost to a halt once more as we worked the endless morning shift back at the sludge face.

The long day dragged on along these lines until we finished the actual cleaning – after some twelve hours of unremitting effort – at around seven that evening. We were all exhausted. We clawed our way out of the deep-tank manhole with what little was left of our fingers and collapsed on the tank lid. We had a five-minute smoko, and then Blom was back cracking the whip.

'Right then. One last push, boys. Home stretch now. Giewy, you clear up the gear. NotNorman, put away the lights. Windy, you put the tank bolts in and the manhole back on, and I'll organise for the tank to be pressure-tested. Go!'

'What?' I exclaimed. 'All those bolts and the manhole back on? I'll be here all night!'

'Character-building stuff, Windy. A job all to yourself – real responsibility for you. Do a good job of this, and I'll get Ahmed to put aside some dinner for you. Chin up! All part of growing up and being British. I'd love to help, but if I don't get showered up quick I'll miss dinner myself!'

And with that the three of them nipped off to do their one-minute jobs, laughing all the way. I was really peeved. Why couldn't they have helped? Four of us could have done the job in under an hour. By myself it would take three. It was totally unfair. I kicked the 'tween-deck bulkhead and hurt my foot. They would all be in the bar swilling away by eight, and I would be out here till ten finishing off their work for them. Crowd of dogs. I kicked one of the manhole bolts and would you believe it, the bloody thing went straight down the hole into the tank. I would have to go and get it back. And it was their fault.

'You BASTARDS!' I screamed, and kicked the bulkhead again, but nobody heard. I was alone in the tween-deck. Then I realised that the lights had been pulled up from inside the deep-tank. I'd have to set some back up again just to find that one bolt. I imagined Blom was standing there. I pointed my finger accusingly at him. 'Nuts to you, mate. And nuts to setting all the lights back up just for one bolt!' I roared sternly. 'It'll just have to stay there. Either YOU get it yourself,' I poked his chest firmly to punctuate my point, 'or your precious manhole cover will just have to make do with forty-nine bolts instead of fifty.'

I was brilliant. Masterful and succinct. I was firm and assertive and yet not unnecessarily aggressive. I can be pretty devastating when my opponent is out of earshot.

I settled down to the tedious, finger-scraping job of

bolting the tank lid and forty-nine fiftieths of the manhole cover back on, grizzling and grumbling the whole time. I eventually finished at 10:15 and tramped off to get showered. I could hear them all in the bar, but I was not interested. I just wanted to turn in and get the worst day of my life behind me.

The next morning was sunny, and I was surprised to find myself in a good humour. I suppose somewhere in the back of my mind it had registered that the last deep-tank was clean. There could be no more. Whatever the day ahead held for me, it would surely be gloriously clear of deep-tanks and coconut flavouring. I looked out of the porthole and watched the untethered Caribbean Sea flowing by. I felt cleansed and free. If leaving places was going to be hard to come to terms with, the freedom of the oceans in between them and the welcoming embrace of the next unknown new world was going to provide an equal and opposite excitement. Breakfast. There was my next worldly opportunity. One of my first chances to have breakfast in the officers' mess.

I walked off, proud and happy in my crisp white tropical uniform, but I quickly became aware that I was unable to walk in a straight line. It is quite normal to have problems walking against the pitch and roll of the ship. One moment your nose is on the deck and you are crawling up hill, the next you are involuntarily belting downhill at a run, hoping to God that the ship rolls back before you hit the rapidly advancing bulkhead at the other end. More often than not, as you walk along a corridor, you will be entertained by a person failing to make the turn into your corridor at the far end. Instead, they slide past from left to right in the Snoopy-skateboarding pose. They wanted to turn, but they couldn't. Instead, they disappeared completely out of shot but for their fingers desperately clinging on to the bulkhead. Then they appear sideways around the corner as if they are climbing over a wall.

But today was different. As I navigated the first

corridor, which should have had me staggering from side to side into the bulkheads, I found myself slowing down and beginning to fall over backwards. Then, as I headed across the ship along the second one, I found myself scraping along the left bulkhead. The ship was down by the head. Most definitely down by the head. Quite alarmingly down by the head. If breakfast had not been continuing unabated, I would have thought we were sinking.

'We're a little down by the head, wouldn't you say?' I asked the assembled throng on the navigators' table.

'SERIOUSLY down by the head,' said Blom. 'There's a search party out now, and the big guys will be out there as well after breakfast to find out why. Seems we might be taking on water somewhere.'

The 'big guys' Blom was indicating with his fork full of egg on toast consisted of a captain, a chief officer, a chief engineer and a second engineer, eating their food as if it was the last supper and discussing the problem of the ship's angle in the water in hushed tones.

'What will they do?' I asked.

'The problem is,' began the third mate, a cheerful London lad, known for some mysterious reason as 'The Famous Dick Wrigley', 'that to come down by the head by so much in such a short period of time means we must be taking on considerable amounts of seawater from somewhere. It's got to be pretty serious. They've already sent a deckside party out into each of the holds to look for signs that she's taking water on board, and they'll have an engine-room party check that all the pumps and valves are right. They've already altered course for the nearest port and put out a general call for any ships within four hours of us to head our way in case we're going down. This is really heavy, you know?'

'Good grief,' I said. 'If I'd known the ship was going to sink, I wouldn't have bothered cleaning that deep-tank yesterday. We could have had the day off to prepare for our funerals!'

My joke was the rambling of a nervous child. I

wanted to ask if there were sharks round here, but Blom asked me a question before I could embarrass myself.

'What time did you finish last night? You didn't come to the bar.'

'No, I didn't fancy it. It was gone ten o'clock thanks to you lot. Oh yes, by the way. One of the little bolts fell into the deep-tank, so I put the manhole back on without it.'

'Eh? Sorry? Say that again,' said Blom. All three tables fell silent. All the jaws had stopped chewing and heads were raised from their plates to look at me. Open mouths full of half-chewed food were on view everywhere. It was a dentist's nightmare. I didn't see the point, but I repeated myself.

'I just said, one of those silly little bolts on the deep-tank manhole cover fell into the blasted tank. I thought forty-nine of them could do the job of fifty, so I put it all back without one.'

All eight diners spat egg and bacon across the table as if they'd received a simultaneous and full-blooded whack in the small of the back. Disgusting way to behave, I thought. Uncivilised. They should save that sort of thing for late-night bars. But that was not the extent of it. There was more. All eight leapt from their seats and formed a disorderly scrum around me. It was like being on the Underground in the rush hour, the difference being that in my experience of the Underground, the nearest man does not lift me by the lapels, call me a stupid, STUPID bastard, pass me on to the next guy and run from the room, as was the case here. The next officer did the same thing, as did the next, and so on through the group, until I reached Blom at the end.

'You stupid, STUPID bastard,' he confirmed. 'Go to the poop deck and hide under the spare propeller. Do NOT come out under any circumstances. These guys will tear you limb from limb once they've got the ship back on an even keel. I'll bring you supplies. Do not come out for anything. Your life depends upon you remaining undiscovered.'

He dropped me on the floor and rushed out after his companions.

Now, we Baboulenes are quick on the uptake. I had a hazy idea that I might in some way be to blame for the ship hobbling along at an angle of 45 degrees, and although I wasn't sure quite how, it seemed to be the news of the deep-tank bolt that had given them the clue they needed.

'Can I come out yet?' I asked Blom as he arrived with my tea and biccies at eleven.

'No, no, no. Not if you want to live. Ages yet. They're still pumping out the 'tween-deck and hoping to rescue some of the cargo. It will take some forgetting, this one.'

'So let's go through it again. Once we'd finished last night, you went off to get them to pressure-test the tank while I put the manhole back on, right? That means they start a pump with a 'torque knockoff'. The pump filled the tank with water, and would have automatically turned itself off if the tank was sealed, right?'

'Right,' said Blom. 'But some stupid, STUPID bastard left a bolt-hole, so the pressure never got up to the point that would turn the pump off, so water fountained out of the tank up into the 'tween-deck ALL NIGHT – filling half the ship with water, and nearly drowning us all. The engineers never cottoned on to it, because never in the history of shipping has ANYONE been stupid enough to leave a hole in a tank which is being pressure-tested. As stupid bastards go, you stand alone. You are head and shoulders above all the other stupid bastards in the world. You are the king of the stupid bastards, and no, you cannot come out yet. Don't move a muscle until we get to Jamaica where you can run off up the road.'

I sighed heavily. What a life.

The bolt-hole incident went to the top; to the captain, or

THAT SINKING FEELING

'The Old Man', as he is most commonly known. I had hardly even seen him as yet, and had only communicated with him in terms of the odd shrieked, 'Yes, SIR!' in urgent response to one of his authoritatively bowled instructions. I was fetched from beneath the spare propeller by virtue of his summons to attend a personal audience. I had already been in trouble over one or two things I have neglected to tell you about – most notably, a teensy oil spill in the Houston Ship Canal which might, I guess, have been my fault. Now this. It felt rather like, for example, being called by the headmaster to account for the matches found in your jacket pocket ten minutes after the Chemistry lab goes up.

Captain Benchmerson sat me in the corner of his day room to sweat it out while he calmly completed a few items of paperwork. His glasses reflected the light so I couldn't see his eyes. They looked like two mini-TV screens. Eventually, he took a deep breath and stood up. I was already aware that he came in the family-size model, but as he emerged from his seat, he looked as if he was being inflated beyond capacity. The rate he was going, I didn't think he would ever stop emerging from his seat. However, at around eight feet he tailed off in the vertical plane, continuing to around four feet in the horizontal. He didn't look overweight though – just huge.

Until now, every time I had seen him he'd looked sort of angry, but now I faced him close up his demeanour was more pained. Put-upon. He put me in mind of a bloodhound who has just heard the words 'vet' and 'neuter' in the same sentence. He put his fingertips together and began to pace. When he eventually spoke, it was with the round, authoritative tones of a Victorian headmaster.

'I have heard your name once or twice already,' he began as if reading a prepared statement, 'and it seems you have set about involving yourself in an extraordinary range of monkey business in an alarmingly short space of time. Following today's episode, it now seems we have lost a goodly amount of valuable cargo in a flooded 'tween-deck, and it is only through the merciful grace of God that we have a ship left under our feet at all. You know, if you continue along these lines, you could quite possibly bankrupt the entire shipping line single-handedly. That would admittedly be an impressive effort, but ask yourself, what would be the benefit? Is our downfall your intention, Mr Baboulene? It certainly seems to be. You seem quite single-minded of purpose.

'Maybe you are a fiendish doppelganger from one of our rivals sent to spread as much discord as you possibly can. Are you a fiendish doppelganger? Whether you are or not, I'm sure you are capable of realising that, from my viewpoint, it is hard to come to any other conclusion. When I take my inventory of cadets I find myself noting "Cadets: Engineering – one; Cadets: Navigating – two; Doppelgangers: Fiendish – One." I can't help myself. There's no other rational explanation. Unless of course, you are simply a fruit-cake.'

He paced thoughtfully around his desk as he considered the possibility that I was a fruit-cake, his voluminous white shorts following shortly behind him like flags in his wake. He decided to confront me directly with it. He turned and looked me directly in the eye. 'Are you a fruit-cake? Because fruit-cake or fiendish doppelganger, it is my job to encourage you to see the error of your ways. To see the light. I would like to persuade you that there is a better life, and that causing the collapse of shipping lines is not a route to happiness – particularly not mine. Oh sure, in the short term it may appear to have glamour, but one really needs to take the broader view in these matters, don't you think?

'So what would you do in my position? What would you do to correct wayward fruit-cakes and doppelgangers?'

He stopped and leaned on his desk, looking at me through TV-screen lenses. Then his trousers caught up and his entire persona was attentive behind the desk. I got a foggy idea that maybe, for the first time, he actually wanted me to answer one of the questions he was letting off towards the skies. I had learned through a fairly arduous school career that the best policy under pressure from authority was to sit tight, say nothing and hope that they'll give up in the end. I sat tight and said nothing, and he set off westward once more from behind his desk, presumably for another chin-rubbing circuit. A second or two later, his shorts set off after him, and soon the entire captain was on the move once more.

Eventually, he came to his decision. 'I have a few jobs that need doing, so you shall do them for me in your spare time. That way I can train you to do one job without creating fourteen others and give you less time to yourself in which to destroy the shipping line. This is a light punishment. If you do indeed transpire to be a species of charlatan, sterner measures will befall you. You are on thin ice, Mr Baboulene, and I want you to take particular care of your deportment during the rest of the trip. Each time you find yourself upon this carpet, your fate will become less and less pleasant until you will eventually find life insupportable. I hope I have made myself clear. Report to me the next time you have a few hours off, and I will take half of them from you. Good day.'

And with that he and his entourage of temporally displaced clothing collected itself back into his seat like a flock of birds landing in a tree.

I wasn't quite sure what to make of him. I couldn't understand him half the time, but what I did know was that he was sinister and frightening in a very different way from the mate, and that I had had enough of both of them. I was determined to render myself anonymous from now on. Neither of them would hear a peep out of me ever again.

Chapter 5

JAMAICA

*Rising above racism. Windy becomes a Great Man. Philosophy? –
Baloney! Fall follows pride all the way back down to earth.*

A S WE APPROACHED Jamaica, there was a special
buzz of excitement amongst those present in the bar.
The lads were like children on their way to a funfair.
None of them had visited Jamaica before and we had made
the pleasant assumption that the island would be similar to
Barbados in its prospects for frolics; the thrill of the
unknown added to the licking of lips and the rubbing of
hands.

We arrived at four in the afternoon, and channelled our
excitement into getting the berthing operations done as
quickly as possible so that we could get up the road that
night. However, our first contact with the shore-wallahs
soundly placed a damper on any such plans. The ship's

agent (a local company employed in each port to act on the shipping line's behalf) brought aboard, amongst other things, a sheet of printed paper for the attention of each of us. It said that owing to the racial tension in the area, it was not wise for white men to travel alone around Kingston, the capital. If we intended going ashore at all, it should be in groups, and only to the safer beach areas. Any unnecessary travel into Kingston should be avoided.

I was astounded. Jamaica is only round the corner from Barbados. From where we berthed, Jamaica looked every bit as picturesque, exciting and full of buzz as Barbados. It seemed to be just as full of Caribbean wonder and rhythmic promise as Barbados. Could it really be as bad as they said? As one who had experienced racism at home in South London (albeit from a white perspective) I was confident that I could win over any situation with my positive attitude and strident anti-racist feelings. I even felt a certain kinship with Jamaican culture and music. Maybe this was My Moment. Armed with my experiences from Brixton, I could be an ambassador, bridging the gap between confused peoples. I felt I had to stand up for what was right, and I had watched enough American movies to know that courage of this nature might just kick-start a change. I would do what I knew was right. I would not be intimidated by ignorant oiks posturing and bullying people. The Empire was not built by people shrinking away every time half-a-dozen cowards took over the town on some trumped-up pretext! I was a civilised Englishman, and I would damn well go where I pleased. Let them try to stop me.

The bar was already staging a heated debate by the time I got there, and I chimed in loudly with my views. We would be in a large group, we would not be looking for any trouble, and there was no way we should allow racism – which we all deplored – to stand in our way. It was agreed. We put on our happy clothes and set off defiantly for the town.

OCEAN BOULEVARD

As we left the port area and walked purposefully towards Kingston I felt good. There were ten of us, and we looked pretty damn scary ourselves, I can tell you. I was a member of a strong, united force of hairy-arsed sailors, standing up for what was right. Nobody in their right mind would tangle with us. We had agreed that if there was any trouble, we would stand shoulder to shoulder and fight as one. No-one in their right mind would take on a crack unit like us. In fact, I felt pretty damn hairy-arsed myself. Sure, we were attracting attention as we marched towards the city, but nothing we couldn't handle. Black men hung out of long flat cars and drawled out incomprehensible abuse alongside weirdly insulting finger configurations. We couldn't hear what they were saying over the volume of reggae music emerging from their cars, but the message was clear. We weren't welcome. Those who weren't threatening – ladies with children, workmen, granddads – stopped in the street to watch us go by. I curled my lip at people who stared at us, and nodded threateningly at anyone who held my gaze. I've got your number, John. As we continued on our way, some of them even turned around and started to follow us. It was incredible that we were attracting so much attention. What was the matter with these people? Didn't they have better things to do than stare at us? It was early evening, and the sun was shining through the dust kicked up from the dry roads. I felt my mouth go dry. I didn't know if it was because I was thirsty, or if it was that I was beginning to feel somewhat threatening. Maybe it wasn't such a great idea going out in a large group. It seemed to be inciting Jamaica to form into groups of its own; including one ever-growing group which was now following us along the street. Almost nobody was ignoring us. Everyone had an opinion and seemed to want to make it known. I tried to dismiss them from my mind. We'd be in a pub soon, and out of sight. If we could bond with a bar owner interested in our money, we'd probably end up having a great night. One of the best ever. The problems would all be over as soon as we got off the street.

However, as we proceeded, I became uneasy about just how many large black people were dropping into step behind us. They were not pretending to look the other way under the power of my unwavering stare, or scattering before us as we marched purposefully by. They were gathering in a disorganised pack behind us, like sharks building up their numbers before a feeding frenzy. What was worse was that they were behind us. It wasn't cool to look anxiously over our shoulders at them, but it was also impossible not to. Paranoia won out, and each of us in turn would sneak a worried look back at the mounting numbers following us.

This was not in the plan at all. At worst, I had expected some verbal abuse from groups of lads who were more scared of us than we were of them, but what we were getting was more akin to psychological warfare. As the numbers gathered behind us, they started a chant. The chant built louder and louder – and I felt less and less hairy-arsed as the intensity of their presence and volume built to unbearable proportions – until finally they all suddenly screamed at once. It was like being shot with a blank. Then they all hooted with laughter at us and shouted crude derision in exaggerated pidgin English before the seeds of another chant began to take root.

I was unsettled to say the least, but what could I do? What could we do? There were already about a hundred of them, and they did not seem to know that they were supposed to show a deferential and automatic respect for our British superiority. We could not possibly turn back – our way was blocked – we didn't know where we were headed and their numbers were growing all the time. I considered ducking off from the main group. There were occasional alleys on both sides, but would I fare any better alone? I would probably be in more danger. I could feel panic beginning to grip as the latest spine-chilling chant built to an overwhelming volume. HELP!

The group of followers was getting closer to us all the time as their numbers swelled, and it did me no good at all to see that tough, self-assured and worldly engineers like Skippy and Crate were looking decidedly sweaty. The leaders of our tormentors were almost breathing down our necks and the intimidation was insufferable. I had tried to move myself to the front of our group, but it quickly became apparent that I was not the only one with the idea of appearing to be a leader of men. I felt self-control leaving me and I broke into a trot to get to the front. Before I knew what was happening, we were all running flat out, rushing along unknown roads, with the baying mob bearing down behind us in hot pursuit. The trees and buildings swirled around me as I tried to keep running, and frantic shouts from my colleagues penetrated my sensibilities enough to keep us together. We rounded a corner and my heart was filled with dread. Ahead of us on the street was another large group of dangerous-looking black youths. They were not expecting us, but they quickly managed to add two and two, and set about cutting off our path. We were outnumbered by about two hundred to one and would have to fight for our lives. The situation was –

'QUICK, IN HERE!' I heard Jinx shout through my panic.

I swung round and saw a large wooden door, through which local civilians and petrified sailors were retreating like rabbits into a warren. The door slammed behind us and a cast-iron key the size of a tennis racquet turned reassuringly in the lock. I dived in gratefully, but our troubles were far from over. Inside was a bar with around a dozen pool tables and about twenty bemused local lads. The shouts and boom of a hundred angry men hitting the outside of the sturdy door all at once rang through the air, and the fears of those locked inside – both black and white – took over. A frantic battle broke out, and the frustrated army outside expressed itself by throwing heavy objects through the (thankfully) high windows, and pummelling the door.

I observed (from my position in a corner behind a fruit machine) that a pool room and bar is a particularly unfortunate place to indulge in violence. Ready to hand are cues for splitting heads, broken bottles for removing layers of incorrectly-coloured skin, and heavy, hand-sized pool balls for attracting attention across a goodish distance. At the height of the battle, I actually noticed people desperately searching for the correct change to insert into a pool table in order to secure a fresh supply of ammunition.

Eventually, the fight on the inside became a stand-off, with the white men hiding behind the drinks counter at one end of the room, and the black men behind a line of upturned pool tables, each speculatively hurling bar-room items at the other. Bleeding individuals struggled for cover, there was even a girl lying in the centre of the bar. I have never been so scared in all my life.

Outside, the police had arrived, and were calming the mob with batons. Suddenly, the door caved in and dozens of police swept purposefully through the mêlée. We were grateful to be arrested, bundled roughly into the back of an armoured van and taken off to prison. Emotions ran high as we were questioned through the night about the incident. We were held without charge or justification, but that was fine. We were very, very lucky to be arrested.

That night there was trouble in Kingston, and a man was murdered by muggers when he decided he would stand his ground and fight for his wallet and passport.

The atmosphere was heavy and grievous in the cells. I couldn't sleep at all, I had so much adrenalin and fear coursing through my veins. I just lay on my cell bunk in the dark and reflected on what had happened. I was hollow and drained with shock, and my stomach heaved as I contemplated what might so easily have been much worse. Here was I, a fun-loving easygoing kinda guy, without an ounce of malice in my soul, and here was a frenzied crowd of people who didn't even know me, prepared to tear me limb from limb simply because of the colour of my skin. In South London I had thought I understood what racism meant for those suffering from it. In reality, I had no idea, and my new-found understanding shook me rigid.

The next morning the captain came down and

negotiated our release. We did leave the ship again, but not to go into Kingston. We did as we were advised, and took cabs up to the safer beaches as far from Kingston as we could get.

A day or two later I was discussing my new-found morality with an English vicar I met on the north shores. He was a splendid old chap, living in a beachfront house near an amazing place called Runaway Bay with his family. We sat out on his veranda for two long, hot evenings watching the props guys lower the orange sun and pull up a perfect moon. Runaway Bay was nothing short of paradise; it wasn't just a long way from Kingston in miles, it was as far from that dreadful night as it was possible to be. We listened to the sounds of the night and the waves lapping at the coral-white beach. We drank iced vintage whisky and talked to the stars about the problems of the world.

Reverend Hall was a wise and worldly man. He had been living here a long time, so he had managed to integrate and make a safe life. He knew all about Jamaica, but I did a lot more talking than listening. Time and alcohol were curing my cowardice. I had discovered a new and better inner-me, and I was keen to tell people how soulful I was. The prevalence of evil and wrong-doing had come home to me on my travels, and I now realised that it behoved me, as an educated, civilised human being, to rise above the general desperation of the world and give something back. To educate others, to lead by example, and to give up material things. Compassion was the answer to the world's problems, and I would, from now on, devote myself to the teaching and practice of higher goodness.

And with the whisky glowing passionately behind my eyes, I meant every word.

I was becoming rather pleased with what a well-rounded chap I was becoming; intoxicated not only with the whisky, but with the depth and breadth of my capacity to forgive, to lead a good life and to resist mindlessness. I told him how forgiving I had been to the other cadets as they left me alone to work on jobs that they should have helped me with. How understanding I had been of NotNorman's puppy-like ignorance. How patient I had been with the mate despite his megalomania. Good grief – I was virtually a saint already.

Reverend Hall raised his glass to the stars. 'Good lad,' he said, 'you're a good lad. If only there were more like you. I could lose my faith if I didn't meet the odd spark of hope like yourself. Do you know what? Only today I took delivery of a brand new Mini-Moke, and it seems some dirty dog has been out joy-riding in it before I've even touched the dashed thing. There's 200 miles on the clock, a big dent in the front, the gearbox is like a bowl of porridge, and the engine's had six bells thrashed out of it. Now why can't more people have your attitude and show a little respect for their fellow man? Can you answer me that?'

For some reason, I couldn't.

Chapter 6

THE PLANTING OF SEEDS

Eavesdropping pays a scary dividend. Why mules die in Panama. Fear of David Attenborough. Making money from Colons. The mules live on!

FTER JAMAICA THERE was a general buzz that always accompanied a change of scene. We had finished with the Gulf of Mexico and the islands of the Caribbean, and were heading for pastures new in the agreeable shape of Australia. All that lay between us and the Lucky Country was an interlude by the name of the Panama Canal, and an impossibly vast quantity of seawater. Not only that, but we had managed by a minor miracle to be clean enough by 8 a.m. to attend breakfast in the officers' mess.

THE PLANTING OF SEEDS

Breakfast is a major event on board ship, attended by men who have already clocked up a couple of hours behind the plough before the eight o'clock bell. In the case of us apprentices, we would generally have been out working on deck since six, meaning an appetite is built up, and a quite astonishing quantity of food can be devoured at the first opportunity. A stream of waiters flood endlessly out of the kitchens and throw food in our faces like clowns in a circus, the only difference being that the food does not splatter amusingly – it gets swallowed whole.

Breakfast consisted of five full courses. Reading from left to right, they lined up as follows: To begin, we ingested some variety of fruit. If we were in a tropical port, this would be whatever weird and wonderful dongly things could be found and picked from the trees in the surrounding area at sunrise by hungover cadets. At sea it seemed exclusively to consist of half a grapefruit. Half a grapefruit-worth of endless giggles for the more childish amongst us as the acidic citrus content caused its recipient to curl his lip in an involuntary Elvis impersonation.

Next came a cereal course - an innocuous matter of milk, sugar and cereal, occasionally given a sinister mobility if some insect species had set up home in the cereal store. Pouring the milk on the cereal caused all livestock therein to panic and strike out for the shore. An off-guard first-tripper (mentioning no names) who is used to his cornflakes remaining relatively sedentary during the process of being eaten, might quite understandably fall off his chair and bang the back of his head on the floor before leaping up and down in a busy dance routine involving pointing at the offending breakfast bowl and rhythmically choking on the contents of his mouth. All good fun for the old sea-dogs, who are quite used to shovelling insects into their mouths and are grateful for the extra protein.

The first-tripper insect-dance course was followed by a fish course: variety, freshness and acceptability dependent upon region and season. After this we had 'eggs to order' in any one of their myriad manifestations. Assuming you were able to impart to the Asian chief cook (via several intense tutorials) the detailed specifications of your eggs, the sky, as they say, was the limit, your wish his command, and Bob a close relative. However, Asian chefs do not normally cook eggs British-style, and if you failed to communicate the essential data, this course was more prone to being a globular mess somewhere between an omelette and a road accident.

Fourth came the meat course. Yes, we are still at the breakfast table. Each day saw maybe liver, or pork chops, or steak, served with one of the equally myriad manifestations of potato.

The whole affair was then topped-off with tea (or coffee) and toast with marmalade, (or jam) and a discussion of the day ahead, with the relaxing music of the twelve-man Indigestion Concerto heaving away mezzo-forte in the background.

On this occasion, as NotNorman and I squared our elbows and assumed the position, only the captain, the mate and the chief engineer were at the captain's table. We nodded a cautious and respectful 'Good morning'.

NotNorman and I chatted self-consciously through our Elvis and insects, but by the time we were attacking our globular mess we had fallen into silence. An onlooker would think we were in that quiet, introspective mood which is so often a feature of earnest men with an honest day's toil ahead, but they would be wrong. Our ears were like satellite dishes, our eyes wide with disbelief, and our concentration intense.

We were eavesdropping.

'Surely things have improved since then?' the captain was saying. 'It's been five years since I last went through the Panama Canal, and it was so bad then that I complained to the High Commission. I understood something was being done.'

'Apparently,' continued the mate, waving his fork about and forcing a giant bolus into each cheek to facilitate speech, 'apparently, it's getting worse 'cos the ships they have to pull are getting bigger and bigger. It's certainly no better than the first time I came through twelve years ago. The mules still get pulled into the water, and they still can't get back out again 'cos of the Canal's steep sides. I was here last year and I saw two get pulled in. Dreadful it was. Really dreadful.'

'Ooooh, I know,' said the chief, who, despite his enormous size, had a voice like Sybil Fawlty, 'but things have improved. They used to just let them drown. At least they shoot them now.'

As the conversation continued in this vein, NotNorman and I ceased our mastication and stared at each other in silent horror. I was aghast. I'm not saying I was scared or anything. No, no. It's just that some of life's harsher realities – especially those involving the struggle of dumb animals against lethal forces they don't understand – reduce some people to tears. And I don't just mean the kind of things we all dread, like the yelp of a puppy in time with the bump under the car wheels; the three-legged mouse hobbling pathetically away from the cat; the zing! of the Flymo blade as my dad sliced the top off our hibernating tortoise with the lawn mower. It can be far more subtle than that. It's nothing to do with being macho – strong men can be sensitive too, you know – but just the sound of David Attenborough's syrupy narration has me reaching directly for the remote control. You can be sure his slavering tones will accompany slow-motion pictures of a pack of wild dogs tearing into an exhausted zebra, or big cats chasing helpless little bambis about. I can't take it at all, I just feel... excuse me a minute.

Sorry. Ahem, someone at the door. Anyway, suffice to say that the thought of watching drowning mules getting shot caused me to worry for the lads. Some of them might be squeamish. But there was worse to come.

'You'll never get –' gulped the mate, stopping mid-sentence to force what looked like a sideboard down his throat, '- you'll never get any change as long as it costs them nothing to use mules to pull the ships through the canal.

We have to feed 'em, so they cost nothing to run. If one breaks down they just eat it and wheel in a replacement! No problem! Basic economics – you'll never get any change.'

'Ah, but you obviously haven't seen the latest 'M' notice, have you?' said the captain. 'They are definitely tightening up. The new directives insist that from now on, all mules, while physically engaged in the towing of ships, have to wear a hard hat.'

'Oh good,' I thought. 'At least somebody is doing something.' I don't know how I thought a hard hat would help a drowning mule, but I was desperate for any hope I could cling to, and so was all for it. I could tell from NotNorman's demeanour that he had been shaken by what we had heard, poor chap. He looked a little sick. To be honest, I don't think NotNorman is really man enough for this line of work. We exited stage left with our breakfast unfinished and depressing pictures of what the next day would hold haunting our minds.

There was only one night's stop at an overexciting Panamanian port by the (rather apt) name of Colon, before our passage through the Canal. I was on cargo watch all night, so missed out on the trip up the road, and – being macho and care-free – once I'd heard what Jinx had schemed up for this evening, I was dreadfully disappointed to find myself unable to attend. They were all going out for a penguin dance.

The story goes that a cash-dollar profit could be made by handsome young sailors who were not afraid to be a little cavalier with the heart-strings of Colon's substantial homosexual population. Apparently, an eyelash-fluttering cadet could, without too much expertise, tempt a woopsie Colonite to part with twenty dollars simply by leading him suggestively by the belt up a side alley. The cadet then holds the gaze of his victim and drops sumptuously to his knees while slowly undoing the victim's belt and fly. With all the promise of the moment, the cadet licks his lips and slowly draws the Panamanian's trousers down, then in one lightening movement he does the belt back up round his victim's ankles and runs like the clappers, clutching his ill-gotten gains. Working on the principle that a cadet with his trousers up can run faster than a Colonite with his trousers down, our protagonist is a swift twenty dollars up on the evening for ten minutes' work. An ingenious basis upon which to start a business, but not, I would imagine, one for the faint-hearted. The expression 'penguin dance' arises from the limited but energetic range of motion achieved by an angry Panamanian trying to give chase with a belt done up around his lower legs.

So as the lads headed off up the road with such money-making adventures in mind, you can probably appreciate my chagrin at being stuck on a midnight-until-six cargo watch. I would love to have gone, of course, but I had to work. Great shame and all that, but there you are. And don't concern yourself on any moral grounds over such an unprincipled money-making scam. These things have a way of balancing out. For every Colonite left hopping about trouserless in an alleyway, suffering from unrequited love and a lightened wallet, there was a sailor getting just as thoroughly laundered by one of the local ladies. As with most professions, the girls who put the most into their work reaped the greatest rewards. The most enterprising would, for an increased fee, spend an entire night with the sailor on his ship. She would then put a great deal of effort into delivering her goods until the hapless victim was reduced to a complete standstill, then delivering again until he could give no more and was begging her to stop, then delivering yet again until he was smiling but unconscious. The next thing said victim would know, it was morning. Girl? Gone. Wallet? Gone. Credit cards? Clothes? Luggage? Jewellery? Sextant? Toothpaste? Keys? Shoes? Light bulb? Toilet paper? Carpet? You name it, it was gone. Clever girl – stupid sailor. And he'd paid her as well.

Colon is one of those serious sailors' ports, where all the worst sailors' stories are acted out for real every night. Debauched, licentious, criminal, drunken, fighting nights out with no holds barred. Some make money, others lose heavily. Some are hunters, others are prey. Some are street-wise and slick, others are Giewy.

The Famous Dick Wrigley and I spent the greater part of our cargo watch leaning over the side watching the intrepid adventurers come and go in their various states of dishevelment. In between returning heroes, I took the opportunity to ask him about the mules at the Panama Canal.

'Ah, you've been told have you?' he asked.

'I heard the old man and the mate talking about it. Is it true that the mules fall in and get shot? It sounds dreadful.'

'Yip. I'm afraid it is. They use mules because they are free to run. The ship has to feed them as we go through, so the service doesn't cost them anything to provide. I know it's harsh, but most countries work their animals. They don't have pets like we do in Britain. The real fun, though, is that YOU are the murderer! It will be your job to feed the mules and try to stop them going in. The chief steward will give you a bucket of food, and you have to use it to tempt them to move. Don't give them any – just let them chase you – that way, they pull the ship along. If you give them too much, they just stop and go to sleep. Give them enough to know what's in the bucket, and to get their taste buds fired-up, then run off so they follow you. Simple.'

'But what about when they get pulled in?'

'Well, when the ship begins to tug them towards the edge, it's your job to try and tempt them inland with the bucket. If you do your job properly, they ought to be OK. But don't lose any sleep over it. It is devastating to watch them desperately struggling to avoid drowning only to get shot, but so long as you've done your best, nobody will hold it against you. Try not to blame yourself – it will be a miracle if none gets pulled in.'

This was dreadful, and I had plenty more questions, but we were interrupted by the noise of a returning sailor. Whoever it was, he was trying to get back on board without being noticed, so our curiosity naturally took us to the top of the gangway to meet him. It was 3:30 and it was Giewy. He sidled through the shadows towards the gangway. When he eventually saw us, he winced visibly at being discovered.

'Giew!' he said pointedly in reply to our raised eyebrows. 'I do NOT want to talk about it!'

We were puzzled at first, but as he got closer the course his evening had taken became clear.

He was clutching twenty dollars and was having considerable difficulty in walking properly.

Once the ship had freed itself from outrageous Colon, the canal and all the horrors it represented lay ahead. I tried to wangle myself a bridge watch for the passage in order to secure an interesting and active role at the centre of things, (without any mulean death-throes to witness) but it was no use. Blom came down from the mate with the expected bad news.

'Right, Windy. Go to the chief steward and get a bucket of apples. You are on the fo'c'sle for a forward stand-by looking after mules. NotNorman, you're amidships with a bucket of carrots. Cookie Short of the Full Biscuit, you're down aft – sprouts. Right, before you go, let's run through a quick mule tutorial.'

So Cookie Short, NotNorman and I exchanged shrugs and began to learn the techniques for our most vital of roles: stopping mules from falling into canals. Through a series of role plays, with one of us playing a wayward mule (by bending over, using our hands as ears and braying) and another as a cadet, we learned how to extract maximum effort from them while giving up a minimum of groceries. We also learned how to tempt the mules away from death through expert proffering of the most succulent produce. For real emergencies we were additionally equipped with a strategic Hobnob in the back pocket.

Two hours later as we approached the first cutting, I was fully prepared. I had a handsome bucket of large green apples and a giant pooper-scooper (apparently first-trippers are also responsible for tow-path hygiene).

'They're in there!' shouted the mate, pointing to a metal shed-like structure on the quay. It didn't look much like a stable, but there you are. These were foreign parts.

We exchanged lines with the shoreside crew, then it was time for me to take up my position on the quay. I climbed down the ladder and walked up to the shed with my bucket of apples and my pooper-scooper. I walked all round the shed. Then all round it again, this time scratching my head. There didn't appear to be an entrance, let alone a proliferation of mules.

'COME ON, WINDY!' screamed the mate from the fo'c'sle. It sounded like he was right next to my ear. 'Let's get a wiggle on down there!'

'But there's no entr –'

'JUST GET ON WITH IT!' he roared, his tonsils waving in the wind. I was becoming conscious that the whole operation was waiting on me, so I walked round again. There were various knobs and switches here and there on the shed, so I thought I'd best try a couple to see if a door would open, but as soon as I touched the shed, I regretted it. The shed exploded into life and roared at me like a lion with a V8 engine. My head swam trying to get a grip on things, then the entire building jolted a couple of feet, and set off towards me like some unearthly monster. I had heart failure and stumbled backwards shouting something along the lines of 'WuaahOOOOARGGHH!' I then fell on my arse, and the sky became a mass of apples and pooper-scoopers. When it cleared, my world consisted entirely of delighted, laughing faces and snapping cameras. Even the pilot was doubled up, shrieking with laughter on the bridge wing.

The realisation that the 'mule' was a machine was just dawning on me when, just audible over the sound of my cardiac arrest, there was a boom from amidships, a cry of surprise, and I saw NotNorman leap backwards, flailing his arms and legs around. He too sat on his pooper-scooper, distributing carrots hither and thither. Then there was an

THE PLANTING OF SEEDS

even more distant boom from down aft where Cookie Short of the Full Biscuit was having five years removed from his lifespan and was giving a bucket of sprouts the gift of flight.

I couldn't shout at anybody, because there wasn't a soul on board who could function properly for laughter. These 'mules' are in fact dirty big engines that run on rails to haul the ships through sections of the canal. Why I didn't notice the rails I shall never know – I tripped over the bloody things enough. We were forced to pose in front of these contraptions with our buckets and vegetables as if trying to feed them, and behind them with pooper-scoopers as if awaiting a parcel, and proper pillocks we looked too.

As if this was not enough, there was an additional blight to compound my misery. There is a code of practice on board ship regarding practical jokes, the thrust of which being that the sucker (i.e., me) has to buy each of the perpetrators who have been successful in catching him out (i.e., everybody else) a case of beer. This is in addition to the humiliation at the time and the incessant ragging from the moment the trap is sprung until the last ever human being finally leaves this planet, wiping his eyes with mirth at me getting duped into feeding impostor mules six hundred million years before.

Chapter 7

BUTTERFLIES

A humble butterfly frightens the bridge watch. The homicidal nature of the washing-lines Grimm. A cross-eyed sack monster frightens the bridge watch.

THE PANAMA CANAL took a few days to negotiate, and although some points were man-made and perfunctory and others positively dangerous (on account of the warring factions on either side throwing explosives at one another), long stretches were extremely beautiful. With steep-sided hills climbing skyward, and teeming with tropical plants and wildlife, it is definitely good on the eyes.

I was on the bridge during one such section and life was cooking along most acceptably. Although I hadn't spent much time on the bridge yet, this was where I would spend most of my professional life as a navigator, guiding my ships across the seas of the world, and I liked it very much. I particularly liked the charts and positioning work. The charts were maintained by the second mate – Cranners – and the correct charts for our location, all marked up with the planned routes, were always laid out on the chart table at the back of the bridge. Over the charts were the only lights allowed on the bridge. In front of the chartroom on the main bridge, it was always natural light, and therefore pitch black at night. I loved that too. At the centre of the bridge was the helm and auto-pilot, with a seacunnie – an Asian helmsman – at the wheel. To the sides were the radar, depth sounder, direction finder, VHF radio and telephone, the tachometer and Commodore log, the engine-room controls, or 'telegraphs', the chronometer and clocks, an Aldis lamp (for transmitting Morse by light) and lots and lots of other lights, bells, alarms, and whistles that I didn't fully understand yet. I was still at the stage of adoring the 'Clear-View Screens'. These were two forward-facing 'windscreens' with circular sections which spun rapidly, clearing the rain instantly and allowing a 'clear view'. I just loved that they went round and round. The bridge was my home.

My watch for the canal transit was an early morning day watch. It was a bright, cool day, the air tasted fresh and the light was clear and beautiful as the sun rose, sending warming beams slanting sideways between the Panama hills. The captain was strutting about keeping an eye on things, Cranners was showing me how to fix positions on the chart, and the pilot was looking through his binoculars and giving helm commands to the seacunnie on the wheel. The various animated gadgets whirred and clicked reassuringly, and efficient activity ruled the bridge.

Now follow me closely here, because in two shakes things moved on from this scene of nautical bliss to one of chaos and discord as our mood was shattered by the entrance on to the bridge of – a butterfly. It flew in through the bridge-wing doors without so much as a by-your-leave. Well, as I am sure you can appreciate, our reaction was one of outright panic. We are but simple people, and out of the blue, as cool as you please, in flies a butterfly to ruin our day. We all screamed in unison and dived for cover as if the butterfly was packing heat.

Yes, I did say butterfly; but this was no ordinary butterfly. This thing was massive. I thought it was a pterodactyl. A pterodactyl looking mighty cheesed off about something. Maybe it had just found out that it became extinct five million years ago. Whatever – I thought it was going to eat me.

One low flap of its mighty wings carried it about two hundred yards, and it definitely looked hungry. I wrapped myself as close to the back of the radar as I could and put my arms over my head.

'Er... get that, will you, Cadet!' commanded the captain from his position on all fours behind the chart table.

You know what you can do, I thought, peeping out from behind the radar. I couldn't see anyone. The bridge was completely clear of people and no one was steering the ship as she steamed serenely along the narrow channel of the Panama Canal. More importantly, there were no monsters flying about. I shook my head and looked again. Nothing. If it existed at all, it must have flown directly across the bridge and cruised straight out the other side. I raised my eyes cautiously from my position of safety at the same time as other people's eyes were emerging from theirs. The eyes of the seacunnie appeared from where he had dropped to the floor like an Italian soccer striker behind the helm. The second mate's eyes appeared from behind the door that led to the rest of the ship – he'd actually left the bridge – and the pilot's eyes peeped out from his position crammed into the cupboard. The captain's then appeared over the chart table as he summed up the question being asked by every pair of eyes.

'Has... er... has the bloody thing gone?'

A tentative look round seemed to establish that it had,

so we emerged sheepishly from our hidey-holes. We straightened our clothes and dusted ourselves off, feeling a little foolish at our reaction to what was, after all, a butterfly. It had all been so sudden. It was hard to believe it had happened at all. If there hadn't been so many others suffering the same soiling sensation as me, I would have sworn I'd imagined the beast.

As dignity returned once more and the ship was brought back on course, Cranners said that he hadn't really been scared, he'd just left the bridge by coincidence to visit the gents. Then the captain said he hadn't been scared, he'd only jumped because of the way we incompetents had reacted, and he told us all off for deserting our posts. Then the pilot said he hadn't been scared, he'd just gone to the chart cupboard for something (and presumably decided on a whim to leap in and close the door behind him) and the seacunnie said he had fallen over. I was therefore blamed for my ridiculous overreaction to a piffling butterfly, and told that if I couldn't uphold basic professional standards I wouldn't be allowed on the bridge. There was no one below me in the hierarchy I could blame, so I just had to swallow my pride and apologise, swearing under my breath at the injustice of it all. Why did the buck always seem to stop with me? I sulked away at the situation and determined to punch Giewy after my watch, but then a dastardly plan crawled into my razor-sharp mind. I was reminded of a night out just before I joined up, and I began to hatch a delicious plot.

It was back at home, just a few months earlier, when my friends and I were all sixteen and terrorising the town on our mopeds. We were indulging ourselves in the usual way, riding from one pub to the next, getting steadily less steady. As the evening drew towards its ridiculously early close (well, you know what British pubs are like) the gathered multitude of tipsy teenagers was not yet looking for bed. We wanted more from our Saturday night. It wasn't even midnight yet, and there was plenty of dancing left in our legs and plenty of thirst yet to be quenched. So it was with sincere urgency that questions began to circulate concerning whose parents were away, and whose house could therefore be commandeered for partying purposes. And it was with one arm forced up her back that a girl by the name of Tracey Grimm admitted to her father's absence from the family home until at least 3:00 a.m. Sir Isaac Newton would have been proud of the equal and opposite enthusiasm that the masses generated to counter Tracey's reluctance, and before you could say *Philosophiae Naturalis Principia Mathematica* (which we couldn't) the take-away beers were being taken away, and the mopeds were eating up the mile and a half to Tracey's house.

Tracey had a rich father and an impressive house in a private road. However, those of us who knew her dad also knew how he got his money. With a string of betting shops, a company which repossessed cars, and a dodgy loans outfit, he ran a sort of mafia and was not a man to be messed with. Those who did not know him personally knew him by reputation, so despite the apparent joy at the prospect of a party, there were private fears that 'Grimbo' might return.

Anyway, like true drunk teenagers, as the music boomed, the lights went down, and Grimbo's drinks cabinet decanted itself into our brains, we quickly forgot our concerns and the party was soon doing a roaring trade.

At about 1:30 a.m., I was dancing in a huge room with a couple of hundred others when Tracey, who was looking anxiously out of the windows at the front of the house, saw a car enter the drive. None of us had cars – most of us were too young to drive anyway – so two and two quickly made four.

'Daddy!' she cried, and despite the enormous noise of the music, the whole party froze, the music ground to an ominous halt, and the only sound to be heard was that of jaws hitting the floor all around.

'Oh, man!' said somebody. 'He'll kill us!'

It was with focus and determination that the entire company set off for the French doors at the far end of the lounge and legged it off down the garden at the back of the house.

The combination of a brain full of booze and the pack mentality of dozens of people running desperately down the garden like an Olympic 100-metre final made things rush, so I was ill-prepared for strangulation, but that was what I got. Being particularly scared of Grimbo (I upset him once with a foot-pump and a Jewish parrot, but that's another story), I made good time over the first half of the course and was one of the first to make it to the washing-line that was stretched across the garden but invisible because of the dark. I was running as fast as I could when it took me perfectly by the throat. It stopped me dead in my tracks from the neck up, swinging the rest of me up in the air until I was horizontal, some eight feet off the ground.

'YEULK!' I said sensibly.

The next thing I knew my whole body from my ankles to the back of my head hit the ground with a sickening thud, the impact knocking all the wind out of me. My body convulsed and choked as it attempted to begin breathing again, and all around me my fellow revellers were: (a) being taken by the throat; (b) yeulking heartily; and (c) causing the ground beneath me to shudder as they arrived prostrate on their backs.

But my thoughts were not with them. I knew that any second now, a large and violent Grimbo (his suspicions aroused by the sound of nearby yeulking) would be round the back looking for party-goers to castrate with a rusty knife. I summoned all my strength, and with the supreme willpower of a true Baboulene, dragged my shattered body into the hedgerows. By the time the footsteps and long shadows emerged along the side of the house I was watching intently, hopeful that one of my good friends who didn't have the strength to hide would be caught and beaten up so I could nip off. However, things are not always as they seem, and, as the shadows moved into the light, I saw that it was not Grimbo at all. The footsteps, shadows and car belonged not to the Brother Grimm, but to one Pat Gallagher. And he was not a Mafia hit-man. He was one of us. He had arrived late in his father's car. An eighteen-year-old kid had frightened the daylights out of one hundred and forty of South London's coolest dudes, and red faces were the fashion accessory of the evening. We crawled sheepishly from our hiding places and trudged back to the house, our pride and throats in tatters.

We sat around talking for a while, waiting for our hearts to slow down, and decided that what we had done was pathetic. Not only were our bikes lined up at the front and our coats in the house, which made running away pointless, but there were also dozens of us, and only one Grimbo. We decided that even if he did return, there was no point in running away, we would just leave his stupid house, dismissively saying 'Yeah, yeah, yeah. Wotevaaahh,' to his rantings and amble off into the night. There was nothing he could do about it – he would just have to lump it. Thus decided, the party began to move again, and soon it was back up to full speed.

By 2:30 a.m. the beer stocks were getting a little low, so my mate Nick and I decided to ride off to my house to pick up some more from my father's supply. We set off into the night air, and as we hurtled along the lanes on our mopeds, an idea gripped me. I looked sideways at Nick, and could see from his gleeful expression that the same idea had occurred to him, too. We stopped and organised our strategy, then swung the mopeds round and headed back to Tracey's. As we approached the driveway, we adopted the agreed formation, side by side with around four feet between us thereby giving the appearance from the house of an approaching car. It worked like a charm. The faces of all the brave young men who were going to tell Grimbo to shove his Rolls Royce where the sun don't shine looked decidedly anxious as they whizzed past the hall window towards the French doors. As we turned off our engines, the night air was full of the throttled cries of young men yeulking – it was like a holiday in Austria – and the driveway shuddered beneath our feet as those brave yeulkers hit the unforgiving ground under the washing-line. We adopted the gruff, angry tones of a Mafia murder cell and marched purposefully around the side of the house. Desperate young men were trying in vain to drag themselves towards cover and were praying that another might be chosen. The bushes all around the garden shook at our approach, the ground beneath the washing-line was strewn with crippled bodies, and red faces glowed like Christmas lights from the trees and hedgerows all around. It was tremendous.

Nick and I needed those mopeds after that, I can tell you.

So, as I say, the reaction of the brave warriors on the bridge reminded me of Tracey Grimm and her party, and a similarly devious plan formed in my mind. After my watch, I collected NotNorman and he played Igor to my Frankenstein as we spent a constructive half-hour creating a monster butterfly. We used a black plastic bag filled with gunny sacks. Great, big, flappy, cardboard wings, hinged to bounce up and down realistically; massive, unearthly, crossed eyes on the ends of long, wobbly antennae, and a big, angry mouth full of pointed yellow teeth. Then, while I snuck up on to the monkey island (the area of exposed deck above the bridge) Igor beetled off for his camera. I attached about six feet of thin rope to the brute's back, tied the other end to the rail above the bridge wing door, and awaited NotNorman's thumbs up. He positioned himself to take a prime shot through the bridge-wing window, then gave me the green light. I took the hideous beast and threw it upwards and outwards as if setting it free. It set off for the sun until the rope became taut, then it changed its angle of attack and peeled off in a beautiful parabola for the bridge-wing door beneath my feet, like a World War II Spitfire beginning a strafing run. It was perfect. The creature flew directly on to the bridge with good speed, at the perfect height and although it entered the arena bum-first (which may have been MORE frightening) it righted itself in time to present its fangs. I heard the simultaneous cries of five alarmed men in fear of their lives, and there was a bit of a scramble. With the sounds of panic filling the air as the assembled officers squeezed up tight together into the limited cupboard space, I made good my escape and met NotNorman in the bar. He said that the pictures would be fantastic, featuring five men with their mouths open and their eyes on stalks as good as the butterfly's, every one of them about a foot off the deck, petrified by a cross-eyed sack and some cardboard dangling in the background.

Ha! I was definitely getting the hang of this Merchant Navy lark. I could play with the big boys when it came to this joking around stuff. These boys would have to get up pretty early in the morning to catch this puppy out, and anything they tried would spring straight back in their faces. I was definitely feeling GOOD.

Chapter 8

WATER, WATER EVERYWHERE

The sea is big, Windy is small. The recalcitrant nature of propellers. The significance of bicycles in space. The mate's underwater brethren. Windy leaves his post. Nobby Clark and the indignity of suddenly being curried.

AS CENTRAL AMERICA sank slowly into the sea behind the ship and the depth-sounder reported unbelievable information regarding the quantity of water below us, the sheer enormity of the Pacific Ocean began to dawn on our feeble brains. You will remember, of course, what fun it was earlier to concentrate on the one word 'Blom' until it lost all its meaning and shape, and went completely crazy on you? (I hope you're joining in the participatory bits, now...) We were getting the same sensation, only magnified one thousand-fold, by leaning on the rails and trying to imagine the ocean as being full of cars instead of water, or as a quantifiable mass of water – say, if it was all in buckets. It blew our finite minds to smithereens before the concept even halfway hit home.

Using a measure such as 'gallons' to describe the Pacific doesn't even begin to get the thing over, and the more we thought about it, the more our heads swam and the worse it got. Apart from anything else, as that great ocean threw the ship hither and thither like a rubber duck in a bathtub, I began to realise that a 12,000-ton ship is small and insignificant. I realised that the dozen or so mere mortals running the ship, in whose trust we placed our lives, would have no answers should Mother Nature choose to wipe us out. I felt humble and insignificant, and this was before we had even lost sight of land. I would need to multiply the amount of water I was unable to comprehend here by several thousand miles and nearly twenty days before we would be in Australia. I don't know if I'm getting my message across here. There simply are not the words to convey accurately the experience of being completely surrounded by – and at the mercy of – a phenomenal quantity of water. My sense of propriety was completely deranged by the mighty Pacific.

Apart from becoming spaced out at water volumes, the first few days out of Panama were relatively calm as we settled in to our first long haul. People seemed to hide themselves away for a day or two as if taking stock and preparing for the trek ahead, so although there was a fair degree of jollity and merriment of an evening in the bar, the tone was low-key, and the atmosphere noticeably more, well, pacific.

The lads still found time to rag me however, and I had already heard plenty about the dreaded Crossing the Line Ceremony. Apparently it is traditional for anybody crossing the equator for the first time to 'declare their allegiance to King Neptune' through some sort of ritual. Specifically, a humiliating and painful ritual. The subject is also required to make a 'sacrifice', whatever that meant.

WATER, WATER EVERYWHERE

Nobody was very clear, but they delighted in showing me some of the disgusting array of stinking artefacts and steaming potions they were preparing for the big day. There were paint drums full of unspeakable muck, ropes and chains were being rigged, and, worst of all, a bottle kept under lock and key in the bar (but on view through the cabinet's glass door) was gradually filling up – and had been throughout the trip – with sperm.

Yes, you're right – that's what I thought.

With my limited navigational skills stretched to their utmost, I kept an eye on the approach of my opportunity to suffer. It would not be long – just a couple of days to go – and the lads were building into a sadistic frenzy. The bottle was becoming more disgusting by the day and we four first-trippers were becoming increasingly convinced that a career in insurance would have been a wise move. However, a couple of days out of Panama we ran into a problem which set the crossing of the line back a little while – in fact, it almost wiped it out completely.

The well-oiled machinery was pushing the old girl along at a game 17 knots, and all was running as smoothly as a Swiss watch. (The Swiss have asked me to point out that they have never made any giant, rusty, shit watches. Ed.) Three or four of us were leaning on the bulwarks watching the sea go by and making ourselves ill trying to comprehend how amazing it was that the water level rose the world over, albeit by a minimal amount, every time someone threw in a pebble (on which basis we decided that one of my dad's belly-flops could wipe out a Greek island) and whether, if you took all the sponges off the sea-bed, the sea level would rise. Ahmed – the lucky man who was looking after our every need – had brought us tea and biscuits at 3:30, and we were having a five-minute break for ten minutes. Half-an-hour later the mate was taking up his post on the bridge for his four-to-eight watch (and was therefore unaware of our whereabouts) so we could safely settle down for an extra ten minutes, watching the endlessly fascinating turmoil of waves, foam, iridescence, flying fish, birds and the fathomless shades of blue and green surrounding the ship as she cut a furrow through the ocean. An extremely civilised way to spend an hour or two, and the perfect backdrop for a discussion of the world's problems, a quiet sharing of our personal and emotional issues, insight into our various political standpoints, or – more probably – bosoms. Whatever the topic on this occasion, I have good reason to have forgotten it. Because the peaceful scene I have painted for you was ripped from the canvas, torn up and slung unceremoniously into the rubbish bin.

Ships are fundamentally designed to move in the horizontal plane, roughly in the direction in which you point them. The repetitive, easy pitch and roll can become pleasant or even forgotten completely. It becomes a part of the day; the same as the constant engine noise, the mate's hollering, and curry for lunch. It's just there.

So you can imagine our disappointment with our grand vessel when she began to vibrate. Now, I don't mean the kind of vibration that a car might exude at high speed on a motorway. Dismiss this imagery as less than representative. Maybe you can picture the discomfort experienced by a road worker attached to the upper regions of a pneumatic drill. Cast such wimpish analogies from your mind, because although the vibrations were as rapid as the excitable end of a pneumatic drill, they were covering a much greater distance. Each vibration was not merely a shift of an inch or two. Or even a foot or two. We are talking about a ship here, with vibrations covering a displacement of a couple of yards a time at one hundred oscillations per minute! Each of us became a fifteen-foot blur clinging to the rail for dear life as it thrashed up and down.

Having quickly discovered that there was nothing I could do about the shape of my face under these conditions, my next thought was that life could not be supported for long, and that I should shortly be cashing in my chips with this crowd and moving on to less exciting worlds. Under these conditions I'd be pleased to see an end to it all. It was to this end that I was in the process of trying to get my head in the way of one of the rails on its upward thrash, when some bright spark had the idea that turning off the main engine might improve matters. It certainly did. The vibrations abated, the ship became dormant and strangely silent as it floated along on the great ocean. We were adrift and out of control, but at least the vibrations had stopped.

We cadets stumbled off in the shaky style of newborn giraffes towards the engine-room to get the score from the men in the know.

By the time we got there, the detective work was already well under way, but no delinquent component was immediately apparent. Soon engineers were emerging from every orifice of the great old engine, shrugging their shoulders and shaking their heads. Everything seemed to be in perfect working order. A test run of the engine was organised – to see if we were all dreaming (and to allay rumours of that giant octopus you see in all the old paintings) – but was quickly aborted. At only 'slow ahead' the vibration was appreciable, and by half ahead we were all milkshakes again. There was only one thing left that it could possibly be. The propeller. The problem here, however, was that the prop is not an easy chap to check up on. He has free rein to get up to whatever spinning mischief takes his fancy without fear of observation from above. With the ship fully laden and down by the stern, it is at least fifteen feet under water and – more importantly – another fifteen feet under the transom stern. Harder to get at than a nasal hair with a pair of garden shears.

It was decided that a lifeboat would be lowered into the sea, containing a special group of volunteers led by the mate. The team could then motor round to the stern of the vessel, where one brave volunteer would dive down with a mask on and observe the condition of the propeller. The probability was that if the cause of the crazy vibes we were all digging was the prop', then there would be something fairly obvious wrong with it.

All jolly sensible. Naturally, I volunteered, with vigorous support from the mate who helped me to secure one of the places (by my earlobe). Giewy genuinely did volunteer (he was grinning inanely at me as if I was Santa Claus, I mean, what is the matter with him?) along with Benny the Dog to man the lifeboat engine. Before you could say 'I'd love to help but I've got a dentist's appointment' the lifeboat was unshipped from its moorings, the davits swung out, and I was standing uncertainly at my assigned post in the stern of the lifeboat, the baying crowd a-whooping and a-cheering at the exciting prospect of severe injury befalling us.

As the boat began its descent down the side of the ship, the hullabaloo of the madding crowd became a distant buzz and I caught a glimpse of the mighty ocean rolling hungrily beneath us. My mind was suddenly awash with clear and unequivocal realisations. The first bombshell was the sheer scale of the component parts making up my predicament. People who think a 12,000-ton ship represents a large and intransigent object are fools. They should be given a wide berth and sent somewhere secure as soon as possible. Twelve thousand tons can be tossed about by the sea like a rag doll in the jaws of a Doberman. Those who consider a thousand miles to be no great distance are similarly insane. Ask them to consider such a distance – which was our distance from the nearest land – in shipping terms. In a car there are hundreds of other drivers sharing the road, as well as access to motorway services, breakdown services, police, ambulance men and overnight stops. There was no help for our ship; just a dozen or so rather strange blokes and the feeble abilities they were so pathetically arrogant about. On shore we are so reliant upon the 'authorities'. We do not see them as consisting of mere people with failings and uncertainties. The authorities are there, endlessly providing a God-like safety net, present at every turn to help us through life's crises. We had no authorities on board. No police. No paramedics. No breakdown services. No mummy or daddy. Not even passing fellow-travellers. Just me and Benny the Dog, and Cookie Short, and... Oh, Jesus. It suddenly dawned on me how ludicrous it all was. A motley bunch of us pitting ourselves against the mighty oceans; completely out of our element and trying to steer a floating metal platform across the Pacific. Absolutely ridiculous. It's not natural for human beings to leave terra firma in the first place, and it is especially stupid to take on the might of the sea with nothing more than a rusty piece of tin.

The Pacific was not particularly rough that day, but the waves no longer looked friendly. The crests, which had resembled white horses, suddenly seemed to lick at hungry lips. And this was just the surface. It went down and down and down. Five miles down. I tried not to think about all that deathly nothingness beneath our floating platform, and my dead bones lying at the bottom. I felt a rush of foolishness. Whatever ego I had was crushed by the sheer insignificance of my being. My muscles? Laughable. My brain? Insignificant. My opinions? My desires? My anger? The sea would not listen. Why should it? I felt I was falling through space with all my old beliefs and opinions regarding what was good and fair completely unhinged. A good analogy for going to sea on a ship seemed to be that of an astronaut travelling a mile or two away from his spaceship on a bicycle.

As the lifeboat started her jerky journey down towards sea level I had the job of patrolling one of the ropes. Two ropes are attached to the davits on the ship and coiled into the boat – one at each end – but they are not attached to the boat. They are knotted at regular intervals and, once the boat is in the water, provide, during the boat's intended employment, a means of boarding for late arrivals. It is therefore necessary to feed out these ropes as the boat descends, because if they get caught on anything, they can upset matters considerably (and literally).

Giewy was feeding out the other rope. He was grinning inanely as if we were on some sort of fairground ride. He obviously had no grip on the inadequacies of civil authorities, the colossal nature of the phenomena we were up against, or the significance of bicycles in space. However, even he was forced to display a modicum of human awareness by what followed. When we were approximately halfway down to the sea we heard shouting from above. Looking way, way back up to the bridge wing, I could see The Famous Dick Wrigley shouting and pointing to the sea.

'WOW! Look at the size of that bastard!'

I leaned carefully on the gunwale of the lifeboat and peered gingerly into the sea below. There, cruising patiently beneath us awaiting his lunch, was a huge shark. Although my sensibilities were already in shreds (as were my underpants) a fresh wave of desperation washed over me, but the roar of the mate about two inches from my left ear still managed to penetrate, and I returned to my post. Then we hit the water. Or I should say, the water hit us. The crest of a wave suddenly swept us upwards. The boat came away from its retention hooks and we were in. Immediate and undiluted fear climbed all over my desperation, and stood victoriously above my insecurities. I clung to the rope with catatonic strength, frozen in horror. This is not a clever thing to do, as the rope had a separate agenda from that of the lifeboat, so there was a good chance that I would be left dangling there once the boat had gone, like a punter stranded atop his pole.

I know it sounds barely credible, but I don't believe I was thinking straight at this point, and the screamed instructions from the mate were entirely wasted on me, so it was fortunate that a fresh wave of shouts went up from the gathered audience above. The shark! I let go of the rope and leant over the side once more. This time the water level was about six inches from me, and four feet away was the deep, black, penetrating eye of a massive hammerhead shark – one of the most efficient killing machines on earth. I remember it as being the same length as the lifeboat, which would make it thirty feet long, so even allowing for fifty percent exaggeration, it was still a fifteen footer, and there was nothing between me and this incredible monster except the flimsy wooden sides of the lifeboat. I tried to turn away, but I couldn't. That fathomless eye had a stronger grip on me than any straitjacket could. I thought how feeble human beings are in the water, how superb sharks are, and how large this one was.

From somewhere I became distantly conscious that the mate was shouting something, but I could not hear. I stared into the shark's eye and I found no compassion. I found no hope. I was transfixed. In the age it took for the shark to pass and to release me from its grip, Benny had started the lifeboat engine, and the boat was beginning to move. I shook my head and came back to life with a start. The rope I had been feeding out was now hanging in the water about ten feet behind us, and the forward rope, which Giewy had been feeding out, was coming towards me. I caught the mate's eye. It matched up perfectly with that of the shark, and it hit me: They were brothers. This was a conspiracy. I suddenly knew who was going to be the volunteer who would be diving down to look at the prop'. Giewy's rope had just past me and was leaving us at the aft end of the boat. I ran two strides to the back and leapt as hard as I could over the open water for the life-saving rope. My legs splashed in the water, feeling all dangly and eatable, but I just made it to the rope and the shark didn't get me. I climbed the forty feet back up to the boat-deck in about three seconds, accompanied by the jeers and derision of my companions. I didn't care. Safety is a relative thing, and I knew where I wanted to be. As far as I was concerned, my life had just been saved. We cowards should stick together, rejecting all those who do daring things simply because they are not brave enough to be cowardly. We should form a society and practise jumping at our own shadows. Where does swashbuckling get you? OK, apart from money, girls, status, respect, self-belief, friends, satisfaction and confidence? Exactly – nowhere. Follow my advice and turn chicken.

Despite my begging to the heavens that the mate would lose a couple of vital organs to this Nobby Clark, things went without a hitch. In fact, the water was so clear that they could see directly from the boat to the prop' simply by leaning over the side with a mask. And the problem with the propeller was so obvious even from there that a closer inspection wasn't necessary. Don't ask me how or why, but the prop was missing a goodly portion of one of its blades. Although baffling and mysterious in itself (although doubtless I would be getting the blame) it did explain the vibration.

And before I become deluged by those who were paying attention earlier, I know there was a spare propeller – I had spent the entire journey living under the bloody thing – but it was no good. Not purely because it would involve too much upheaval for me to remove all my personal effects from beneath it, or because it could not be changed at sea – it had been done before – but because we were too heavily laden. To change the propeller required us to be at least close to light-ship. As we were, the damaged prop' was too deep irrespective of how we altered the stability. Light-ship, the broken prop' could be almost entirely raised out of the water just by making her bow-heavy by filling all the forward ballast tanks and emptying the aft ones. The propeller can then be changed over using the cargo derricks. Unfortunately, sharks or no sharks, this was not possible here.

The politics and global administration of a shipping line were soon flashing around the planet in Morse code. Where were we close to? Central and South America. Both bad news for dry-docking, and still ages away at our new cruising speed of around four knots. Back to Panama? No good dry-dock services there. America? May as well continue to Australia. Yip, that was the way to go. We would take a month at four knots, but the problem could be easily handled there, and it would keep the cargo – the lifeblood of the shipping line – on course for the paymasters.

The engines were fired up again and people returned to their normal routines, the only differences being that the ship was going appreciably slower and we were looking at a full thirty days more at sea, rather than the expected fifteen.

WATER, WATER EVERYWHERE

During the period that the ship was drifting serenely from wave to wave awaiting further instructions, the crew had not been idle. They knew from experience that sharks follow the ship, and they were ready to ambush the earliest arrivals. There are several theories as to why sharks follow ships, one of which is that the thrashing of a distant propeller in the water gives sharks the impression of a creature in distress – the equivalent of a dinner gong to our fearsome friends. Another theory is that they have learned to associate ships with the discarded scraps that are thrown overboard. Being scavengers, this too gets their saliva flowing. For whatever reason, if the ship stops deep-sea, it is soon caught up by numerous nobbies, all looking for a free lunch. But as is so common in nature, the hunter can quickly become the hunted. The crew stuck half a pig on a dirty big hook and slung it in the sea on a 22-millimetre runner wire. They followed it in with a few buckets of blood and offal to stir up the emotions, and before you could say 'Allez oop!' a dirty big nobby – not stopping to question what half a pig was doing swimming around mid-Pacific – had been plucked from the water and plonked on to the deck. So while I was climbing forty-foot ropes to escape the sea-born scourge, the crew was busy bringing it aboard for me.

When I saw the first shark they'd caught, I was fairly preoccupied by other matters, so did not dwell too long on the slow death they were inflicting upon it, but as the day wore on, I could see why they had not been quicker about dispatching it to the great sea in the sky. After they'd landed it, they sharpened up their knives, tucked in their napkins and waited for each other to curry the thing. However, a full half-hour later it was far from dead, and they didn't seem to know quite what to do about it. It lay there on the deck, apparently deep in thought, but nobody could get near it. For some reason it seemed mistrustful of its hosts. Every time someone went within fifteen feet of it, there was a whirring blaze of flashing teeth and the approacher would turn tail and run like the clappers to a safe haven where he would anxiously enumerate his limbs. After an hour or so, I was astonished to find this drama still being played out to the same script. I have no idea how it stayed alive, but every time they thought it was definitely dead, someone would venture too close with a carving knife, and Boo! It was after them again.

After a while this entertaining spectacle was simply a part of the day, and we were becoming used to the poke-the-nobby-and-leg-it routine that was by now a familiar feature of the afterdeck. So it was a surprise to return from a short diversion to find that the shark was gone and all the crew were mooching about with rotund bellies and curry round their mouths. I scratched my head in disbelief. One moment there is a shark terrorising the neighbourhood, the next moment they've curried the bloody thing and are offering you bowls of it.

I can't help but feel a little sorry for sharks really. It must be strange to be a nobby – stalking aggressively around with the gang, in your leather jacket and sunglasses, killer of the deep and all that – casually going about your normal mid-week schedule, when all of a sudden someone comes along and curries you. Most embarrassing, at the very least.

From that day forth, I vowed never to stand still too long in the presence of the chief cook. However, I would gladly submit myself to a convention of chief cooks rather than ever have to undergo the Crossing the Line Ceremony again. However hard we tried, even the combined navigational incompetence of NotNorman and me could not put the position of the ship at what might be termed a comfortable distance from the dreaded equator. We knew that the day was almost upon us when we would discover the purpose of the chains, the ropes, the stenchy potions and acid cocktails... and that unbearable bottle of congealed, contaminated, accumulated sailors' sperm going rancid in the cabinet in the bar.

Chapter 9

A GIFT FOR KING NEPTUNE

Crossing the Line. Windy shows disarming and unexpected bravery.
Spit or swallow? Cookie Short lets the biscuit out of the barrel.

THE CROSSING THE Line Ceremony is every good first-tripper's opportunity to declare his allegiance to Neptune upon crossing over the Equator for the very first time.

Thus far, I was somewhat hazy as to what form this ritual would take, it being very difficult to distinguish the wheat from the chaff when speaking with our torturers. Most of what I was told was so unspeakably hideous that we first-trippers nervously agreed it could not possibly be based on fact, but what certainly seemed to be common to all the incidents recounted was that we would be asked to endure a number of pagan rituals, pay various forfeits, suffer numerous punishments for our sins, oh... and have every hair on our body – yes those ones as well – shaved off and committed to the deep. What the hell Neptune wanted with four sets of adolescent pubes I shall never know. From my very first day aboard *Global Wanderer*, and on every day since, everybody with whom I had spoken, upon finding out that I was a first-tripper, had shaken their head and sucked their teeth sharply.

'Oh dear, dear, dear, first-tripper, you say? You don't want to be one of those. You'll have to cross the line, you know. You want my advice? Get off NOW. Go home while there's still time. RUN AWAY!' and so on along those lines.

Similar encouragement to make with the ankles came from the various activities going on around the ship as the trip progressed. The engineers were slowly but surely building up a five-gallon drum of thick, black crud with grit in it. I couldn't help but notice that it was not being thrown away with all the other waste when the opportunity presented itself. One day I came across Jinx stirring the steaming brew.

'Eurgh! What is that?' I asked, retching on the fumes.

'It's to do your hair and fill your pants with when you cross the line,' he said cheerfully. 'It's highly toxic, lead-based and quite extraordinarily poisonous, so try not to swallow any. Could be lethal. Mind you,' he added conspiratorially, 'your mouth will be brim full already, so there shouldn't be too much danger of eating any of this! HAR-HARHARHAR! HAAAR-HARHARHARHAR!'

His laughter haunted my nights as his enigmatic words took me back to the worrying developments in that bottle locked in a glass cabinet in the bar. Its contents initially looked like some sort of mucus culture, and it grew as the weeks went by. Eventually you have to ask. You know you are going to regret it, but you have to ask.

'Oh, that,' replied Sparks, the radio officer, blithely, 'that's the bottle of sperm we're building up especially for you to eat as you cross the line. It's a part of the ceremony.'

A GIFT FOR KING NEPTUNE

'Oh,' I said quietly, wishing I hadn't asked. 'I shouldn't have asked, should I?' Sparky shook his head sadly. 'I should have got off the ship while I had the chance, shouldn't I?'

The head nodded with priestly sympathy, 'You certainly should. No good now, though, is it? I'd love to help you out, but my hands are tied. Tradition and all that, you know. You have to declare your allegiance to Neptune, don't you? Love to make an exception and all that, but, well, rules are rules.'

Suddenly I had a brilliant idea. The old Baboulene brainbox was in top form. I slapped my forehead.

'But Sparky,' I lied, happily, 'you can let me off! Didn't I tell you? I went to Australia a few years ago. I've already crossed the line! We're saved!'

'Well that's wo-o-o-nderful!' sang Sparky, brightening, the heavy responsibility for my educational advancement lifting from his shoulders. 'All you have to do is show us your certificate and you're off the hook! I am pleased! This means you won't have to suffer that hideous abuse, or have your head shaved, or eat all that –'

'Sorry, er, hold your horses there, old chap... er... did you say, "certificate"?'

'Yes, your certificate. If you've crossed the line, then you've got one, of course, and we can call off the hounds. I am relieved!'

'Ah. Well. I didn't actually, er, bring my certificate with me. You see, I mean, you know how it is. Once you've crossed the line a few times like me, you don't bother carrying the old certif' anymore, do you?'

The weight returned to his overburdened shoulders.

'Ach, I'm sorry. We're back where we started. I wish I could help, but if you've crossed the line as often as you obviously have, then you know all the rules. No certificate, no reprieve. Love to help and all that, but my hands are tied, you know.'

And so it goes on throughout the time one is in

hemisphere A. The slow but effective build up, irrevocably squeezing with a cold grip, like piano wires tightening round your heart.

On the dreaded afternoon that we crossed the Equator, the lynch mob got itself organised in the bar and built up a good head of team spirit before setting out to find us first-trippers. NotNorman was quickly tracked down to the anchor locker, but that didn't mean he could easily be led to the slaughter. He was well bedded-in, armed to the teeth, defending the small entrance admirably and was, for the moment, beyond extraction.

KiloWatt – the second electrician who was also a first-tripper – was clinging to a bulkhead twenty feet up in the engine-room. He had worked his way out along a structural girder, and was clinging on to a metal bar welded to the bulkhead. His was an effective refuge in that it was almost impossible for the enemy to get at him; however, the precarious nature of his position meant he was continually expending energy just staying up there. Like NotNorman, he too was, for the moment, beyond abuse, but time would surely find him out.

Cookie's hiding place was indeed, Short of the Full Biscuit. He was tracked down to a toilet in the accommodation. The lock was forced, and he was shortly to be found with two heavies attached to each limb, kicking and screaming his way to the ceremonial altar on the foredeck.

And me? Well, I am proud to tell you that the mob was quite taken aback to find me lying casually on my bed with my hands behind my head, indulging in a pre-ordeal snooze. It put them right off. In fact some of them were visibly perturbed. They didn't seem to know quite what to do.

'Good grief, Windy! I would have put money on a turkey like you trying to hide!'

'Yeah, we thought you'd have been hiding for a fortnight, being such a girl!'

A GIFT FOR KING NEPTUNE

'Go on Windy, you're spoiling it for us! Run off and give us a chase. We'll give you ten to get away. What do you say?'

They were at once bemused and impressed by my stone-faced bravery, and it quite threw their uncivilised antics. I could see one or two of them shifting uneasily from one foot to the other as I rose above their savagery. I was prepared to take my medicine like a man and here they were demonstrably humiliated by my moral fibre. They looked like half-a-dozen priests caught dancing round a brothel with their pants on their heads.

As they dragged me bodily from my bunk and carried me roughly out on to the deck I could see that their hearts were not quite in it, and as they chained me up next to Cookie Short they cheered weakly, not feeling quite as pleased with themselves as they had supposed they might. They were unnerved by my resolve, set so firmly against the winds of adversity as I faced up to them with self-respect and pride. They could not look me in the eye and left quickly, preferring the less conscience-searching job of hunting down one of the proper first-trippers – those ill-equipped with moral fibre – cowering in their principle-free hiding places. They wanted the thrill of the chase as well as the ritual humiliation, and I was spoiling things for them. We Baboulenes are made of stern stuff you see, and I was proud to be following in the footsteps of my ancestors who fought the great battles at Hastings, Dunkirk, Rorke's Drift and Yorktown, engendering new and better morals in the hearts of lesser mortals. They might abuse me this day, but they would not feel good about it. Thoroughly embarrassed, the motley crew left me dangling and set off in pursuit of the cowards, NotNorman and KiloWatt.

Despite the enormous pleasure they got from hunting down their prey, the average drunk sailor still looked upon the hiding first-tripper as an ungrateful child. They felt miffed that all their efforts towards his education were being spurned and they resolved to be firm but violent with him once he was eventually coaxed out.

OCEAN BOULEVARD

KiloWatt was still clinging to the engine-room bulkhead, and the job of encouraging the shy young chap down began. The assembled masses shouted threats, detailing the present extent of the intended violence and outlined a list of special extras to be added should he fail to give himself up. But their tempting sales patter had no effect on the customer. He turned his face away and pretended he was not listening. They huffed and puffed with frustration, and retired to a corner where they huddled together to rethink their sales and marketing pitch. Eventually, they decided on a fresh combination of carrots and sticks and returned to the scene. The original menu of violent intent was shouted out, the extra details were enumerated (this time guaranteeing their inclusion in the programme) and a new list of envisaged atrocities was appended to the repertoire should the current package be rejected. KiloWatt provided the traditional response, chanting the sacred words 'Bugger off' and, for good measure, he threw some nuts and bolts at them as punctuation. Heads drooping, the marauders retired for another strategy meeting, and so we went off around the loop again.

Some first-trippers have achieved legendary status by holding out for many hours – even days – but all give up eventually. On a ship in mid-ocean, there is simply no escape. NotNorman and KiloWatt could have saved everybody – including themselves – a good deal of heartache if they had shown a little good old British spirit and got on with it. I have no idea why some people are so spineless, it really is quite beyond me.

Eventually the hunting party that was expedited to fetch NotNorman and KiloWatt returned empty-handed. The fugitives were holding out. Neptune (more commonly known as Jinx) took charge. He stood up in his fine grass skirt, held his three-pronged cardboard trident aloft and pronounced that the proceedings should proceed (that's what proceedings do). His amassed cronies – in their equally ridiculous and ill-fitting costumes – cheered long and hard at the prospect of some action, and Neptune unfurled his scroll and began to read the solemn ceremonial words written thereon.

The early part of the ceremony was fairly controlled, with the mob chanting back the ritual responses and flexing their fingers as they awaited the opportunity to get at us; but with great tension building in line with their expectations, the whole atmosphere was becoming notably forbidding. There were no jokes or laughter anymore and the thing had an eerie air – more like an execution than a lads' jape.

Soon enough, some physical abuse featured, and another pattern began to emerge. Neptune would sombrely read out an indictment against myself, or Cookie Short, or both. Witnesses from the baying mob would then step forward and read out prepared statements pertaining to the incident in which we had allegedly shown ourselves to be imbecilic. For instance, Jinx – sorry, King Neptune – announced: 'That on the fifteenth inst. of this very month of this very year of our Lord, Windy here spent twenty minutes in the engine-room trying to stop a generator… which was not running. The punishment for one such heinous –'

I leapt to my defence.

'What? How can you say that? How was I to know it wasn't running? It – It was Crate's fault! He told me to! It was noisy in there and you just couldn't hear when I –'

King Neptune put his finger to his lips and raised the bottle containing the ceremonial sperm. I said no more. Crate stepped forward as a 'witness' and spouted some utter tripe concerning the event. I looked sadly at the bottle and said nothing. I was found guilty as charged, and sentenced to be 'taken into custody'.

The mob set about me with determination. My clothes were ripped from me until I was standing in only my underpants. There was a pause as they awaited the green light from King Neptune, who raised his trident aloft. 'Take him into custody!' he shouted and they leapt joyfully into action. My pants were gripped tightly, stretched wide open and the workers began filling them to the brim with cold custard siphoned off from the galley some months before. A generous quantity of chicken tikka masala was added to my custardy pants, followed by a cupful of iron filings. They then stood back to admire my bulging underpants (a whole new experience for me). There must have been two gallons of the stuff brimming out from everywhere when Neptune gave the next order:

'PULL!'

And with that four of Neptune's helpers who were holding the sides of my underpants pulled upwards with all their might. The gunky mixture fountained out in all directions as my pants were brought up under my arms. The penance complete, they all stepped back to admire their handiwork. What a state. Covered in browny-yellow sludge (with chicken pieces), a pair of incredibly well-stretched underpants covering my nipples and a look of grim surprise on my face, I learned that day just what iron filings are capable of when left to their own devices amongst one's more sensitive nooks and crannies.

The gloves were now off. Soon a stream of crimes was being read out, and Cookie Short and I were undergoing an increasingly violent flow of physical abuse. What started as custard down the pants and chilli peppers rubbed on the nipples steadily built as the thirst for blood grew, and British pride in dignity and compassion got drowned under basic animal savagery. Soon the separation between one punishment and the next was indistinguishable and Jinx was reading out crimes faster and faster. The hair under my arms went west, as did one eyebrow and half the hair on my head. To the enormous delight of the onlookers, my penis was painted black and buff (the same colour as the funnel) with a callously ticklish paintbrush, and all my pubes were shaved off. Flowers were stuck in my ears and a dreadful mixture of black gunk and pink gloss paint (seasoned with grit) was slapped all over me.

I looked at Cookie Short and caught his eye between

his choking on the tar they were sticking up his nose and his receiving a monk's hairdo. Like me, he had switched off and was just concentrating on surviving. Like a mouse being toyed with by a gang of alley cats, we had disconnected our senses and were simply trying to hang on as the endurance test continued. I was beginning to have a degree of success in blotting out the present when I was suddenly snapped back to the here and now, because... oh no...

The Bottle was brought forward.

Had I the presence of mind to think about it, I may have tried to take comfort in the probability that my life was about to hit an all-time low and could not possibly get any worse. Then it did. As The Bottle was held up in front of my face, I saw that there was a small green streak running through the contents, like the colouring in a marble. Neptune informed those gathered that the addition had been kindly donated by a 'special effort' from Crate who, despite having caught gonorrhoea in Jamaica, had still got in to the spirit of the thing and come up with the goods. A spontaneous round of applause rippled around the assembly who appreciated the fine effort he had made despite his illnesses, and Crate blushed coyly and kicked a shackle.

At this point I found myself once again going up in the estimation of the lads because I resisted the traditional practice of shouting for mummy and begging for mercy. I have to admit that the reason for this was perfectly simple. The slightest hint of an open mouth and I would be eating the bodily expulsions of many unclean sailors. I was also experiencing an overwhelming desire to be elsewhere.

My problem was that I was dealing with old hands. They had years of practice in helping young lads to eat sperm, so I braced myself for a titanic battle as they tried to force my mouth open. A battle did not come. I opened one eye, and saw no such activity heading my way. Instead, Neptune strolled over with the bottle. I clamped my lips tight and tensed my jaws as hard as they could go. If he tickled me, I was determined not to giggle – matters were far too serious to fall for that kind of stuff – but all he did was to hold my nose. I opened one eye and looked around, suspicious at the lack of brute force. What was going on? Why was he holding my nose? Then I realised that I could no longer breathe.

Oh.

I asked the Baboulene brain to analyse the situation and report back, but as it leapt into action, concentration seemed to elude it. While my body started up sirens telling me it was time to breathe in, my mind did not come back with a perfect plan. Instead it gave me a familiar face from school: Tuckerman. The same Tuckerman who took full responsibility for the Freedom Party following the combustion of the chemistry lab. It was perfectly all right to blame Tuckerman, because Tuckerman was a swot. He enjoyed latin, read books at breaktime, wore string vests and sensible shoes, would fall on his arse if he tried to kick a ball, and had the sole and expressed ambition of becoming an accountant for the same insurance firm as his four-eyed swotty old father. Us streetwise kids used to rag him endlessly for being such a plonker, but now he came back for his revenge. He sat in the corner of my conscience, sitting at his accountant's desk in his warm insurance company office, smiling smugly at me. He leaned across the desk and said, 'You're going to have to breathe now, Baboulene.'

I knew it was true, but to be quite honest with you, I didn't really want to. Breathing had suddenly become a grossly overrated pastime, and the only 'hot' idea the Baboulene brain could come up with was to pretend to breathe in, then stop again, in the hope that they might spill the gunk. I pretended to breathe in twice, stopping again immediately despite the powerful and urgent reflex messages I was getting from my diaphragm, but to no avail. They had obviously met this trick before, and made no attempt to feed me any. They knew that my third breath would be the genuine article and were ready and waiting until I had to drink the stuff down.

I feel sure that even the most committed optimist

could not convince you that my current cloud could possibly contain the remotest sniff of what might be called a silver lining; and as I stood there, naked, chained to a container, covered from head to foot in crap, with my pubes in the sea, an unspeakably bad taste searing through my digestive system, my head and genitals smarting and even bleeding from a clumsy razoring, my poor beloved willy painted black and buff, and iron filings in my most delicate neighbourhoods, I have to admit that the old 'joie de vivre' for which I was so well known seemed to have deserted me entirely. But I have to say that amongst this gunk-cloud there was, indeed, a silver lining. You see, I actually got off lightly. Yes, you read that correctly – I actually got off lightly.

The ordeal seemed to be abating as the savages became bored with their now-unresponsive quarry. We hung ravaged and despondent from the container chains, and they began to drift off towards the bar – their sadistic hunger satisfied, and beer becoming the foremost motivator in their simple animal brains – leaving a couple of sympathetic crew members to wash us down with a fire hose and cut us down from the container.

The ritual left me incensed with the futility of the human condition, and I vowed never to put any future first-trippers through the same degrading ordeal that I had just suffered. I decided to devote my life to the outlawing of the Crossing the Line Ceremony. If I achieved nothing else in my three score years and ten, it would have been a worthy life.

While I was in the shower entertaining these vocational thoughts, NotNorman had been snared with a rope around his ankle. He would hold out for another fifty minutes, but his goose was definitely cooked. And KiloWatt was becoming weaker. He couldn't have been more than a CouplaWatts now; his position teetering high on a ledge on the engine-room bulkhead necessitated the concentrated exertion of energy every time the ship rolled. Alas, although he was a big strong lad, the unrelenting roll of the ship was grinding him down, and he too would not see out the hour. The baying hounds drank there beers and watched eagerly. They knew the time they had to wait for the next act was shortening with every roll of the ship.

That hour was quite enough for the main combat unit to sink an appreciable quantity of additional alcohol. This was gradually making them feel more reckless, more aggressive, less capable of wielding a razor with finesse, and far less interested in the ceremonial details of the event. That hour also gave Cookie Short and me time to get ourselves into some semblance of order. It would take several weeks to get rid of all the gunk, remove the lead-based paints and evict the grit and iron filings from our most tender parts; a further few months to regain anything remotely resembling an acceptable hairstyle, and a lifetime or two to overcome the psychological trauma of eating sperm; but we were able to shower off the worst of it, put dressings on our wounds, comb our tufts, wash out our mouths and find some loose clothing to wear. Our strength was returning and it was beginning to sink in that we had survived the dreaded crossing the line. It was all over.

Cookie Short and I were at once relieved, elated and angry. Revenge may take years, but we vowed there and then to get our own back on each and every one of those diabolical sadists who had played their part in our humiliation. We discussed plans for getting the ceremony brought to the attention of the authorities, we listed the newspapers with the highest profiles, we would contact the –

Blom's head popped round the door. 'Quick lads. You're on!'

'Wha . . ? What NOW? What have we done?'

'No, no. Nothing to be scared of. They've got hold of NotNorman and KiloWatt and are chaining them up now. You lads have crossed the line, so you're on our side of the razor blade for this one. We thought maybe you might like to get involved?'

Cookie Short stood and shook with the emotion of it all. He could barely speak.

'AAAaaaaAARSE!' he shouted, putting things in a nutshell. I couldn't agree more.

'I guess that's a 'yes' then,' said Blom, smiling.

In a blinding flash of realisation, I clearly saw the value behind the ritual. The ceremony was an essential part of a cadet's education. It was character-building and sincere. I was a better person for the experience and, in time, NotNorman and KiloWatt would grow to thank us for what we were about to do. Cookie Short was rushing to put some clothes on, but I was already dressed, so I picked up a razor and headed for the door.

As I rushed passed the officers' bar I was stopped in my tracks by a small party working at the bar. They had The Bottle, and were bent over it in concentration. I remembered. They had used up the whole bottle on Cookie Short and me, so I wouldn't get to feed any to NotNorman and KiloWatt! This was terrible! Maybe we hadn't got off so lightly after all! Surely they weren't trying to recharge it now? I stormed into the bar.

'You dogs!' I said. 'You didn't keep any back for the other two! That's really unfair!'

'Don't panic,' said Benny the Dog. 'We're just making up some more. There we are! Another bottle!'

He held it proudly aloft, and sure enough, it was brim full and disgusting again. The memory nearly made me throw up on the spot. Then my eyes caught sight of the laughing eyes around me, and I looked back at the counter. There, in the centre of the activity, were the essential ingredients: flour, water, lemon, sour cream and gin. The flour was lumpy and thick, and the rest just didn't taste good together. I couldn't believe it. It wasn't sperm at all. My mind flooded with anger and relief. I was beside myself with conflicting emotions and was incapable of doing anything. 'And not forgetting that extra-special ingredient,' continued the Fourth, 'provided through a very special effort by Crate himself...' The Fourth gave the bottle to Crate who produced a teaspoon with a line of bright green Swarfega on it and stirred it gently into the mix. It was unutterably disgusting once more. 'Well, don't just stand there gawping at it!' he said. 'Get out there and frighten the crap out of them!'

'Before you go,' said Crate with all the embarrassment of a big man saying something sincere, 'I have to say that we were all well impressed with your bravery today. None of us have ever seen a first-tripper cross the line with such dignity.'

I blushed and dismissed his compliments with a modest wave of the hand. Just then Cookie Short walked in.

'Unlike THAT limp old digestive,' laughed the Fourth, pointing at The Cookie. 'Not only did he show no bravery whatsoever, the best bloody hiding place he could think up was to lock himself in the loo! Couldn't you do better than that, Cookie who is verifiably short of the full biscuit?'

Cookie Short's lips tightened.

'What do you mean, "hiding place"?' he blurted. 'I wasn't hiding in there, I'd gone in there for a dump! That Baboulene jerk went up to the chart-room this morning, came down and told me there were two more days to go before we reached the equator! I had a great hiding place all worked out and HE would have been wimping away like no other if he didn't have the navigational prowess of a drunk turkey on bad acid. He thought we were still two days away!'

The laughter rang out, and I was sinking fast to my all-too-familiar levels of humiliation. Suddenly my purpose in life was clear. I knew what had to be done.

I took the razor firmly in one hand, snatched up the bottle with the other, and headed off with a purposeful stride towards the restrained and helpless NotNorman and the soon-to-be-earthed KiloWatt.

Chapter 10

FROTTAGE

Muses on exercising in one's pants. The Grand Cranking Competition. We meet SmallParcel and learn of his relationship with the Post Office.

MASTURBATION IS AN issue of paramount importance to seamen. (There is a joke there if you can be bothered with it.) So despite the lowering of the tone, I am compelled by the onerous code amongst honest chroniclers to grasp the matter with both hands, so to speak.

The saying on board goes: 'All men are either wankers or liars' and, speaking from a purely subjective and non-self-committal viewpoint, I don't think there's much doubt about it. However, it is one of the dichotomies that occupy the great thinkers of our time that although all men masturbate, and the pastime is therefore a masculine activity, anyone who is caught in the act is immediately accused of being a Wanker. A scandalous insult, carrying the loathsome suggestion that the accused is unable to secure female companionship, and is therefore less than a real man. In a nutshell, all men masturbate, therefore no man is a man.

So despite a healthy trade in the preferred currency aboard ship – glossy magazines – NOBODY admits to playing the organ, and anybody who is caught red-handed (there may be a joke there, too) has to pay a fine in the form of the other favoured currency – beer. The fine amounts to a case of beer to every person who witnessed the shameful act or was instrumental in catching the instrumentalist. Thus all the men aboard are furiously pulling more than just ropes every day, but the stakes are high, both in beer and humiliation, so when a chap isn't conjuring himself up a quick hand-shandy in the tween-deck of hold three, he is probably poking around the less frequented areas of the ship with a Polaroid camera trying to apprehend others. It was simply not possible to get two minutes' peace without people assuming you'd nipped off to 'rough up the suspect'.

Now why, I hear you say, does a chap with an itch not simply lock himself away in his cabin and scratch it to his heart's content? No good, I'm afraid. It is a golden rule deep-sea that cabin doors are not locked. Rarely are they even shut. Trust in one's fellows is implicit, so a locked door can mean only one thing to a bar full of drunks with the prospect of easy beer glinting in their eyes. Any seaman worth his salt (another there, don't you think?) knows just what to do upon finding a locked door:

1) Run and tell everybody you can find that Bob is masturbating. This will inspire joy and resourcefulness. The well-oiled machine will leap into action. People will run and fetch each other, collect cameras and flash-guns, and gather swiftly

but quietly at Bob's door.

2) While the team is mobilising, go to the mate's office and beg, borrow or steal the accommodation master-key.

3) Return to Bob's door where a good crowd has gathered expectantly, cameras as primed and ready to go as Bob's bits.

4) Gather closely round Bob's door. It is vital to get as many bodies and cameras through that door as you can in the shortest time possible.

5) Turn the key ever so quietly, inch-by-inch so as not to disturb the victim. Countdown using the fingers: Three... two... one. BANG! In we go!

From the bed glossy magazines are thrown skywards by the thunderstruck Bob. He tries to cover himself up, but he is way late. Fifty photographs have been taken, and Bob is instantly in debt to the tune of a dozen cases of beer. An unwilling new hero of the bar photo board is born, and doesn't he look the superstar! Naked and airborne, doing a starfish impersonation a foot above his bed, with glossy pictures floating down around his startled countenance.

Once, Cookie Short thought he was a tremendously clever chap. He borrowed both sets of master-keys before locking his door and setting confidently about choking the chicken. He was well into the home straight when he got the feeling that he was not alone. Looking up he saw a delighted face upside-down at his seaward porthole. We were dangling NotNorman on a rope by his ankles from the boat-deck right out over the side of the ship simply to get the solid photographic evidence we needed.

Another time we burst in on Giewy, but he didn't fling everything skyward and shrivel with embarrassment, he just kept going. He had headphones on with rock music blasting his ears off, and was so thoroughly immersed in the job at hand that he didn't even notice we were there. So with his head thrown back and his knees up, he had no idea that ten other people were standing there in the room with him. The scene could easily have been an officers' cocktail party (but for the presence of one naked person masturbating). We casually chatted of this and that amongst ourselves until Giewy started shouting: 'YES! YES! I love you, Clint!' He opened his eyes to be met by the entire ship's complement applauding appreciatively and awarding marks out of ten on squares of card. He jumped ship, changed his name and moved to Brazil (I wish).

One of the additional incongruities of the shipboard monkey spanking phenomenon was that despite the highly competitive detection organisations and the adamant rebuttal of all accusations concerning the act, there were endless double standards. From the first week on board, a poster had been placed in the bar proclaiming: 'Grand Cranking Competition. Officers' Bar, 18:00 hours, first Wednesday into the southern hemisphere. Full uniform to be worn. Third officer to officiate.'

I was on bridge watches with the third officer for a while and broached the subject. I had visions of a line of sailors trying to start old Fords, so his answer as to the definition of the term 'cranking' gave me quite a jolt.

'Surely nobody is going to bash one out in front of your stopwatch?' I said incredulously. 'You cannot possibly expect me to fall for this garbage, can you?' I was becoming worldly-wise and cautious in my old age and suspected another merry jape.

The Famous Dick Wrigley laughed long and hard. 'Nooo,' he said, 'don't be stupid! Nobody is going to do that! Would you? But this is an absolutely serious, bona fide, pucker cranking race. You'll find one every trip on the first Wednesday after the ship changes hemisphere. It's an ancient tradition and there's an awful lot of beer for the winner.' I furrowed the brow and eyed the Famous One. I was greatly suspicious, but he forestalled my complaints. 'To ease your troubled mind, let me give you some inside info. The lights are turned out for the full duration of heightened sexual activity. Everyone knows the routine and has done it many times before. They'll all join in because the whole thing takes place in the pitch dark; but if you don't want to, don't. First to ejaculate wins six cases of beer.'

I was still far from happy, and continued to quiz people throughout the trip. Their answers always matched. I still had no intention whatsoever of joining in, but, what with the performance of the lads in the ports to date and the kind of activities I was beginning to realise were standard among sailors, the thing was becoming almost plausible. Now, on a slow boat to Oz, the Grand Cranking Competition was almost upon us and everyone seemed to have gone into training. Men for whom the sole normal form of exercise was lifting beer cans suddenly took up jogging and doing press-ups on the boat-deck. I couldn't believe it – they were all taking it so seriously. I was still mighty unsure, but received lots of advice and encouragement.

'Bar profits will put up six cases of beer for the winner,' said MegaWatt, jogging past me on the foredeck. 'SIX CASES!'

'I don't know why I'm bothering at all,' panted Sparky, shadow-boxing on the boat-deck. 'One of you young bastards always wins.'

'Remember,' lectured Cranners, pointing his skipping rope at me as he strode off towards the monkey island, 'everybody will be just as nervous as you are.'

And gradually all my fears and questions were answered. I still wasn't having it, of course, but I could not see the trick in it either. Even if there was some trick, they would still have to give out the beers, and most of these lads were more than happy to show off their sports department for a lot less reason than was on offer here! I couldn't make it out.

On the night of the Grand Cranking Competition, dinner was a sombre affair. Most of the competitors were preparing themselves psychologically for the forthcoming event and men who would normally laugh heartily as they put away a horse or two were studiously nibbling at pasta salad. As we retired to the bar the beers in the fridge remained untouched, and the huge pile of prize-winner's beer in the centre of the room was eyed intently. There was no chatting as resolute men with towels round their necks jogged on the spot and concentrated on their breathing.

Soon we were all gathered and The Famous Dick Wrigley called the proceedings to order. He ensured that all the entrants were seated in a circular arrangement around the cases of beer before reading in clear and solemn tones the contents of an ancient scroll containing the rules. He then had to sort out a small dispute as Sparky accused Skippy, the Australian third engineer, of cheating via premature stimulation. Skippy claimed he was simply 'scratching his balls' in a purely offhand and disinterested manner as he always did at this time of night. The Famous Dick Wrigley resolved the issue by forcing Skippy to stare at a picture of Princess Anne on a horse for two minutes with his hands behind his head. This engendered a second dispute as Skippy had apparently shown a treasonable interest in this picture earlier in the trip. Skippy replied, to the relief of the royalists present, that it was because he fancied the horse, which somehow placated everybody, and The Famous Dick Wrigley was able to regain control and call us to our marks. All round the room men sat back in their chairs and primed their zips ready for the off.

'Upon delumination of the lights,' pronounced The Famous Dick Wrigley, indicating the switch like a game-show host, 'you may commence self-stimulation. I do solemnly declare that these lights will remain extinguished, and I will guard the switch personally in accordance with the scrolls, so help me God. I will rekindle the lights upon one of our number reciting the hallowed words 'Me, me,

FROTTAGE

me' followed by name and rank, in the prescribed fashion. Do we all understand the rules, gentlemen?' He took the lack of response as an affirmative. 'In that case, may the biggest wanker win, and if we are all ready… on your marks…' everyone leant forward and began hyperventilating, 'get set…' the zips all came down in one crisp movement, 'gentlemen, you may begin.' And the room was plunged into darkness.

Now I had been reserving judgement on this affair throughout, and still seemed, for some reason, unable to throw my heart and soul into it in the abandoned way I managed easily enough whenever I was left on my own. Despite everybody's seriousness and preparation, I was still somewhat sceptical even now, but rules were rules and The Famous Dick Wrigley had given his solemn word to keep the lights out under the penalty of buying everybody ten cases of beer apiece. I couldn't see any catch, and when the zips came tumbling down and the noises around me started up, it was quite clear that nobody else could either. A dozen zips all being unzipped in unison is a fairly interesting sound in itself – they should record it and use it on albums – but it was nothing to the noise that followed. An indescribable mix of grunts and moans, blipping and skin, sweat and machismo filled the testosterone-laden air. It was perfectly disgusting, quite unbelievable and absolutely clear that genuine masturbation was going on all around me.

The tension built very quickly, and after only a minute or so the atmosphere was already building to a feverish pitch. I sensed Cookie Short, to my left, was about to burst the biscuit barrel with his beer-winning spasm, but coming up on my right was Giewy, making a noise like an asthmatics' ward, and it was he who was first to fall to his knees.

'Argh! Uh! Uh! Yyeess! Ugh! Ugh!' but the stupid sod was so carried away with his orgasm that he hadn't said the right words by the time NotNorman came up on the stand side with a tremendous last minute spurt.

'Wugh! ME! ME! Wugh! ME!' he cried. 'Not…

Wugh!... Norman – navigating cadet!'

The lights crashed on and suddenly the awful reality hit. In a small circle on their knees in the centre of the room around the beer cases were all the first-trippers (and Giewy) with their shorts round their knees and their excitement in evidence. Everywhere else around the room dignified officers sat back relaxing in comfortable chairs, resplendent in their uniforms, and as innocent as wild flowers. There was a moment of silence as they let the thing sink in for us, then every last one of them started to hoot, cry, roar and roll about with laughter at the depraved spectacle before them. Those that could manage any semblance of order in their lives reprised the groaning and wet slapping noises they had all been making by slapping their cheeks against their teeth. The awful truth was there before us. The officers had all been sitting back in their chairs making wanking noises while all the first-trippers (and Giewy) were masturbating furiously in the middle of the room. What made them doubly delighted was that because of the rules regarding catching others wanking, all the first-trippers (and Giewy) would now have to buy all of those present a case of beer each. Even NotNorman, who had genuinely won six cases would have to part with twelve, so once again we had been suckered.

It was quite brilliantly done. All that trouble we had gone to in order to catch people masturbating – knocking down doors, dangling off the boat-deck on ropes and so on – and we had been tricked into cranking away in the middle of the officers' bar in front of the entire assembly.

I hid myself in about ten pints of beer and spent the night trying to decide what my new name would be when I moved to Brazil.

Before I leave the topic of masturbation, I must just tell you one more story. It's not that I wish to dwell on base matters, but, following the revelations of the previous story, the more people I can drag into the field with me, the less conspicuous I'll feel, if you see what I mean.

FROTTAGE

I have not yet introduced the fifth engineer. His name was Eddie, but everybody called him SmallParcel following the event I am about to relate. The reason you have not yet met SmallParcel is that he didn't really exist in the orthodox, tangible sense. He was alive, but we get into deep water very quickly in arguing the point. He was alive in the sense that cheese is alive.

He was a pale, thin chap with scraggy hair, an unshaven, vacant face and a body you felt you could put your hand straight through and out the other side. Do you remember in Star Trek when the people on the Enterprise got the co-ordinates wrong beaming someone up and they sort of beamed up, but got stuck in a faded and translucent state in the transporter room? That's how SmallParcel looked all the time – half beamed up.

One of the main reasons he was like this was that he provided for himself an almost continuous supply of mind-expanding drugs. And not just one type – he liked plenty of variety in his diet. This meant that any conversation with him was very unlikely to advance matters. For instance, if you came across him on the deck somewhere, instead of saying 'hello', it was always a good game to hit him with a randomly selected word, such as 'radish' or 'theodolite'. If you caught him right it drove his scrambled brain to new extremes of surreal delirium. He would freeze, pole-axed by the word, then jerk his head around trying to make it slot in somewhere. He would repeat the word a few times, rolling it around his mouth as if it was a message from God, a look of wonderment creeping over his face, then he would crack up into raucous, emotional fits of laughter or tears that could go on for hours. You then went on your way, leaving the man reeling from the blatant delivery of a single word.

One night we were having a few beers in the bar when the door burst open and Cookie Short's delighted face poked into the room. 'Stations lads! Eddie's having a chieftain in his cabin!'

We all leapt into gear and two minutes later a crowd of us were sardined around SmallParcel's door ready to burst in. We got ourselves organised for maximum effect, the master-key was turned and, BANG! In we went. The usual glossy magazines went up, the cameras flashed and the laughter rained; the normal, everyday humiliation of a man caught playing with himself. But then someone noticed that there was something different about this particular catch. The glossy magazines that had been thrust skyward by SmallParcel were not the usual range featuring bad, rude excellent girls. There was not a single curvaceous blonde to be found. This in itself was not unheard of – chaps had been caught with every imaginable variation of fetishist material from a Crufts' programme to a medical journal on amoebic dysentery – but SmallParcel was indulging an interest in neither of these. Nor was he a rubber fetishist or one of those guys who likes to dress up like a baby, wet his nappy and get punished by a gothic tractor-mechanic matron wearing flippers. Any of these would have raised appreciative eyebrows without surprising anyone too much; but the shocking perversity of SmallParcel was beyond the experience of even this worldly bunch of sailors.

SmallParcel was sexually aroused – and you must follow me closely here, because it's all rather strange – by letterboxes. Mmmm, letterboxes. And this was no passing fancy or whimsical attraction – he could fall in love with the doors to which they were attached. This is absolutely true, and the evidence was there for us in the glossies being examined with wide eyes. Although the majority of them were the advertising literature from builders merchants on the various front-doors available in the marketplace, the one that stood out above all was an American-published magazine – called something like 'Remember Your ZIP' or 'CosmoPostman' – for people who shared his front-door and letterbox fetish. Inside were contact advertisements for this like-minded, happy-go-lucky bunch to meet and admire one another's mail, advertisements for the various letterboxes you could buy, 'ready and willing' to receive your advances, and stories and letters on the various adventures these people had. (Apparently the American way of life is a particular tease for those sharing SmallParcel's predilection, as American doors do not have letterboxes. These doors were referred to by the magazine as 'prick-teasing bitch doors'. Need I add that trips to Europe were a major advertising feature.)

SmallParcel was disarmingly unembarrassed at being caught in the act. Indeed, he was evangelical in his enthusiasm to convert us to the wonders of his religion. He was more than happy to share his convictions with us, presumably in the hope that he might recruit more members for the clan. He showed us a contraption, which he had made himself, that looked like a sort of hollowed-out cucumber fixed to a flat, rectangular piece of wood. It was actually made of Tupperware lined with polystyrene, and was so constructed as to fit snugly into a letterbox, thus allowing SmallParcel to consummate his love with the door of his choosing. Putting it plainly, this fitting – which he referred to as a 'lobby-shunter' – allowed him the luxury of shagging letterboxes. He told us, in his own inimitable fashion, that this was extremely exciting for him, not simply because of the emotional fulfilment in making love to a door you are fond of – which is rather touching in itself – but because, if there was anybody inside the house he was rogering, there was no way he could know what their reaction would be upon encountering a womb's eye view of the sexual act in the form of a huge Tupperware cucumber wobbling about at the end of the hallway. Nor could he predict what action a householder might take, and the prospect of some overwrought housewife setting about his genitalia with a food processor excited him above all else.

So SmallParcel had become a postman. Wandering from door to door, trying to hide his excitement, it was the perfect job for a man who wished to establish the prospects for love in the neighbourhood. As he posted a letter, he would close his eyes and get a feel for the letterbox – strength of springs, size, make, material, flexion and general cuteness. When he found a good one his knees would turn to jelly. He would pray that the door around it was a beauty and that the view of his bottom from the road was none too clear. Then he would retreat, and the door would quake on its hinges, for she knew that SmallParcel would return after dark to 'do his funky thang' (as Remember Your ZIP so aptly put it). The act of making love to a door was also given its own verb – 'to starfish' – presumably from the splayed nature of the position the Don Juan needed to adopt up against the door.

Anyway, SmallParcel ended up in prison. He had been unable to resist a tempting young 'Pine Mastif' (half-glazed with a brass twin-sprung letterbox) in Southampton, and an old woman – thinking it was her husband – had crept up on him from the inside with a carpet beater. SmallParcel passed out, and woke up in a cell. He was ordered to visit a psychologist who told him his job as a postman exposed him to too much temptation, and that he should try to find an environment entirely devoid of puckering front-doors with teasing letterboxes. He was also told to come out of the closet and tell his friends he was an abuser of letterboxes. He took this instruction to heart and following a sympathetic reaction from family and friends, he went a little too far, going around confessing to people that he'd been shagging their houses. Unfortunately, rather than engendering the sympathetic response the psychologist had envisaged, this had the opposite effect. Irate house-owners threatened SmallParcel with whatever domestic items were nearest to hand... and he became all the more aroused.

SmallParcel felt a burning need to get away to a sex-free environment. The Merchant Navy seemed the ideal answer, but now he was here, he was yearning to be back amongst the knobs and knockers. His enforced separation from his loved ones was too much for him to take.

To try and get closer to his desires he was writing a short story to send for publication in the magazine. He showed it to us and it was a remarkable piece of work, which I would like to share with you here. What follows is the result of a drugs-inspired, half-beamed-up letterbox enthusiast putting pen to paper for the benefit of his fellow worshippers. It is written from the viewpoint of a house-owning couple whose front door is being sullied:

'Dear Sir,

My wife and I were sat at the breakfast table, wondering why the mail was late this morning, when your missive came squeezing through our front door's front door. My front door is now in the post-pubescence phase common in kiln-dried hardwoods, and, for the first time in our experience, showed signs of being in ecstasy. Of course, we were shocked, but mostly we were concerned for the welfare of our front door, so we decided that it would be best for the time being if we blocked up her letterbox with a wet chamois. To our utmost amazement, she enjoyed this more than a Reader's Digest Prize Offer, but we hoped, with the chamois there, she would have no more problems until she grew a little more mature. But then the postman started ringing the bell (our front door enjoyed that too). He told us that he was 'frustrated' by our actions, and that if we did not restore our front door's receptive capability forthwith he would take (a) umbrage, and (b) action. Which we thought was a bit much on top of (c) liberties.

Let me fill you in. It's important for us to protect our front door from the ravages of the harsh world outside lest she become distorted. We want to protect her so she can 'open out' and not feel that people just walk straight through her when she does. You see, she's very young. She may look strong and reliable, but we've seen her come off her hinges a couple of times, I can tell you. She was left on our doorstep the very first day we moved into this house, and we didn't have the heart to shut her out. I suppose we should accept that she needs to be given more space – she's a good seven feet tall now. Do you know, she used to have just a tiny little bell? Now she's got two huge knockers and that letterbox and... well... when we found out what the postman was doing before we were up in the morning, we couldn't believe it. Anyway, we took suitable measures to stop the postman and, as documented above, he got uppity about her chastity. There was nothing he could do though, so things quietened down.

Then, just as diplomatic relations with the Post Office were being restored, our disgust was redoubled by the discovery that this postman – having declared passionate and devoted allegiance to our front door – was indulging himself in a sordid affair with a 74-year-old 'Suffolk Sturdy' round the corner, and a terrace of 'Jewson Reliables' in Kemptown village.

Well, we were distraught. I mean, what with the fear of Dutch Elm disease and Postman's Knock, which are both going around at the moment, we called in a Gyknockologist straight away. He took a look through our letterbox and – apart from telling the old gyknockological joke about needing to redecorate the hall – he said there was a good chance we might shortly be taking delivery of a parcel. Well, that sealed it. We had a furious row with our front door during which she gave us some rubbish about French letters and the postman's forced entry. Her arguments fell flat when we discovered a large battery-powered, vibrating, rubber latch-key called 'The Juggernaut', an inflatable 'Male Yale' and a pair of skimpy lace draught-excluders disguised as a fluffy snake.

These horrific discoveries are every door-owner's nightmare, and it was at this point that we realised just how bad things had become. It was time to get tough. She shrieked and begged us not to get a porch. Anything but that. She accepted that she had let us down and that the whole incident was a stain upon her woodwork, but said she loved her postman and that nothing we could do would change that.

'Love him?' we said incredulously. 'Can't you see he's just junk male? We're getting a porch, and that's that.'

The next morning there was a ladder up to front door's bedroom window and she was not in her bed when we took her up a morning cup of Cuprinol. She and the postman had eloped.

FROTTAGE

We hired a private Timber Merchant, and he did what he could. He discovered that the postman had escaped from a 'home-for-people-who-like-doors-too-much' in Northamptonshire and that he should never have been allowed to become a postman in the first place. He had also heard that our door and her postman were living on a caravan site in North Wales, and that she too was now beyond restoration. She was 'doing parcels' every day, and getting right up the drive on second-class registereds.

So there you are. The postman wins again, and we have lived in a broken-hearted (and draughty) world since then. We haven't received any letters since March because we're too traumatised to get another letterbox.

That's why we didn't receive the summons, Your Honour, and concludes the evidence for the defence.'

So be warned. Learn the lessons of this story. Tell the truth, don't do drugs, and get a porch. You know it makes sense.

Chapter 11

THE ELECTRIC HAMMER

The treacherous nature of electric hammers. The unexpected existence of windy hammers.

FOLLOWING THE GRAND Cranking Competition, the spirits of the majority were extremely high. The company seemed pleased to have wrought wholesale embarrassment on the first-trippers, and the feeling of a job well done in traumatising young men for life was abundant. Even the few who were not directly in high spirits (i.e., the victims) were understandably keen to drown their sorrows, so the flow of beer (all paid for by the victims) and the fact that nobody had eaten much came together to produce a high-stepping evening of some note.

THE ELECTRIC HAMMER

All I remember is that by 7:30 things were going so well that many of those present were once again dropping their trousers (this time voluntarily and under bright lights). I have no recollection of anything after about 8:30 – actually, that's not quite true. I remember, as I fell back on to my bunk at about two in the morning, that my pillow exploded around my head, and that everything became decidedly damp as a result; however, I am not a man who lets trivial matters stand between me and my beauty sleep, so I did not so much as turn a wet hair. The surprise was only enough to give me a faint memory of the event the next day, but I must not become sidetracked into a discussion on the causes and effects of exploding pillows. If you are intrigued by this, you may like to refer to a chapter in *Pacific Highway*, the sequel to this literary milestone, entitled 'Large William and the Nodders', in which your education is advanced to the tune of 'One Hundred and One Things To Do With a Condom, Six Litres of Water and a Pillowcase'.

In fact, what I said was completely untrue, because now I think about it, I have some decidedly hairy recollections of some of the things that were going on when Animals' Night was hotting up. Sparky was out cold on the floor, stark naked. He had a lighted cigarette stuck in his bottom and was having half his beard removed by four drunks. I would have confidently wagered that he was completely unconscious, but when the cigarette keeled over and the lighted end nestled gently into the back of his testicles he proved me wrong by leaving the room in something of a rush.

Two rubber dolls (Clarabel and Elvis) were suffering horrendous indecency and the entire bar was two inches deep in beer. Crate was trying to establish who had so carefully used one of his flip-flops as a toilet (a flip-flop now transformed to be well worth a space at the Tate Gallery), NotNorman and Benny the Dog were having a fight, wrestling violently on the carpet without anyone paying any attention to them, a deputation had returned from a thieving raid on the galley for some munchies, and Cranners was in the hospital attending to Blom who had 'Got some glass in his back playing darts'.

So it should come as no surprise to you to find out firstly, that my pillow exploded, and secondly, that the next morning the bar was found to be in what might euphemistically be referred to as 'a state of disrepair'. Mind you, weren't we all. I have no idea how anyone managed to get me up at six, or how I survived the deck-work until breakfast. I was still thoroughly drunk, let alone hungover, when I went up to the mate for the jobs after breakfast. (A job delegated to me by Blom who was too busy snoring in the rope store to do it himself.)

'Ah, morning Windy!' screamed the mate, delighting in my condition. 'Good night last night, was it? Someone tells me you lads were wanking in the bar while I was on watch. Tut, tut now. Surely not! Hardly the stuff of officer material, eh? Ha, ha, ha! Anyway, I hope you didn't drink too much 'cos I've got an important job for you. Seems there was a bit of a jolly-up in the bar after your performance. The crew have been in for the last two hours clearing up, but there's some structural damage that has to be fixed very carefully. Some of the rosewood panels and trim have come away from the bulkheads and they are very delicate. You lads can spend the morning fixing it all back up again, but BE VERY CAREFUL. See MegaWatt for the correct driver-nails and the electric hammer, and don't set it higher than torque level two. Those panels don't come cheap, OK?'

No, I was not OK, but I nodded in all the right places.

In the bar we stared through bloodshot eyes at the mess that remained even after the strenuous efforts of the crew to clean up.

'Wow!' exclaimed NotNorman, examining some damaged rosewood wall panelling and shaking his head. 'I'm surprised the ship stayed afloat through last night!'

And it certainly was a mess. This was hardly

surprising, however, because little did I know that a team of four men had spent the last hour painstakingly causing the apparent devastation in the bar – not clearing it up – and all for my benefit. They had taken down pictures, ripped off panels, torn down trimming and, just for good measure, completely dismantled the bar. The place looked like a family of bears had been fed a bucket of cocaine each, then given twenty minutes to find the honey.

'Where do we start?' implored Giewy.

I took charge. 'Right. What we need here are some specialist tools.' I rubbed my chin thoughtfully. I was not going to let on that I was just repeating the mate's instructions. 'NotNorman, you go to KiloWatt and get some driver-nails. Giewy, you go and wake Officer Blomstein – you're good at upsetting people – and I'll get the electric hammer. We'll meet back here asap.' And with the heady taste of leadership swelling my head, I set off for MegaWatt's cabin.

MegaWatt was the chief electrician and was a quiet, fairly unassuming Welshman. That was until he got a few beers inside him, when he turned into a loud, angry, aggressive and violently patriotic Welshman. As I knocked tentatively at his door, I knew that I was more likely to be waking the latter Welshman than the former, and I feared he would not appreciate being woken now.

'Cooee – MegaWatt?' I ventured round his door. 'You've slept in, you naughty lad. Ha, ha! Have you got the electric hammer?'

There were some grunts and mumbled swear words, then a growl like an engine starting. He roared through gritted teeth and launched out of bed straight for me with his fingers outstretched towards my throat. One of the things my family has always been good at is reading people's moods. I divined, in the split second it took him to motor across his cabin, that if he did intend to give me an electric hammer it would be in the form of an enema. I slammed the door on his fingers and legged it.

Shaken but unbowed, I decided to try KiloWatt, the

second electrician. He would be on the bottom plates of the engine-room on watch. I sighed and trudged round the accommodation and into the noisy, hot engine-room. I should mention here, for those who are not familiar with ships, that the engine-room is massive. It is fully six flights of stairs from the door to the bottom plates. It is rather like walking around a car engine, with the people equating roughly to the size of a spark plug. When something goes wrong, the engineers can climb inside the engine block and wander about looking for the problem. We are talking sizeable here. As you can imagine, such a beast generates a great deal of heat and noise, so the engine-room was the very last place I wanted to take the kind of hangover you could donate to medical science.

Having negotiated the metal steps to the bottom plates, I was disappointed to find that the electric hammer was not there. KiloWatt told me that SmallParcel had apparently taken it to carry out some essential work on the motor that hauls up the anchor. He could be found on the fo'c'sle head attending to that. I couldn't believe it; that was a mile away, and half of it was stairs! I trudged back up the six flights to the exit, round the back of the accommodation and flopped on to the foredeck for the long haul up to the fo'c'sle head. At least there was the benefit of some fresh air outside and the chance of a peaceful minute or two watching the world go by. It's always a pleasure to taste air that has not even seen land – let alone a car exhaust – and to soothe one's eyes on the passing sea and sky. I was particularly needful of their restorative qualities today because I was tiring fast, and my head felt as if every three seconds or so, someone was inflating a medicine ball inside my brain to a size roughly four times larger than my head, then popping it with a tent mallet. My skull was struggling to resist the pressure to burst like a smashed watermelon on each inflation.

Upon arrival at the fo'c'sle head I was greeted by the gargoyle-like countenance of SmallParcel, looking like the Ghost of the Confused Fo'c'sle Dead Man. He had been hideously drunk the previous night, and stoned out of what he laughingly called his mind, and I could see him struggling manfully with his brain to get it to tell him who I was and whether or not I was a feature of his reality or of real reality. He gave up the unequal struggle and smiled wanly at me. He was waiting to see if I had human attributes or if I was about to turn into a dragon. It was at this point that a well-delivered 'radish' or 'theodolite' would hit home beautifully, but I was short of time so I gave it a miss.

'Mornin' SmallParcel! You all right?' His ears turned towards me like satellite dishes as I spoke, then he threw his head around a bit and snorted, as if trying to get his brain around all those words spoken in one go. I always envisaged his brain as being like one of those children's games where you have to get the marbles to fall into the right holes before anything can happen. When he threw his head about, I could picture them all jumping around and falling back into a new configuration. He would try that one, and if he didn't get a result he would throw his head around some more. Anyway, no answer was forthcoming from this configuration, so I hit him with the biggy.

'Have you got the electric hammer up here?'

He shook a little as if someone had walked over his grave, then looked around his feet at the miscellany he had accrued. The winch was in bits, and lots of tools, cogs, bolts and cables were strewn around the fo'c'sle. He jumped as if he had no idea how all this electrical and mechanical instrumentation had materialised around him. Then he broke into a sweaty panic as he realised he had no idea what any of them was for. This would not do his career any good. How could he be an engineer if he didn't know the purpose of any of the tools? He tried to remember how he got the job in the first place and I could see him fading fast with the enormity of it all. It was not simply that he was drunk or hung over. Sure, he had got wasted last night, but he did that every night. The addition of some more people and some animal tomfoolery in the bar simply blended in with the friends and bizarre scenery his addled brain gave him as standard. No, it was the battle of interacting with other people that was hampering him. My case was especially tough because I'd asked two questions. He had them both stacked up over Luton, and I was beginning to wonder if he would ever be able to land one. Suddenly, he threw his head back and snorted again, as if he'd just received a carpet beater in the 'nads. He had remembered several things. Firstly, that he had clear and specific knowledge on the subject of electric hammers. Secondly, that he had qualified in Mechanical Engineering (Ordinary National Certificate) at Portsmouth Polytechnic in 1972, and thirdly, that eight out of ten cats preferred Whiskas.

'Errrrr...' he began. It sounded as if a little fan had started up in the back of his head somewhere, but there were signs of better things to come, so I nodded encouragingly. 'Errrr... the errr... yeah.' The fan stopped. We were back where we started. His mouth was still open, but sweet words did not fill the air. Then he got it again. 'Errr, electric hammer, you know? It's, like, Not Here. We're talking... somewhere else. Right? Not here.' He nodded vigorously to try and coerce me into agreeing. 'I found something out,' he continued with an air of collusion, 'from a statistical analysis of engineers who own cats, they found that eight out of ten cats that expressed a preference preferred Portsmouth Polytechnic. Chiefy's got the hammer – he's on the boiler flat.'

He spun round to see who had said the last bit. He had no idea it was him. I turned and left him to it. In my condition I could not face quizzing him on felines in further education. Another time, maybe. As I walked away, he was shouting with heartfelt passion to an empty sky, 'Why, WHY oh, why are there no LEAVES on this ship?' He seemed close to tears. 'What are they trying to DO to us?'

I didn't worry about him. I knew that as soon as the ship rolled back the other way, the marbles would all roll into different holes, he would forget the lack of foliage and be happy again. I was more concerned about my personal plight. The boiler flat? I was already getting sore feet and – Jesus my head – and the boiler flat was way, way up in the funnel. I was also aware that by now the guys would be waiting for me back at the bar, so I picked up the pace and battled on.

Getting to the boiler flat was another major distance, primarily involving steep stairs upwards. When I got there I was doubled over and wheezing from the exertion. I was in no condition for all this exercise. The chief engineer stared at me with some concern as I put my hands on my knees and stared at the floor, striving to force the correct words out between my wheezes. I had a feeling he wouldn't simply give me an electric hammer, and I was right. He had used it, and last he knew Jinx had it on the poop deck.

I stumbled down the companionways from the boiler flat, crawled the length of the afterdeck and dragged my half-dead body up on to the poop, only to be told by Jinx that Benny the Dog had it, and that he was on watch in the engine-room.

And so we went on. Benny told me that The Famous Dick Wrigley had just that moment been using it on the bridge, who, it transpired, had given it to Crate who was working on the propeller-shaft. That was back down into the engine-room, down to the bottom plates and out along the shaft tunnel to the very farthest end where the shaft exits the ship to join what remained of the propeller. What remained of me was told by Crate that Skippy had the electric hammer working on the bilge pump at the bottom of hatch number one, right up near the foc's'le then down a fifty-foot ladder to the deck of the hold. And so it went on. Everyone I spoke to had just that very moment passed it on to someone else who always seemed to be at the furthest imaginable point on the ship from the point I was presently occupying. Incredibly bad luck.

Had I the mental capacity to analyse what was happening, I might have wondered if perhaps these cheeky chappies were not being quite as co-operative as they might have been, but a combination of hangover, nausea, and the convincing line in patter of each of the people I had to visit kept me from suspecting that this might all be a merry jape. As it was, I never believed for one moment that the hammer did not exist, which was just as well, really, because it did indeed exist. The only problem was that I was still a long way from getting my hands on it.

Skippy sent me to Sparky up in his 'shack' near the bridge, who sent me to Cranners in the number five 'tween-deck down aft, who sent me to the fo'c'sle rope store, and so on until I had visited everybody on the ship apart from the captain himself. Each person I visited duly sent me somewhere else, then unbeknown to me, went to the bar, where they met up with all the others and tracked my progress. Finally I arrived at the captain's day room, gasping like Chitty Chitty Bang Bang on a cold morning and coughing enough to throw up my legs.

'Good Lord!' he exclaimed. 'Cough it up, there Baboulene; it might be a lung! How can I help you – apart from cardiac massage?'

'The electric... the electric...' I put my hands on my knees and waved at the captain to indicate that I would be with him shortly. Luckily he came to my rescue.

'The electric hammer? Certainly! It's in the top drawer of that desk. Bring it back when you've finished with it – I'm going to have it framed!' And with that, he left the room and headed off to the bar.

I was too weak to be puzzled by his last remark, and too overwhelmed with relief to care what he had said. I had finally got my hands on the bloody thing! I opened the drawer as if I was waking a princess, and there was my jewel, as large as life. I held it up and it shone out like a visitation of angels. To me this was not a power tool; this was the Holy Grail. It was of no consequence that I was reverently holding aloft a perfectly ordinary two-pound hammer with a bit of wire stuck in the back and a three-pin plug on the end. To me, my life's work was over. My quest complete. Simply to behold the electric hammer meant I could die a happy man. With the renewed energy of a mission completed, I headed off for the bar with my prize.

As I opened the door I was about to start talking to the other cadets about what a business I had had trying to find the thing when I suddenly became unaware of which planet I was on, what my name was or how I fitted into the scheme of things. I still remember that feeling every time I see one of the thousand photographs taken at that instant. I see my dumbfounded face registering innocence, ignorance and shock in equal measure. I see the hammer in one hand (PROVING innocence and ignorance) and the pointless plug in the other, just to rub it in.

The delighted chant went up for me to buy the breakfast beers. I had been caught out again. Then MegaWatt hushed the gathered throng and asked me to explain exactly what I thought would happen were the electric hammer plugged in. He took it from me and plugged it in to the wall socket. Then to roars of approval he threw the switch. The hammer flashed up and down, beating the life out of thousands of unseen nails. MegaWatt, his face gripped by fear, held tightly with both hands as the hammer gradually took over his whole body. First his arm, then his head, and soon he was entirely possessed by the manic motion of the electric hammer. He unplugged it just in time and managed to survive the experience.

Which was more than I did. From that day to this, whenever I bump into a member of that ship (or one of the many more who have heard the tale) they pretend to be in the merciless grip of a hyperactive electric hammer, and begin hammering away uncontrollably, shouting, 'TURN IT OFF! PLEAASE!! TURN IT OFF!' Dreadfully boring it is, and juvenile in the extreme.

For years afterwards I tried to get other first-trippers to nip off and get the electric hammer, and not one of them has ever fallen for it. Irrespective of whatever greatness I achieve in life – be it musical superstardom, literary genius, sexual infamy, academic excellence – I am afraid I shall go down in history as 'that donkey who fell for the electric hammer routine.'

The issue came up again about a week later. Giewy was in the doghouse for something or other – being astoundingly ugly while on duty or something – and Harry Tate said to him that as a punishment he couldn't have his timetabled, cushy study afternoon. Instead, he was to collect himself a 'windy hammer' and help the crew who were chipping and painting the foredeck. Giewy furrowed his brow and pushed out his lower jaw. He had never heard of a 'windy hammer' in all his months of experience, and wasn't going to be fooled, and he told the mate so. This led to the inevitable transfer of information and abuse (from close range and with a three-part chorus of tasty saliva) about how the windy hammer was an air-powered, triple-headed power-tool, used in the removal of surface rust and scale from metalwork. It was very noisy, highly unpleasant, and could be obtained from the serang immediately, if not sooner, and was equally effective on recalcitrant cadets' genitals. Giewy's nerve held. He knew the mate would respect him if he stood his ground and avoided the trap.

'Righto,' said Giewy, winking at the mate. He crinkled his nose and added, 'No problem.' Then he patted him on the shoulder, tweaked the mate's cheek and walked happily from the bridge, chuckling with self-satisfaction. The mate was too stunned to do anything about it. In twenty years at sea nobody had ever tweaked his cheek. Giewy cheerfully ignored the orders and settled down on his bunk for his study afternoon. I'm sure you don't need me to tell you that it was not very long before Giewy was lifted bodily from his repose, pinned up against the wall, and requested to explain why he was not in extreme discomfort at the business end of a windy hammer. Giewy also needs no reminding that a windy hammer is indeed a triple-headed pneumatic device for chipping decks. He also knows they are especially unpleasant when employed on bulkheads in the cramped and sweaty confines of the after-peak (another tank, but with no elbow-room) and anchor

THE ELECTRIC HAMMER

locker, and that to make the chipping and painting of such areas your very own responsibility, all you need to do is wink at the mate, pat him on the shoulder and tweak his cheek when he asks you to do something. Simple.

Chapter 12

BRIDGE WATCH

Deep wonderment on a tropical bridge watch.

AFTER ALL THE fun and games of the previous few weeks, it was a great contrast – and something of a relief – to find myself away from the bustle of daily deck work and on the midnight-to-four bridge watch. This is the second officer's watch, and despite the unsociable hours is arguably the most pleasant of the three watches. The twelve-to-four afternoon session is busy and alive, with sun-sights to complete, people coming and going and plenty of business to get through. Then, at the other end of the clock, the midnight-to-four stint is dark and quiet as the ship sleeps, and there is little to do at sea but think deep thoughts and chat deep chat.

BRIDGE WATCH

There is no better time or place to contemplate life than leaning on the bridge wing at 2:00 a.m. in the balmy equatorial Pacific. Without an artificial light for a thousand miles, a million stars twinkle their secrets to you as few men have seen them. The warm breeze strokes your face, and the easy motion of the ship rocks you into a most pleasant mood of happy reflection. The haunting, mysterious darkness of the deepest of all seas contrasts brilliantly with the sparkling iridescence of the moon reflected in the bow wave. Way down aft, a crewman is hunched over the light from his stove, and above him hangs the reassuring presence of a great albatross. This is the time to take stock, to talk in hushed, sincere tones of the meaning of life, and to see it not as a tragedy, but as a miracle and a privilege.

Never have I found a more wondrous place than this. I would recommend to anyone and everyone that they do whatever they must to experience these circumstances at least once in life. It is the eighth wonder of the world, but it cannot be seen or touched. It is a feeling. An aura. A sensation.

I leant on the bridge wing and placed my chin on my arms. I stared out at the stars as they rocked to and fro, and sighed happily. From here I could laugh at the practical jokes and the hard work. And with a week of the midnight-to-four lying ahead of me, and Sydney, Australia – a place I had been burning to visit – sitting just over the horizon after that, the old Merchant Navy began to look as though it wasn't such a bad idea after all.

Chapter 13

HARBOURING GRUDGES

Australia runs off and hides. Argumentative pilots in Sydney. Egg on the face? Lady Luck has a flannel.

ON THE AFTERNOON that we finally arrived on the Australian coast, I was lucky enough not only to be on the bridge, but also to see, first-hand, a stretched and decidedly nervous navigation team at work. The previous day's noon sun-sights had not worked out because of bad weather, nor had the mate's star sights, so our last reliable position had been more than twenty-four hours earlier. In these circumstances, with the ship known to be heading towards a great continent and a cunningly concealed shelf of underwater reefs, the navigating officers understandably tend to become edgy.

HARBOURING GRUDGES

The estimated position put us fifteen miles off the coast. If we were a few miles north of our actual position, we would be about to run onto the reef. A few miles south would give us a similar fate, so tension was high as we played hide-and-seek with Australia. It was still raining and visibility was poor, so two seacunnies, Cranners, the captain, and I were all scouring the veiled horizon, anxiously searching for the first signs of land.

To be honest, I had no real idea what to do, but I had learned that the way to handle these circumstances was to fix a severe expression on my face and march about purposefully as if greatly troubled by the gravity of the situation. In fact, I was greatly excited by the gravity of the situation, but I adopted the acceptable pose and joined the circuit shifting from chart table to bridge wing to radar – shaking my head and tutting at the lack of information – to depth-sounder, to binoculars and back for any clue as to our precise position.

The radar had not been giving us too much information because it was picking up rain, clouds and wave-tops (known as 'clutter') ahead of all else, so no land could be distinguished. I had still been spending a lot of time staring into it because I liked to fiddle with the knobs and watch the pretty green line swing round and round. I was thus engaged when I twiddled the wrong button; the clutter disappeared, and there, clear as a bell, was a headland. I reported my find with due composure (although with hindsight I might perhaps have missed out the 'Geddin, you beaut-eeeee!'). And sure enough, once they had all had a look, relief abounded amongst the cognoscenti as they agreed it was indeed Australia.

Now the circuit shifted to a trot between the radar and the chart to try and match the landfall with a known piece of Australia. Within five minutes another headland blinked shyly into view, and the captain and Cranners needed only a few seconds poring over the chart table before agreeing our position. The headlands were the North and South Heads at the entrance to the Sydney

Harbour itself, and they congratulated each other on a marvellous piece of navigation. To set a course from a position thirty hours previously, taking into account wind and current, and hit the target smack on the nose takes some doing (or so the captain told me) and the old man was not just relieved, he was full of himself. You could see him thinking that the old instinct was still there, that he had done us all a great favour by helping make those key decisions at nine that morning when sun-sights had looked like a washout. He picked up the radiotelephone and spoke with the kind of voice Churchill used to announce victory in Europe.

'Sydney pilots, Sydney pilots, this is the British merchant vessel *Global Wanderer*, over.'

I could imagine the pilots looking at each other and saying, 'Oh Jesus, listen to this Pommie jerk!' before they replied formally – or at least as formally as Australians get – 'Yeah, go ahead, mate. Tell us all your stories.'

The captain took the instrument from the side of his head and looked at it as if it had just run its tongue round the inside of his ear. This was not correct radio protocol, but he batted on regardless.

'Ah good, Sydney pilots, Yes. We have a landfall of two-niner decimal seven, two-niner decimal seven miles east of the South Head and can give you an ETA between the heads of eighteen hundred hours. Is this acceptable to you, over?'

Another gap, then the correspondent came back with the sound of restrained giggles in the background. He sounded as if he was speaking from the centre of a particularly serious drinking session. I imagined the pilots all crashed out drunk on a wharf somewhere.

'Is it acceptable to me? Y'know, I reckon we could fit you in there, mate. See ya later.' And the radio went dead. The captain was extremely unhappy and called them straight back.

'Sydney pilots, Sydney pilots, this is the British merchant vessel *Global Wanderer*, over.' He stood tapping his foot and fuming as they left the customary pause before answering. Then a bored voice came back.

'Yeah mate. Can we do something else for you?'

'You certainly can! Firstly, I am NOT your 'mate', and secondly, you can start using proper radiotelephony protocol in your communications! Really! We didn't invent all these rules and regulations just for you damned colonials to ignore. They may not make a lot of sense to someone of your intellect, but there is a purpose to each and every one, and if you do not begin to employ them forthwith I shall be visiting your superiors as a priority upon my disembarkation. Do I make myself clear?'

I was embarrassed by the captain's outburst, and from what I had heard of Australians thought it would be best to try and be friendly, so I was surprised when he did not receive a stream of abuse back from the other end. In fact, quite the reverse.

'Er, yeah, sorry about that, Captain. Yeah. Er, rendezvous at the agreed location to collect your pilot at eighteen hundred hours. Roger and out.'

The captain snorted as he replaced his receiver and stalked out on to the bridge wing, muttering something about forefathers and the last bastions of western civilisation.

We were about ten minutes early arriving between the heads, so were not surprised that the pilot vessel was not there yet. However, when six o'clock came and went and we couldn't even pick it up within five miles on the radar, the captain began to think they were deliberately messing him about.

'Sydney pilots, Sydney pilots, this is the British merchant vessel *Global Wanderer*, over.'

'Oh, er, roger, Captain. We can't seem to find you. Are you er... having trouble with your position there, eh? Er, over.'

The captain flew into a rage. He snatched up the

instrument and began working it over. 'I have been at sea for over thirty years, both man and boy. I was working with no navigational aids except for a lead-line, a brain and a pair of eyes before you were out of nappies, and I do NOT expect to be treated with anything less than the respect I deserve. WE are in position between the heads awaiting a pilot, and you are nowhere to be seen. I will be on to the Admiralty and you will be struck off before you can draw breath if I don't get a pilot within the next half hour. DO I MAKE MYSELF CLEAR? OVER!' He breathed in for the first time and puffed his chest out like a rooster. Then a new voice came over the radio.

'Good evening, Captain. This is your pilot here. Listen, I've spent TWENTY years piloting these waters. You are NOT where you are supposed to be. We are precisely between the heads, bearings one-nine-two and zero-zero-four, and you are not here. Over.'

Cranners nipped over to the radar and took the bearings, then ran them up on the chart. 'We're in the same place as they say they are,' he said, shrugging his shoulders.

'They are NOT going to get away with this,' said the captain, boiling across to the radio. 'Sydney pilots, THIS is the British merchant vessel *Global Wanderer*, over.'

'Go ahead, Captain, over.' The captain drew himself up to his full height and pursed his lips.

'Now you listen to me. You people had better get your act together pretty damn quick-smart or there will be trouble. I am a reasonable man, and I accepted your apology for letting your standards drop. However, your subsequent behaviour has been abominable. You clearly lack suitable leadership and I refuse to become the butt of your mindless retribution just because I am man enough to point out your failings. You have pushed me just about as far as I am prepared to go, and unless I get some co-operation from you IMMEDIATELY, I am getting straight on to the...'

'Captain!' I called. 'Red light on the port beam!'

'. . . bloody insulted in all my... sorry?' He put down the radio. 'Red light, you say?'

HARBOURING GRUDGES

'Yes, Sir! Flashing red three every ten seconds.'

'Ah, good lad. Let's get a precise position, then two-oh. Then we can sink these scallywags once and for all.' Cranners was poring over the chart table, but no position was springing happily from his lips. In fact, he looked decidedly pale.

'Well come on then, two-oh. You can work a pair of dividers, can't you?'

'Er, yes, Captain. Flashing red three in ten, was it?' Cranners knew how the light felt – he too was flashing red three in every ten seconds.

'Yes yes, that's it. That must be the light on the headland.'

'Well, yes, Captain, but not the headland you're thinking of. We are not between the North and South Heads of Sydney Harbour, sir. We appear to be between a different set of heads, around twenty-five miles south of Sydney Heads, sir.'

The captain's eyes bulged out like boiled eggs, a klaxon sounded from the back of his mouth and his knees clacked together like an alarm clock going off.

'WHAT?' he cried, stupefied. 'You – you mean we are sailing gaily around some of the most dangerous reefs in the world without knowing where we are to the nearest... twenty-five miles?'

He had hit the nail on the head. That was exactly what we were doing. We had mistaken these heads for Sydney's heads and were talking on the radio to Sydney pilots, who were twenty-five miles away. It was nothing short of a miracle that we had not run aground on the reef and sunk the ship in shark-infested waters. The enormity of our mistake – and our escape – hung heavy in the air. Nobody spoke for some time and Cranners self-consciously changed the charts around for the ones we needed now.

Suddenly the radio crackled into life. '*Global Wanderer, Global Wanderer*, this is Sydney pilots. Come in, over.'

The captain had gone white. He made no move to answer them.

'Good God,' he said, falling into the pilot's chair and wiping his brow. He was shaking visibly. 'I... I... could have lost... lost the ship – maybe some crew. I could have killed everybody! Get me a glass of water, cadet. My lord, what a thing.'

'*Global Wanderer, Global Wanderer*, this is Sydney pilots. Come in, over.'

The captain looked mournfully at the radio.

'Whatever am I going to tell them? My career will be in tatters once they get blabbing. This will be in the papers tomorrow. Tell them I'm unavailable two-oh. I can't face them just now – but don't tell them anything! I have to think.'

Cranners walked silently to the radio and picked it up. He did not know what he was going to say.

'Sydney pilots, this is *Global Wanderer*. Go ahead, over.'

'Ah, good evening, *Global Wanderer*. This is Captain Mollineaux here. I gather you've been having a few problems tonight, over?'

'Ah,' said Cranners. What could he say? He gulped and was about to say something vague in order to play for time, when Captain Mollineaux came back.

'Yeah, well, I'm real sorry about what you've been put through tonight. I don't know how to tell you this, but I've just turned up for my shift, and the blokes here are all drunk. They had a big win on the horses earlier on, and they've been, er... celebrating. I don't know how to apologise, and I'm sure you must be raging out there, but what can I tell you? The guys are all lying around here – they say they came out there but couldn't find you.'

We stared at each other dumbfounded while the radio continued apologising. 'These things happen, eh? Ha ha. We were all boys once, eh Captain? So listen, I'll be coming on board tomorrow with an invitation for you to come back here to our offices and I'll help you with the formalities of your complaint, but until then I've pulled the pilot back in, so I'm going to have to ask you to put down an anchor, Captain, and wait until we can get a sober helmsmen to bring the pilot out to you. I know this is disgusting behaviour, but I don't see any other way round it.' I could hear the poor chap wringing his hands as he spoke.

Our captain, on the other hand, seemed to have found a whole new lease of life. He strode once more to the radio, a fully restored, belligerent old bastard. He picked up the radio, stuck his nose in the air, and spoke in clear, majestic tones.

'Sydney pilots, I shall give this matter my deepest consideration. What has happened tonight could well have had grave consequences, and you have been fortunate to get away without disastrous results. I shall expect a pilot here at oh-six-hundred hours, and I shall want to talk to you first thing when we come alongside. Over and out.' He then turned to Cranners. 'OK, two-oh. As far as I'm concerned, we have not yet arrived. Plot a course for Sydney and put the ship there as if nothing happened. In fact, as far as you are concerned, nothing DID happen this evening, OK?' He looked at me, then Cranners. 'Good,' he said. 'If anyone wants me, I shall be in bed.' And he left the bridge looking decidedly older than he did when he'd arrived.

I shrugged my shoulders at the second mate, who was looking a little bewildered. He went out on to the bridge wing and stared at the hulking shadow of the continent of Australia on the misty horizon. He spread his arms to the looming land mass and shouted into the vastness, 'Will the REAL Sydney Harbour please stand up!'

Chapter 14

THE WIZARD OF OZ

Australian workers don't work. The appropriate treatment of a gift horse. Windy gets a life in Sydney. Lessons in adjusting the sobriety of beautiful girls while maintaining the condition of one's shins. Meeting the parents.

AUSTRALIA IS A wonderful country. Let's have no doubt about it, it is a wonderful, wonderful country. I suppose one could argue that anybody who has been incarcerated on a fifties ship for thirty-six days with a bunch of animals would find any land relatively wonderful, but I hope to convince you that my love for the Lucky Country was based on more than the fact that it was somewhere other than the *Global Wanderer*.

It may also be argued that my view was tainted by our

having run out of fresh water. We had drinking water but were showering in seawater and, rather like the ship herself, we were all struggling to get up a good lather. So as we plodded across that famous natural harbour towards the Opera House and that great coat-hanger of a bridge – leaning on the tugs like a marathon runner being helped the last few yards to the finishing post and with a hundred colourful yachts dancing attendance like butterflies around a fragrant bush – we were more than just a little bit fragrant ourselves.

I suppose anywhere would have been a blessing, but we, by virtue of our broken propeller, were heading for a dry dock in one of the planet's high spots: Sydney, Australia. I got a rush just saying the words, but there was more good news to come.

The ship flopped into the Cockatoo Island dry dock as if it were a hospital bed. A long gangway made its incision from the shoreside on to the foredeck, a drip-feed of mains electricity was brought aboard, and the *Global Wanderer* had her generators switched off. She fell into silence for the first time in years. She was put to sleep for her operation, and it was just as well because I think she would have taken her own life had she seen the surgeons. Dozens of laughing, crude Australian workers came ambling on board, full of self-assurance and caustic wit. They were in charge now. *Global Wanderer* was our ship – we were there to provide the tender loving care – but now that she'd been placed on life support, our role was suspended. It was a strange feeling really. Like being possessed. I had invested a lot of time and effort in her wood and brass; we had been through a lot, and crossed half the world together, and here was a bunch of insensitive invaders making jokes at her expense because she was an old girl. I felt sad and impotent.

Whatever else they were, they set about their business with vigour, and by the next afternoon they had whipped the old propeller off. Happy estimates of a week in dry dock and a week alongside for cargo were bandied about as if there was no conceivable way things could go wrong. But they had not accounted for the good old Aussie unions.

We cadets were on the boat-deck end-for-ending the lifeboat wires and slagging the mate off for not allowing us the day off. We were spotted in our endeavours by a couple of Australian workers skiving off for a ciggie. They saw us at our labours and, to our utmost surprise, called an immediate strike. That was it. All out. Some someones were doing some work, and those someones were not Australian someones, so they all marched off the ship. Gone. Within minutes the place was like a morgue. This was at 9:30 on the Tuesday morning. The captain could not even find anybody to complain to; they had all disappeared. It was Wednesday before he managed to find out what the matter was and desperate negotiations with a committee of bolshy union representatives could begin.

Marooned in dry dock with no propeller is not a strong negotiating position, and after a spittle-laden diatribe on the subject of colonies, forefathers and the last bastions of western civilisation, the captain signed his name to the effect that if there was ANY work to be done, an Australian would do it. The captain headed for his cabin to lie down in a darkened room, the union man ambled off to the pub to bring the poor, injured workforce back, and the mate came up to the boat-deck shouting and screaming at us.

'Will you STOP WORKING!' he roared. 'STOP IT THIS MINUTE! And don't let me catch you bastards working AGAIN! You've caused enough bloody trouble as it is, so just KNOCK IT ON THE HEAD!'

His words did not quite sit right at first. We stared blankly at each other as he stomped off, then we shrugged our shoulders and began to pack up, discussing what sort of a practical joke this could be.

The union man didn't have too much luck getting the shore-wallahs back on board. They were deeply scarred by the rough treatment meted out to them, and, poor sensitive lads that they were, they didn't return until the Thursday, and then only with an air of great reluctance.

Their hearts just did not seem to be in it now that the trust was gone from our relationship.

They mooched about kicking stones and staring off into space, unable to thrive in this atmosphere of conflict and discord. The captain was at his wits' end. Every hour that passed was costing the company thousands of pounds, and there didn't seem to be anything he could do about it. The captain tried bribing someone, but he turned out to be a stoolie and news of the bribery spread like wildfire. Before you could say 'More than my job's worth, mate' the gangway was once more alive with departing workers. The captain, in a rare moment of inspiration, shouted to them that it was not a bribe, and that he was going to give everyone the same thing; it was a gesture of friendship, no less. They all turned round and marched back aboard again, forming a queue outside the captain's cabin and wasting another half-day collecting their 200 ciggies and a bottle of whisky each. Things were looking grim for the captain at this stage. He was steaming mad, but had to pretend that he was delighted to give these fine men their gifts. What he actually wanted to give them was a chainsaw in the stomach each, but he kept his face in a rigid smile.

Finally his patience was rewarded when one of them revealed to him what the problem was. It seemed these lads were sad because all their friends in the pub were out of work. They were ship painters and maintenance men and they had no work for the full duration of the *Global Wanderer*'s time in dry dock. The captain kept his fixed smile and spoke through clenched teeth, 'Well if you get on and swap the propeller over, then the next ship can get in and the poor wee petals will all have work again, won't they.'

The informant was not fazed by the captain's attitude. 'Tell you what, mate. I've got a better idea. The lads would be employed immediately if you were to ask them to chip and paint this ship, wouldn't they?'

The captain knew he shouldn't have sworn like that, and jumping up and down on the spot and throwing a tantrum is for children, not ships' captains, so he offered his sincerest apologies to the deputation that finally returned to the ship on the following Monday (Sunday being a religious celebration amongst propeller-swappers, who place a high value on their worship time) and agreed to have the entire ship painted. By the following Tuesday, there were five times as many Australians doing as much nothing as the original number managed in half the time. It was amazing.

The mate was so agitated he made a bit of a faux pas too. The day after we'd received the order to down tools ourselves we went up to the mate to ask what we should do. He hadn't thought about us and was under great pressure. Recently, everyone he had shouted at had stuck their noses in the air, grabbed their mates, and stalked off the ship in a huff. He welcomed the opportunity to shout at us because we couldn't follow suit. Unfortunately, he was not careful with his choice of words.

'WHAT CAN YOU DO? You can BUGGER OFF, that's what you can do! Do what you like. I don't give a shit. Just get out of my face – AND DON'T DO ANY WORK! I don't want to see ANY of you ugly bastards until... until...' he paused, huffing and puffing, and scrutinising his watch. 'Until December! Now BUGGER OFF!'

We buggered off to our cabins in disbelief. It was November the third. A meeting was hastily convened in Blom's cabin.

'Right,' said Blom. 'You heard the man, we've got to bugger off. He will greatly regret saying that when he next wants us for something, so we have to act fast. We have to pack some kit, get off the ship and not come back at any cost. We mustn't sleep in our bunks or drop by for meals. Nothing. We must leave the ship now and stay away for the next twenty-seven days. Meet here fully packed in ten minutes. We have to sneak off together. GO!'

This was incredible. We trotted round the alleyway to our cabins all chatting at once. We packed a backpack each, and ten minutes later we were back in Blom's cabin. Blom had bribed Ahmed to trace the whereabouts of the mate so we could nip off unseen, and as soon as we got the signal we went over the side like the SAS and off into the city as quickly as we could. As we left we could see the mate high on the fo'c'sle shouting at some people. Soon we were disappearing into the anonymity of Sydney's happy throng for the holiday of a lifetime.

I knew it was called the Lucky Country, but I didn't realise that the luck was all mine. I looked around at the bustling city and my heart flew high in my mouth. I got that pit-of-the-stomach sensation you get when something exciting is about to happen. I didn't know exactly what was going to happen, but that was what was so exciting. I didn't even know where I would be sleeping that night. For twenty-seven glorious days – and nights – we were out of the mate's grasp, on full wages, and totally free.

So what do you do when you unexpectedly find yourself young, free, single, randy, rich and at large in the most vibrant paradise on earth? Add to that brim-full of self-confidence and very, very determined not to go back to the ship, and you have yourself a Windy Baboulene, all revved up with all sorts of places to go.

By lunchtime the four of us were eating happily on Manly Beach without a care in the world. It was indeed paradise. I felt so adult. I was completely in charge of my own destiny. Nobody knew where I was. Nobody would be telling me where to go or what to do and even I did not know what was going to happen next. All I did know was that it would be my choice. It was the most deliciously exciting feeling, and I could make all the hairs on the back of my neck stand up just by thinking about it.

However, as the afternoon wore on, it became evident that my optimism and excitement were not entirely shared by all. There was concern over such mundane issues as where we were going to sleep, what we would do and what might go wrong. I was at once disgusted and amazed at their lack of adventurous spirit. I was not remotely interested in sleeping, was fizzing with life because I didn't know what was going to happen, and knew precisely what we should do.

'We find the local groo-oo-oovy kids and PAARRRTTEEE!' I enthused, pushing home the idea. 'If you haven't got laid by the time everyone else has, you sleep here on the beach. Loads of people stay here all night, eating and drinking and dancing and smoking and licking each other. No problem!'

NotNorman was happy with this, but a distinct uncertainty radiated from the more twitchy Giew. NotNorman and I went through the entire 'You-only-live-once-seize-the-day-climb-every-mountain-live-life-to-the-full' routine, but Giewy decided Sydney was boring and that it was high time we were getting back to the ship. He said he'd seen it all before, and that he wanted to get some work done rather than prat about with children like us. He set off back for the ship despite our gentle coaxings, our convincing line of argument and our very best chicken impersonations.

So, from left to right, Giewy was scared, Blom was off to visit his nan in Brisbane, I was covering my insecurity with blind enthusiasm, and NotNorman didn't need to be scared or excited because he'd met a girl a couple of nights before and was already sure of having stuff to do and somewhere to sleep. He'd organised to meet his new-found love in town, so, having agreed that we would meet at midnight in case either of us (i.e., me) needed help, he too headed off. By and by, they each went their own way and I was left alone.

There were dozens of people enjoying the day on the beach – in and out of the sea, buying drinks and ice-creams, playing around in the sand - but I was completely and utterly alone. A bevy of butterflies flitted around in my stomach. The world was my oyster and I was determined to make the most of it. I wandered among the people, revelling in my invisibility. Everything would be exactly like this even if I were not here. I was anonymous. I watched and shared.

Soon, if things went well, I would become involved with some people. I would be affecting their lives, changing the course of their evening. What they said and did would be different because I was there. I moved among them like a breeze, an unseen force. I felt I could have walked into people's houses or ridden in their cars without their noticing me. I caught a ferry back into downtown Sydney and watched as the city and its people moved from afternoon fun to the evening's more serious intentions.

As fortune had it, the third engineer on board was an Australian. His name was Clive Walker, although we'd rather predictably nicknamed him Skippy. He was born and raised in Sydney, and he told us that the place to be of a night was The Rocks. Things have changed a little in recent times, but then The Rocks was a bohemian quarter, lying between the Harbour Bridge and Circular Quay, and slightly off the beaten track for anyone who was not looking for it specifically. The Rocks was the unadvertised rendezvous for the young, trendy and musically adroit. This was a perfect description of me, so with the look of a man who knows what he wants out of life, I swaggered into Coolsville.

No one noticed me even now that I wanted them to. The area hardly seemed very lively, and I could feel myself deflating by the second as the dark buildings and closed doors pointedly excluded me. From Skippy's description I had expected a sort of street party to be rocking along. I fancied that hordes of young people – recognising me as a kindred spirit – would rush up, ask me how I was doing and gather me into their fun-lovin' gang. It wasn't like that. I could have found more life in a railway sandwich.

It was still only about nine o'clock, but I couldn't see any way this dull scene could ever explode into the hub of the universe. Then a door opened. Some people spilled into the street, and although they were not rushing up to welcome me personally, they were certainly young and good-looking, and the splash of light and the music that accompanied their departure indicated revelations within.

OCEAN BOULEVARD

As I stared at this door and listened to the music – trying to decide if I was brave enough to enter – another door opened further down and four or five more people moved into another splash of light with a rush of music. Now I was beginning to get it. I walked the length of the street and back. The venues were all renovated wharf and industrial buildings. They were old and imposing and the doors were faceless, but open almost any one and the chances were it would open onto a neon café or hi-fi bar full of groovy groovers grooving. Some bars were hidden upstairs, some were underground. Some were forbidding, with bouncers blocking the entrance and high-fashion poseurs peering disapprovingly down their noses at you, others were enticing because tremendous live rock music flew down and roared at you as the door opened.

As a rock connoisseur, I chose the bar with the best live music and headed for the door. (Actually it was the door through which five short skirts had just disappeared, but the music sounded OK too.) More deep excitement. More butterflies. Behind the door were steps leading downwards. The throbbing party increased in volume with every step. I reached the bottom to be greeted by just the scene I wanted: a cookin' rock band, beers flowing and hundreds of people dancing, chatting and laughing.

I found a seat at the bar from where I could survey the scene, drink copious quantities of hideous cold, fizzy lager, watch the crowd and listen to the music. I smiled winningly at a few passers-by, but nobody stopped to talk. I could see them trying to work out if they knew me from somewhere because of the way I was smiling at them like one of Santa's helpers, but I didn't mind that nobody stopped to talk. I was once more enjoying my private excitement. I was in no hurry. Besides, I had been in a band at home and I knew there was absolutely no chance of a worthwhile conversation while the guitars were letting rip, so I sat back and satisfied myself with watching the people and listening to the music.

After a while some order began to emerge from the

THE WIZARD OF OZ

chaos before me. I began to recognise where the cliques were, and who was with whom. There were some stunningly attractive girls around, but I wouldn't dare talk to them. They could kill me with a single dismissal, and besides, they were never alone, not for a second.

When the band took a break I looked around. All the people I wanted to talk to were gathered into seated groups. Impossible to break into without the strong possibility of extreme embarrassment. Perhaps things were not going to be so much fun after all.

It's strange how hard it is to talk to someone who is with other people, isn't it? The Americans are best at it. Anywhere you meet strangers in the US – on a train, at a bus stop, in a queue – they will talk to you. If the lift is going more than three floors, the chances are that you'll make a friend for life. In England, if a stranger talks to you at a bus stop, you begin to shift uncomfortably and look for a policeman. In the US, it's the person who won't talk to you who arouses suspicion.

So here I was, being English and reserved. I had visions of drinking myself into a stupor until they threw me out at sunrise, and crawling defeated back to the ship. Then it hit me. The band! Of course! It is socially acceptable – even in England – to talk to members of the band without a formal introduction, and once you know them, you're in the top tier. Most of the band had already headed into the adoring crowd to accept their adulation, but the bass player was replacing a string and was alone on the stage. Perfect! I was a bass player myself. I strode right up there.

'S'cuse me, mate, is that a Bernie Goodfellow bass?' I knew it was, but a GB Bass is an unusual, expensive and tremendous bass, so I reckoned on his having a lot to say about it. I smiled winningly for the four-hundredth time. He looked up, then jumped to his feet, threw his bass to the floor and started stomping towards me with his fists clenched.

'Will you FUCK OFF!' he shouted.

He was a big sod who clearly had no use for

159

Baboulenes. I assessed the situation and froze decisively to the spot. My whole body had turned into stone, I became incapable of taking evasive action even though I fully realised that the stage placed his boots close to my face-level, and I was about to get the inside of my skull beautifully lined with steel-toe-capped leather. It's one of those situations you rehearse in your bathroom: yob coming at you full-tilt, you roll with his punch, grab his arm, sling him over the bar and put your arm round the nearest frightened maidens ('Evening, Ladies'). Any of the things James Bond does without ruffling his shirt. Then you find yourself in precisely those circumstances, and all you can do is stand there spoiling a perfectly good set of underwear.

To my utmost relief, however, he pushed past me and stormed across to one of the tables. A bloke there was evidently chatting up his girlfriend, and he did not like it. In broad and clear Australian terms he informed the gentleman that: (a) The young lady did not wish to receive his overtures; (b) The young gentleman had been putting him off his bass-playing by pressing his suit during the first half, and he would appreciate any effort the chap could make in desisting during the second set; and last, but by no means least, (c) If he did not remove himself to another area of the country, he would be left with no alternative but to fillet his shins for him.

The low-life scuttled off to a dark corner to assimilate this information and to ensure his shins were kept safely out of the way. The bass player returned to the stage, this time grinning at me from ear to ear.

'It's relentless, mate. She gets that crap all the time.'

I was not surprised. She was, without any shadow of a doubt, one of the most beautiful girls I had ever laid eyes on, but I thought it prudent to perhaps keep my opinions to myself on this occasion. 'So, what were ya saying? You like the old axe, do ya?'

And with that we launched into a deep and meaningful discussion about pick-ups and string gauges, amps and effects, heroes and riffs. By the time Rip had to get back on to the stage we were male-bonding furiously. As he dressed himself with his bass and the band prepared to fire up again, he threw in just what I wanted to hear.

'Listen, mate. You doin' anything afterwards? We're having a bit of a jolly-up back at my place. You wanna come along?'

'Sure would,' I said. 'I'll help you load the gear up.'

'Tops, mate,' he replied, supplying me with a catchphrase I wouldn't shake off for years. Then he seemed to think for a moment. He got out from behind his guitar, knelt down by the stage and spoke quietly to me. 'Tell yer what, mate. You wouldn't do me a favour, would ya?'

'Just name it, old friend. Your wish and all that.'

'Yeah, right. Well it's my little sister there. If you wouldn't mind sitting with her, those other bastards'll lay off. Mum gets real mad with me if I leave her alone, 'cos she gets a bit wild with a couple of vodkas in her. I'd be dead grateful. What do you say?' I couldn't say anything at first. God may move in mysterious ways, but I never expected him to start a dating agency for me. 'Say, Lucy! Loose! This is a friend of mine, er... Windy. He's a Pom, and all that, but he's all right. Windy, this is 'Loose'. Windy, Loose, Loose, Windy.'

She was an absolute vision. And the vision was of a stockings commercial. She was tall and slim – probably only in her mid-teens – but with a certain surprising curviness easing out whenever she moved. Dangerous curves. There wasn't a man in the place who wasn't spending more time looking at her than at the band, and I had just been put in the chair beside her. I looked from her to the stage, where Rip was smiling at me as he put his bass back on, then back to her again.

'Er, I don't suppose,' I ventured innocently, 'I could get you a vodka, could I?'

Now life was beginning to look worthwhile. I was getting comfortably drunk and Loose matched each of my small beers with a large vodka. We chatted amiably and she laughed at my jokes. She really was very nice, and with a delightful weakness for vodka that I found utterly charming. Each vodka made my next joke twice as funny as the last. Soon enough her eyes were full of admiration and various parts of my anatomy were clamouring to be released into the open, anxious to be admired too. She believed all the garbage I was spouting, and even laughed at dreadful chat-up lines like 'You're eyes are like spanners – they tighten my nuts.' Not only was I on course for a damn good rogering, but at the hands of a beautiful girl rapidly approaching optimum drunkenness. And, as if things were not perfect enough already, we were going back to her place for a party. Her parents must be out... she must have a bedroom...

'Another vodka?' I asked, my voice cracking as the butterflies that had been resident in my stomach all day now flitted away in my underpants.

After the gig, I helped Rip clear away his bass gear and we loaded up the truck. It was still only midnight and The Rocks were still rolling as we pulled away in a convoy of 4x4s. The three of us sat in the front seat with Rip driving, me in the middle and Loose beside me. All the way home she made advances towards me, and it was as much as I could do to avoid reciprocating, but I kept getting twinges in my shins when I thought about what Rip might do with his filleting knife if I touched her, so I kept backing off. This only served to encourage Loose to redouble her efforts to excite me. Once again I found myself in a car with a rampant young lady desperate to help me lose some weight, and circumstances forcing me to sit on my hands.

Rip chatted away, and thanked me for looking after Loose. I said it was nothing, but he must have been the stupidest guy on earth not to notice that I couldn't keep my mind on the conversation or my eyes off his sister. He was also too polite to ask what was wrong with my voice.

We got to their house, high up on the north shore – and not a moment too soon as far as I was concerned. I was beginning to feel that to be put through a little shin-filleting would be a small price to pay for as much of a kiss as I could manage in the time it would take Rip to stop the car and set up his shin-filleting equipment. It was just as well nobody was interested in unloading gear, because I could only walk using a very restricted subset of my usual range of perambulatary powers. I desperately wanted to get Loose on her own, but had to be discreet because, well, my shins are two of my finest features, and I wanted to keep them that way.

Rip on the other hand, wanted beer. We wandered through the house to the back garden where the view across the bay to downtown Sydney was stunning. It was high summer, the breeze was balmy, the stars were a three-dimensional canopy that seemed to start with the spangled, twinkling lights of the city and work all the way up into distant galaxies. Good grief, it was perfect. Within a couple of moments beers were fizzing open, music was in the air and we were all chilling nicely. Soon the warm night and cool beers began to weave their spell. People were interested in talking to me, the new kid on the block who had nowhere to live, and I looked about as far away from a session with Loose as I was from frenching a horse.

She kept brushing past me, and I got the occasional tantalising glimpse of the creamy bronzed thighs that lay beyond her short skirt. I became conscious that something else was going on in the world and dragged my senses back from my trousers to my brain. Rip was talking to me and, for about the fortieth time, he had received no response as I sat open-mouthed and bewitched by his sister.

'Oi, Windy! Windy? Come on, mate, you're losing the plot here. Your brain's gone up the pictures, eh? Tell you what. Why don't you go through that room, up the little stairs at the back and into the diner. There's some beer in the cupboard, get us one each and stick another dozen in the Esky, will ya?'

I was pleased with the excuse to go. Even Rip, who seemed completely oblivious to what was going on right under his nose, was bound to notice sooner or later. 'Oh, and Loose,' he added, 'you go up there with him and give him one for Christ's sake, before the poor bastard cums in his pants. I knew the Pommies were reserved but you'll be all year if you wait for him to make a move!'

Uproarious laughter followed me as I walked across the living-room towards the diner. Of course they'd noticed! Good grief – how could they have failed to? I'd been sitting there all evening dribbling down my shirt. Fortunately, I didn't have time to dwell on the embarrassment of being the butt of the local humour, because no sooner was I into the diner than Loose was in after me. There was no lock – in fact there was no door, just a curtain pulled across – and I suppose we could have gone off to find a bedroom somewhere, but neither of us gave a fig. We tongue-wrestled one another to the floor and span around like two fish caught on the same line. Anyone peeping through the window would have thought a murder was going on, with suffocation the principle aim. It was frantic stuff. Clothes were torn and furniture was knocked over. Suddenly the rolling stopped. She sat on top of me, pinning my arms to the floor, her hungry eyes looking at me as if I was a plate of sausages. She kissed my lips, then my chin, then my neck. She tore my shirt aside and kissed my chest, then slowly moved down to my stomach, then kissed her way ever so slowly towards my navel. She undid my fly and licked her lips, then... the curtain whipped back. We both shot up and stared at the imposing figure standing there. It was a policeman. A huge policeman.

'Daddy!' exclaimed Loose. 'What are you doing here?'

It was a huge policeman who was Lucy's father.

I looked at the gun on his belt and prepared to die. He surveyed the debauched scene and shook his head slowly. My testicles, sensing they might be unfairly blamed for all this, withdrew to a position behind my Adam's apple. He began to walk towards the fridge and I had visions of him force-feeding it to me. Then the most extraordinary thing happened. A smile grew across his face, and instead of the roars and limb-tearing activities of an outraged father about to commit justifiable homicide for the honour of his youngest daughter, he addressed us in dry, humorous tones.

'You been on the vodkas again, Loose? Who'd have bloody daughters, eh?' He lifted a box from the fridge and held it up. 'Forgot me nosebag,' he said, and disappeared.

I breathed for the first time since he had appeared on the scene. Great laughter emanated from without. The boys had hugely enjoyed omitting to warn us of his approach. Good grief, this lot were worse than the bastards on the ship. But events had managed to dampen our ardour – cardiac arrest being somewhat unromantic – so we adjourned to the garden to grab a beer and to try and slow down our pulses.

We sat together with cold beers and laughed at the adventure of it all. We were young and rebellious. This was the kind of wacky event that happened to us dudes. I excused myself and went to the bathroom where I heaved a sigh of relief, splashed water on my face and tried to stop shaking. That was too close for comfort. No more sex for me. Beer is the thing. Beer and music. Sex is just not worth the aggravation.

Back outside I voiced this opinion to the lads and we sat around talking this point out. Apart from anything else, we agreed that we would all have been top session musicians were it not for the time and effort we wasted chasing girls. Any bloke who wants to make it in life should have his organ lopped off first. He'd be a millionaire within a year. A life without women suddenly made perfect sense.

Funny how these things work though, because before long I was looking at Lucy's lush pastures and quite fancying a private chat with her again. Strange thing really, because I couldn't so much as look at her a short while before, and now I couldn't for the life of me remember what the problem had been. Her dad was long gone and we knew that he didn't care anyway. Before you could say 'Who wants to be a millionaire anyway?' Loose and I were heading off for the diner once more.

Having checked the cupboards for members of the constabulary, we were soon at each other again like fighting dogs. This time I was domineering and masterful. I wanted no nonsense. Within seconds I was as naked as an Englishman gets (standing proudly in my watch and socks), and after a brief grapple her clothes were off and we were rolling around in demented lust once more. The moment of sweet surrender had arrived and I closed my eyes, prepared myself for heaven, and... the curtain whipped back. We both shot up and stared at the imposing figure standing there. It was a woman. A shocked and distraught woman.

'Mummy!' exclaimed Loose. 'What are you doing here?'

A shocked and distraught woman who was Lucy's mother.

'Oh my Goooooood!' I said, not wishing to be left out. At least she wasn't wearing a gun. But this time there was no wry smile. Quite the reverse. There was a fire of hatred burning in her eyes, a shaking, crooked pointing finger, and fury in her quivering voice.

'YOU evil, EVIL girl... I warned you! I WARNED you!' she growled. 'Well your day of reckoning is upon you. If Beelzebub is to have your soul, then now is his time. You must pay, wanton Jezebel! PAY!'

With that, she began to hurl things from the top of the dresser at her daughter. The air became thick with pictures, cutlery, vases and profanity. They were like some sort of flying game-show prizes – for a moment I thought I ought to memorise them all.

I was rather hoping she would fling me my underpants. The Old Campaigners were hanging on the corner of the dresser just handy for her admirable pitching arm, but she seemed to be giving preference to heavier objects. I weighed up my options and, being an astute sort of chap, deduced that the atmosphere was no longer conducive to an easy life and more importantly, that my chances of intercourse with young Loose had taken something of a knock, so while a continuous stream of household items wheeled and span around my head and smashed and crashed into the wall behind me, I occupied myself with hopping around on one foot trying to put my jeans on. It was every man for himself, so I abandoned my underpants to whatever hideous fate awaited them, left headfirst through the window, and accepted an invitation to join a departing vehicle full of retreating musicians.

I sat in the open back of the 4x4 as it bounced away from the house and watched two silhouettes inside fighting behind the curtains, framed by the clear night sky and the distant city skyline. My weeks of freedom in Sydney had begun.

Chapter 15

THE GRASS

An agreeable life. Giewy is a party-pooper. Windy begins a relationship. Windy begins another relationship. The bizarre world of drunken reprisals. Poachers and gamekeepers. The tables turn.

FOLLOWING MY RAPID exodus from Lucy's house, I stayed the night at the flat of the guitarist in the band. Steve lived alone and was the serious musician in the crowd so there were no girls in his life and I could crash on his sofa. Thus the die was cast for the next week or two. I went out with the band to their gigs and social events, woke late, spent all day on the beach, had a couple of great nights out with Loose, grew slovenly and unkempt, drank more than is generally accepted as polite, and settled snugly into a lifestyle which can only be commended. I can think of nothing which it does not have in its favour and can't understand why anybody in the world would live any other way. All I needed to do was find a way of jumping ship without the authorities cutting off my pay cheque and my goolies, and I would be set. So it was particularly nauseating when Grim Reality came swaggering back into my life.

We were playing soccer on the beach in the boiling sun. Everybody for a hundred miles in every direction was in beach gear, except Grim Reality. Grim Reality was walking towards us in black Oxford bags, (with a three-inch belt), stacked black and red shoes, a jumbo-collared nylon shirt (unbuttoned to the waist) and a face like a smashed crab. The soccer game fell apart as one by one, the footballers stopped to stare at this apparition.

'What in the name of sweet Jesus is that?' asked Steve.

I knew what it was, and it did not bode well.

'Hello Giewy,' I sighed. 'You cannot be here for any good reason.'

He was smiling in a weird, twitchy sort of way, as if he was trying to keep a family of live fish contained in his mouth against their will.

'Giew,' he said, predictably, 'a quick end to your games, Windy. Harry Tate says you gotta come back. There's work to do and he didn't mean you to bugger off all month. I'm to bring you back to the ship.'

He was so pleased with himself. I rolled my eyes to the heavens.

'Why did you go back to the ship? You knew this would happen if you did.' The idea of going back to the ship was repulsive enough, but the thought of doing what bloody Giewy told me to do was against everything I stood for. He waved his head around as if the wind had suddenly got up and smiled the weaselly smile of the school grass. The football had stopped completely now, and my new-found friends were gathering round to see what the trouble was. They had never seen a specimen like Giewy before and were curious to know what it was.

'Jeez, Windy, who's yer friend? Did he just crawl out of the sea?'

Giewy ignored them studiously. He was enjoying watching me squirm. He put his hand on his hip and gave me his ultimatum.

'You coming or what?' he smarmed. Rip noticed the spiteful edge to his voice.

'You all right here, Windy? Is this geek giving you strife?'

'Strife like you wouldn't believe, Rip. Listen, Giewy. See these boys, here? They are only out of the prison hospital for the day, and would take great pride in rearranging your face for you given the slightest provocation – wouldn't you, lads?' The boys duly pulled the wild, psychotic faces of a group of unstable men close to the edge. 'So you would be well advised to pretend you couldn't find me today. What you are going to do is be a good friend and tell Harry Tate that you think I went to Willigolonga to visit my dying grandmother, aren't you? You're going to pretend this meeting never happened. You never saw me today, did you? Now off you go, and do the right thing, there's a good lad.'

I could tell by the blank look on what passed for his face that the threat of violence was completely wasted on Giewy. Actual violence might penetrate to his decision-making processes, but I was being way too subtle. What he did manage to divine was that I didn't intend to go back to the ship.

'Ooooo! Are you ever gonna be in trouble when the mate hears about this!' He laughed through his nose and snorted like a pig.

'Listen Giewy, if the mate gets to hear about this, then I promise – absolutely PROMISE – that you will be caused physical and mental torture worth at least double that which you cause me, OK? That's a promise. Now get yourself a life and stop spoiling other people's.'

THE GRASS

'That's you done,' he said ignoring my remarks entirely, 'now I've got to find NotNorman.' And off he waddled, walking like a contraption that a mad professor might have built to wash the car. Talking to him was as pointless as talking to a plant. At least I knew he wouldn't be able to find NotNorman. I was due to meet him for lunch so I'd be able to warn him of the impending Giew.

Some thirty minutes later I was aboard the hydrofoil as it rounded the Opera House and pulled into Circular Quay. I love the different hydrofoils and ferries that buzz around Sydney. I looked at my fellow passengers with envy. This was their everyday bus, used to get across the harbour. They all seemed to find it normal enough, but I thought it was wonderful.

As we rounded the back of the Opera House, NotNorman waved happily from behind his drink as he awaited my arrival. There were tables and chairs on the peninsula behind the Opera House where tea and cakes were served, and from where it was possible to pass a happy hour or two looking out across that endlessly fascinating harbour. NotNorman was looking particularly pleased with himself, possibly because his left arm, adorned beautifully by his girlfriend, was now balanced rather perfectly by a second young lady beautifully adorning his right arm.

'Hi man!' he cheered as I rolled up. 'You've met Cindy...' I recognised her as the love of his life, '...this is her friend, Jackie.'

He wiggled his eyebrows up and down and hung out his tongue in a way I took to mean that she was my blind date. Normally, I would be way too cool to face a member of the opposite sex in broad daylight without the aid of alcohol, but having scored with a girl as beautiful as Lucy, I felt almost happy at the arrangement. Besides, she was smiling cheerfully and looked like the kind of girl whose parents live a long way away and don't wear guns or join in on those special romantic moments.

The four of us chatted away over lunch and three fundamental truths began to emerge. One was that as a

171

foursome, we could certainly have some fun together, two was that Cindy and NotNorman were utterly in love, and three was that although Lucy and I were kind-of-sort-of-maybe an item, I felt a strange and powerful compulsion to do sordid, filthy, despicably rude things with young Jackie.

We spent the afternoon at Taronga Zoo, and the evening watching another band. Then it was back to the flat the girls shared (and that NotNorman had adopted) in the classy suburb of Vaucluse. I saw NotNorman as a completely changed character. He was almost Norman. He had found the girl of his dreams and he didn't care who knew about it. As far as he was concerned macho values were ridiculous, and love and trust were the food and drink of a rich and happy life. And she was equally dippy about him. They were quite pathetic to watch. They didn't stop touching all day – it was as if they were joined at the hip – and they didn't stop touching all night because they were joined at the hip. They couldn't see past each other for the multitude of blue lovebirds flitting around their heads, and they could hardly hear anything for the violins playing everywhere they went. They didn't get a moment's sleep (as proven by the creaking bed all night) and yet were as fresh as daisies all day. They were running on pure love.

So my highly agreeable life was augmented by the occasional foursome, and the addition of Jackie to the daily roster of sexual bouts with Lucy. The only dog-ends in the beer glass of my life were the nagging irritation of Giewy tracking us on behalf of the mate, and the disgusting spectacle of watching NotNorman and Cindy licking each other. Jackie and I began to feel somewhat inadequate in the face of the Olympian standards being set by the competition, but we persevered admirably. So life was about perfect. I had a dozen activities to choose from every hour, and none of them could remotely be described as unpleasant.

One night, I met Skippy in town. Having grown up in

Sydney, he too was well pleased with the enforced sabbatical here. His parents lived on the river a few miles inland, in a superb house with a boat at the bottom of the garden. This was magic. Whizzing in to the city centre on a speedboat is something people in Huddersfield and Croydon rarely get to do, and it's quite a buzz.

Skippy and I found ourselves together late one night, roaring drunk and wandering the streets trying to get a cab. The drivers took one look at us staggering about and zoomed off, so we started walking. He told me that the mate knew I wasn't visiting my gran in Willigolonga, and suspected I was roaming the town and living it up at the company's expense. I told him that the mate would have been blissfully unaware of my antics were it not for that stoolie, Giew. Skippy – who also had painful experience of Giewy's smarmy ability to irritate – ever resourceful and with local knowledge, had a cunning plan.

'You wanna do him?' he asked, beaming with evil intent. I nodded emphatically. 'Right. Giewy drinks at Monty's Bar, just over Pyrmont Bridge. Everyone's a defect in there, so he feels at home. It'll be shutting pretty soon, and he'll be coming out, so let's go and steal a car.'

And with that he strode off, a man with a mission.

'Steal a CAR?' I cried, running to catch up with the striding Skippy. 'You have GOT to be joking!'

'No worries, mate. Don't panic. We are gonna borrow a car. Giewy is gonna steal a car.'

I expressed doubts that this subtle distinction would wash with the authorities. I could clearly picture us running fruitlessly in mid-air, subtle distinctions lost on the large policemen holding us up by our collars. Skippy cheerfully ignored me and I was none the wiser when we got back to his house where all was quiet. His parents were already asleep. We slid silently along the side of the house and in through the back door. I've always fancied myself as a burglar – one of those stylish, classy ones, dressed all in black who leaves a velvet glove and drives Inspector Grinder of the Yard mad by always keeping one step ahead – and it was a powerful feeling as we stole noiselessly through the house like shadows. I could definitely do well at this game. The newspapers would call me The Cat and women would feel a powerful thrill – a mixture of fear and excitement – anticipating that The Cat might visit their boudoir in the night and...

Once Skippy had helped me up and fetched me a plaster for the bump on my head (low beams and cat burglars don't mix), we found the car keys and ghosted through to the garage where we pushed his dad's Volvo estate out into the road. Once we were well clear of the house, Skippy started her up and we beetled back, drunk as proverbial skunks, towards the city centre.

At Monty's Bar, I confirmed Giewy's presence by pulling myself up at a window. He was indeed inside, so I crossed the road back to the car to find Skippy hot-wiring it.

'Aha!' I exclaimed. 'I geddit! Giewy's going to steal this car!'

'Well done, Bullet. You're on the case. Now, here's the technique. You drive up to Giewy as he's walking back to the ship and offer him a lift. You tell him it's my car, and that it has to go to the ship anyway. Then you say that you're too drunk to drive, and that he can keep the car and take it back for you if he drops you off at your bird's house first. While you're doing that, I'll call the police and tell 'em my car's been nicked by a sailor. They'll be waiting to pick Giewy up when he gets back to the docks on his own. See? Piece of cake. Giewy gets thrown in the chokey, and the police will want to know if I want to press charges against the bastard who stole my car. I get Giewy to promise us the world before I get him out. Pretty smart, eh?'

Now if there's one thing anyone who knows me will tell you, it's that if you want to expose the weaknesses in a plan, then I'm your man.

'If there's a hole in it, Windy will find it,' they'll tell you. 'It looks all right to us,' they'll shrug, 'but you'd better take it to Windy if you want to be really sure.'

THE GRASS

And I have to admit that this little scheme had all the makings of a rock solid, watertight, belt-and-braces, safe-as-houses, dead cert. Flawless is the word. A peach. And Giewy the victim. Perfect.

So with the project passing all stringent assessment tests with top marks, I enthused warmly and we moved swiftly on to phase two: swift and clinical implementation. I began to think that maybe I'd missed my vocation. Perhaps burglary was not my calling after all. A career in undercover work seemed more 'me'. As Giewy emerged from the pub, passers-by could have been forgiven for thinking he was being trailed by Dirty Harry. I let him stagger a hundred yards, then rolled up beside him in the car.

'Giewy, my old mate! D'you fancy a lift? I've got Skippy's car.'

'Giew!' he said, trying to focus events. 'Yeah, all right.'

This was like shelling peas.

'Great! Hop in this side. You can drive – I'm too drunk. Just drop me up the road here, then you can take the car back to the ship for Skippy.'

'No way, pal. You can fockin' drive. I'm too drunk to fockin' wark, sod alone drive.'

This was not in the plan.

'Oh for God's sake, Giewy! Why does everything have to be so difficult with you? I'm way drunker than you are, so just drive the bloody car.'

'Are you as buggery as drunker as what I am,' he dribbled, 'I'm – belch! – I'm well wrecked, me.'

We stood outside the open door of the car for some time with the conversation continuing in this vein. Now, many a lesser mortal might have crumbled along with the plan at this point, and it is at times like these that the possession of the quick-wittedness for which we Baboulenes are so renowned gives us the edge over our adversaries. Despite the tide running against me, I swiftly devised a contingency plan that would allow me to slide out of the driving seat, and for Giewy to drop himself in it.

The crux of the matter was that we needed to establish who was the more drunk, so I suggested a simple test. Now those of you who are following closely will recognise that I was not as drunk as Giewy, and will worry that I might lose any test to establish degrees of drunkenness. Fear not. I knew what I was doing. You see, the master stroke in my devious-but-simple plan was to deliberately fail all the tests, thereby appearing the more drunk, thus forcing Giewy to drive the car. Always one jump ahead, us Baboulenes, that's the secret.

So, to the utmost astonishment of the two policemen watching us from the shadows across the road, we started going cross-eyed trying to touch the ends of our respective noses with an outstretched finger. I convincingly poked myself in the eye, shrugged sadly and looked at Giewy. I was amazed at just how incompetent the bloke was. He missed his nose by a mile, insisted on a second attempt, and then missed again! He could hardly locate his whole head, let alone his nose. I wanted to locate his head with a baseball bat. We argued for a time, then decided the test had been inconclusive. We would try another one.

Across the road, the policemen were mystified. They had received news of a stolen car over the radio, and here it was, as large as life, with the thieves performing some sort of street-cabaret alongside it. They didn't want to move in and make an arrest until they'd seen us more obviously involved with the car, which presently seemed to be playing nothing more than a cameo role in the proceedings. They looked at each other and shrugged as we put our right hand by our respective right ears, balanced ten coins on our elbows, then attempted to catch them all with the same hand. I lunged at the coins, spreading them impressively across the road. I knew there must have been a couple of dollars on my elbow, but it would be worth losing the money to get this farce over with. I failed to catch any of them. I shook my head at Giewy.

'Sorry, mate. I'm too drunk for all this. You have a

go.'

He balanced ten coins on his elbow, and, with his mouth wide open and his tongue sticking out with concentration, watched helplessly as they fell sideways before he'd even tried to catch them. Most went down a drain, so we had to spend a minute or two crawling in the road and accosting passers-by to get ten more coins for Giewy to fail to balance on his elbow once more. He couldn't even manage the balancing bit, let alone the catching. He was utterly pathetic. Had he no co-ordination whatsoever? Soon he had lost all the coins, so I declared the test null and void, and we began arguing again. I was now ready for a straightforward fight, but with so much to gain from getting my way, I kept control and suggested one last test: who could do the longest handstand.

People walked around us on the pavement, and the car ticked over patiently as I made my attempt. Up I went, did a fine job of pretending I couldn't hold it, and collapsed in a heap. I insisted on a second attempt, but with a convincing cry, toppled sideways into the car. I shook my head sadly and passed the floor to Giewy.

Giewy took a couple of exaggerated breaths, then went for it. He had barely touched the pavement with his hands when he stacked his entire weight on to his face and concertinaed his body into the back of his head. This was accompanied by a totally unconvincing animal cry of 'Giew!', and the penny dropped. This cheating dog was not making any effort whatsoever to beat me at these tests! He was failing on purpose! Good grief! Was there no depth to which this scoundrel would not sink? What was the point in having these tests if he wasn't even going to make a proper attempt? I put my accusations squarely to him, and a raucous argument developed.

I was rolling up my sleeves and flexing my fingers as Giewy frantically explained that we were going about the thing all wrong. The answer was to do the same tests again, but giving the trophy to the demonstrably more sober of us. Whoever could do best at the tests would be deemed the winner, and the drunker of us, being the loser, would have to drive. This policy seemed perfect. A solution would certainly be achieved, and I knew I was more sober than Giewy, so the thing was as good as in the bag.

With a laughable improvement in co-ordination, Giewy touched the end of his nose with equal dexterity to me, so – being fresh out of loose change – we moved directly on to the handstands. The policemen in the shadows were treated to the spectacle of the two of us standing on our hands on the pavement beside a stolen car, arguing furiously. I knew I could stand on my hands for ages, but thought it a bit of a farce that Giewy, who had just a few minutes earlier collapsed like a house of cards, was standing on his hands arguing back at me. The bloke had no shame. I decided I would hit him. I padded across on my hands, then discovered the flaw. I was standing on the equipment I wanted to employ in punching. Giewy was equally ready for fisticuffs, but neither of us was prepared to lose the test by coming down before the other one, so, as passers-by passed by with question marks over their heads, we stood upside-down and back-to-back, with our heads arched round trying to look at each other, flailing our legs around in a scorpion-like effort at having a fight. The policemen decided that enough was enough, and moved in.

Two hours later, Giewy and I were woken in our cell by one of the screws (as we hardened crims call them).

'Wakey, wakey, boys. Got a visitor for you.'

In waltzed a beaming Skippy.

'Yip, these are the ones, Constable. Can I have a moment alone with them, please?'

The screw left and Giewy and I both started talking at once. I was wondering how Skippy was going to get me out and leave Giewy in.

'OK, boys. This is the deal. I have some disappointing news for you. I'm only here to pick up the car. Neither of you is getting out now.' Giewy and I what'ed and why'd in high-pitched voices. He calmed us once more. 'I'm sorry lads, but you have both been duped – by ME! I've put you inside, Windy, because the mate promised me six cases of beer if I could catch you. I put you inside, Giewy, because you're a complete wanker. I want you to use your time in here to think about how you might become a better person in life and find a way of resisting telling people's wives about their girlfriends. I left a note on the mate's door telling him there was a surprise awaiting him in the cells. He'll be here first thing in the morning to pick you both up.'

Skippy smiled the smile of a good night's work, rubbed his hands together, and got up, ready to leave. This was a disaster – and not just for me. There were two girls out there who needed my body, I had a starring role to play in a beach football match in a couple of hours' time, and I was working with the band that night. I had a life! The mate would be down to pick me up shortly, and if he got hold of me I'd be grounded for sure. This was catastrophic.

'Skippy,' I said urgently, 'I will give you TEN cases of beer to let me go. Tell the mate you couldn't find us. Tell him –'

'Sorry, Windy. Can't be done,' he replied, heading for the door. 'A deal's a deal and all that. Take comfort in the knowledge that if you ever do a deal with me, I won't do the dirty on you. See you back at the ship tomorrow!'

'You snake!' I called cuttingly. 'Filthy, miserable impostor!' I can be pretty direct when the need demands. Just then, two screws came back through the door and blocked Skippy's exit.

'Impostor, eh? Sounds about right to us,' said one to the other as they took Skippy by an elbow each and invited him to take a seat. 'We want a word with you. We've just had a phone call from another Clive Walker, claiming he is the owner of that Volvo, and that it has been stolen from him. Now you told us you are Clive Walker, and that the car belongs to you.'

'Ah,' said Skippy, smiling as ingratiatingly as he could. 'I can explain that. Ha, ha! Er... that Clive Walker is my father – we have the same name.'

'Right. So you are not the owner of the car?'

'Oh. Er, strictly speaking, no, I suppose not. But he's my dad! I may not be the owner, but I'm his representative. He would –'

'Oh, really? Then why, may I ask, does he seem to think it's been stolen?'

'Oh, well. I took it without his knowledge. No, that sounds worse than it really is. What I mean is –'

'And why did you hotwire it if you are his representative?'

'Ah. Well. What we were doing was er... Windy! Yes! Windy here. He knows what we were doing! We were just having a bit of fun, that's all! Ha, ha, ha! Explain to the officers what we were doing, Windy.'

He turned to me with the most imploring of faces. I looked honestly into the faces of the men in blue and shook my head slowly.

'I've never seen this man before in my life. He seems hell-bent on getting me and my friend here into trouble, and we never even touched his car. Ask the arresting officers. We were larking about on the pavement beside it.'

'That's right,' confirmed Giewy. 'We never even touched the fookin car. That bloke took it. He just told you so!'

This interpretation was born out by the arresting officers, and the screws were definitely tiring of Skippy.

'OK,' said screw A, 'time for some musical chairs.' And with that he unlocked the cell door and the incoming Skippy hung his head as he took over from us beaming pair of departing inmates.

'You lads can go,' said screw B. 'You may be a pair of tossers, but if that was against the law we'd be well fucked on space around here. You want a lift home?'

We accepted a lift, and much to Giewy's surprise, I

came back to the ship with him. No, I had not gone soft. I had a job to do before heading off to Jackie's house.

When he awoke, the mate found a note on his door. A handwriting expert could have told him that although it was signed by Skippy, it wasn't written by him. It said:

'Windy is in New Zealand visiting his cousins. He knows nothing of your desire for him to return to the ship. I suggest you call off the hunt. You'd better keep your beers.

Lots of love,

Skippy.'

Chapter 16

MEAT AND TWO VEG

Emotional departure from Sydney. Run for your wife! The stowaway. An evening with Big Phil. A narrow squeak.

AFTER THIRTY-TWO DAYS – and nights – I left Sydney with a tear of sadness in my eye, vowing to apply for Australian citizenship and immigrate to Sydney as soon as possible. I'd spent my last evening with Jackie a night earlier than the ship was due to depart. I'd lied to her, saying that it was going the next morning. The coast was then clear for Lucy to stay on the ship for our actual last night in Sydney, which I enjoyed happy in the knowledge that Jackie thought I was at sea by then. However, Jackie heard on the grapevine that the ship was in port another night, and thinking an overrun of cargo was causing the delay, she popped down to give me a nice surprise in the morning...

I was sleeping soundly in my cabin when there was a frantic knocking on the door. Loose and I sat up a-who-ing and a-what-ing, trying to get our bearings as Cookie Short stuck his head in.

'Windy! Quick! We need you urgently on the bridge!' He was winking and twitching like he had a toad in his pants.

'Are you all right, He who Lacks Bicuits?' I asked. 'What's the matter with you?'

'There's a problem with the, er, fitting-limitation squadron-linkage frig-monitor... valve... oil... persecutor.'

'Eh?'

'You know, the wobble-mayhem wop-lolly cat-winkler has gone again. The... oh, just come ON, you tosser!'

'Ah, right.' I looked at Loose, who looked baffled. 'Shan't be a mo'.'

I leapt out of bed and hopped out into the corridor on one leg with the other trying to find its way into a pair of shorts. It sounded quite urgent and important, and the poor chap clearly thought I could help, but to be honest, I didn't know exactly what a fitting-limitation frig wobble wop lolly thingy was. He grabbed me by the elbow and lifted me round the corridor as he gave me the news: 'Jackie's here! She's waiting at the gangway!'

'Jackie? Jeeeeez, no! Why do people always arrive when we have problems? We'll never get that... oil persecutor hibble thing fixed. Listen, Cookie. Do you mind sorting it out by yourself while I deal with Jackie? I don't want her to meet Lucy.'

He looked at me with exasperation. He needed my help and I hate to be tough on people, but I had problems of my own. He would just have to fix his wobble-mayhem without me on the bridge.

'And they say I'm not the full biscuit,' he sighed. 'OK, Windy, forget the doodah. We'll do it later. Let's take Jackie to the bar. I'll try to distract her while you tell Loose the boat is leaving and she has to go. Once Loose is off the ship, you're in the clear. Oh! Here's Jackie.'

I put on a big smile and opened my arms to her at the top of the gangway. 'Hiiiiii, Jackie! You cheeky thing, surprising me like that!'

'I heard that the ship was still around,' said Jackie, 'and you left a shirt at my house, so I thought I'd drop in on you for a quick goodbye shag, and if you do a good enough job I'll give you your shirt back.'

To be honest, I was looking forward to getting away from all this physical stuff for a week or two. Both Jackie and Loose liked to ensure they got their fair allocation of time and effort, and I wasn't sure I could muster yet another grand finale of the type worthy of winning a shirt. I decided to try to keep Cookie Short around me at all times as a chaperon.

We led Jackie round to the bar. NotNorman and the chief engineer were already in there. Notters was looking a little strange and the chief was reading a book. It was certainly an unusual atmosphere, particularly so early in the morning – there was usually nobody in the bar at this time of day – but we had a problem. The ship was due to leave in a couple of hours, and there were strict instructions that all 'friends' should have left the ship before midnight the previous night. The chief was not our boss, but he was top brass and would certainly not sit by while we broke the rules.

'Ah. Morning Chief! This is Jackie. She's, er, she's, er –'

'From the agents,' interrupted Cookie Short, 'she's here to... to clean the bar.'

'What?' said Jackie. 'Clean the – ?'

'There you go,' said Cookie, grabbing a cloth and some cleaning fluid from behind the bar and shoving them into her midriff. She was mortified, but the chief was looking at her over his book so she began to play along, cleaning the bar with the exaggerated acting skill of a cheap television commercial.

'Right,' I said, 'see you later,' and before Jackie could complain, Cookie Short and I made a run for the door. As soon as we opened it, our way was blocked by the imposing figure of the mate. He looked down at us as we cowered in the doorway. His suspicious nose smelt the heady pong of rat, and his lips twitched at the edges as he scoured the scene for information.

'Why are you lot all in the bar at this time of day, eh? What's going on, then?' He grabbed my shirt and began to lift me up. 'You bastards are up to someth – oops! S'cuse the language, Miss. Didn't see you there.' He smiled uncomfortably at Jackie. He wanted to set about us with his standard, undiluted brutality, but he didn't know who she was.

'Can't a bloke get ten minutes with a book?' said the chief spreading his arms to the heavens. 'I might as well go and sit in the road.'

'You're right,' said NotNorman getting up. 'C'mon everybody, let's leave the chief in peace. Off we go!' He headed for the door making ushering movements, but the mate wasn't budging, so there were now four of us in an awkward scrum, bunched in the doorway.

'I dunno what you bastards are up to,' said the mate through clenched teeth, 'but when I find out what's going on here, I'm gonna –'

'The captain's looking for you,' I said to the mate. 'I came here to find you and tell you. He's out on the foredeck. Says it's important.'

'Well, why didn't you look in my cabin, yer fool? What would I be doing in the bar at this time of day?'

'Exactly,' I said, 'but I did find you here, didn't I?'

The mate furrowed his brow. 'But... you weren't looking for me – I just came to you.'

'Yes, you're right, I did,' I said shaking my head.

'It was the same for me,' said Cookie Short, nodding enthusiastically.

'I wasn't looking for you either,' said NotNorman, 'and I found you here too.'

'Will you lot stop talking shite?' implored the chief. 'I'm trying to read my book.'

'The captain's out there. Now. Waiting for you.' I did my best to coax the mate out. He was very suspicious, but began to leave. I knew if he went that I would only have about one minute before he would be back to torture me for sending him on a wild goose chase, but I had to distract him somehow. He turned and left, looking back at us as he did. Cookie Short and I gave him an angelic little wave, shut the door, gave him a few seconds then opened it again to leave. There in the doorway was – Loose. I let out a little scream as she came in, and I dived behind the door. The thought of Jackie and Loose finding out about each other turned my bowels to water as I bravely adopted the strategy of hiding in the corner. Jackie could see me and was about to ask an awkward question, but Loose couldn't, so I tried to pretend to Jackie that I wasn't hiding while, well, hiding from Loose. Loose looked puzzled.

'NotNorman, what's going on? Windy seems to have –'

'Darling!' gushed Cookie Short. Sensing Jackie's rising interest at a half-dressed girl mentioning my name, he dived across the room and put his arm around Loose. 'How great to see you!' He kissed her on the lips.

'Awww, bloody hell! I'm trying to read a flamin' book here!'

Loose had only met Cookie Short a couple of times, so the kiss was a little unexpected, and he was definitely keen to make the most of his opportunity. She spluttered as she got her mouth free from his.

'What the bloody hell do you think you're –?'

I knew about her temper, so I had to stop her or the chief would go crackers, so I jumped out from behind the door. 'There, fixed it! Oh, hi there! You're... Lucy, wasn't it? Pleased to meet you. Nice, er, night-dress. Now then, I'll only be a second. Lovely day. What's for breakfast? It's done, lads. I fixed the mayhem wobble. Let's go and report to the mate!'

'Ten minutes with a book, that's all I wanted.'

'Who is this, Windy?' said Jackie. 'Aren't you going to introduce us?'

NotNorman, seeing the look in Lucy's eye, suddenly dived over and put his arm around Jackie. 'Darling!' he pronounced. 'Didn't I introduce you?'

'Ten bloody minutes, that's all. Not a lot to ask, is it?'

'NotNorman!' shouted a new and unexpected voice from behind the sofa. We all looked around as Cindy popped up angrily from behind the sofa. 'Get your hands off her!'

'Whoa!' exclaimed the chief jumping two feet in the air and throwing his book across the room as Cindy appeared behind him. 'What the – ?'

'Ah! Hi Cindy!' said NotNorman weakly. 'You remember Jackie?'

Cindy was half-dressed. She and NotNorman had obviously been interrupted by the chief as they were saying a spicy goodbye in the privacy of the ship's bar when the chief had come in for ten minutes' with his book.

Loose was puzzled. 'Why were you hiding behind the door, Windy? And why was that girl hiding behind the sofa? And why was that cleaning girl asking you –'

'Ah, now Lucy, this is Jackie, she's from the agent and she's cleaning the ship. I was just fixing the persecution monitor behind the door here, and this is Cindy – pest control. How's it all going under the sofa there, Cindy?'

The chief stood up. He had had enough. 'Persecution monitor? Pest control?! What on earth are you talking about? I don't know what sort of madness is going on here, but –'

'Ah-HAAA!' The mate shoved his head through the

porthole from the deck, right behind the chief, who hit the ceiling. 'Try to get rid of me, would you, Baboulene? You're going to suffer like never before, you –' he looked around at the assembled troupe of cadets and half-dressed girls. 'You bastards stay right where you are. I'm coming round now!'

His head disappeared and we all dashed about pointlessly in all directions in the style of a bedroom farce.

The mate came piling in. 'Right, you bastards! What's going on?'

We all stood, frozen to the spot. I felt it best if I got in first, in case uncomfortable truths were revealed, so I answered as clearly as I could:

'This is Lucy, she's my cousin from New Zealand who has lost some money; this is Cindy, her mentally unstable lesbian girlfriend, and this is Jackie from the agent's who is worried about all of us, so we're having a tea party in order to...'

Whatever I said was simply a desperate attempt to keep talking on the basis that it prevented the mate from getting his turn. And in a way, it worked, because I genuinely believe he didn't quite know what to do. In the end he simply ignored me.

'YOU,' he shouted, pointing a shaking finger at Lucy, 'should have left the ship last night! Get your things and GO! The rest of you, I want to see ID, or you leave too! Windy, get these people off the ship then report to me in my cabin in ten minutes.' But his heart wasn't in it. We were finally beginning to get to him. He wiped the spittle from his mouth and left, head bowed. He was utterly at a loss. He wasn't even able to rant effectively.

I led Lucy back to the cabin, made another set of excuses and headed back to the bar. Eventually I managed to get Jackie on her own. I began to explain but Jackie just laughed at me. I had forgotten that Cindy was her best friend. Her NotNormie had told her – Cindy – my adulterous secrets, and Cindy had, of course, grassed me up to Jackie, who told me not to sweat it. 'You and I both knew you'd have to leave,' she said, 'but I didn't see a problem with me using you while you were here. Did you? You blokes are so ridiculous, you know, thinking you have a monopoly on straightforward sex.'

And she gave me the shirt she had brought me, and we said goodbye again, this time with added respect from me. Loose never knew any different.

Great sentiment also flowed between the band and me as the goodbyes rang out. I had found soul mates here; kindred spirits who lived life as it should be lived. I couldn't wait for the day we would be reunited. But, like true teenagers, we didn't exchange addresses, we simply agreed to 'see ya round' on the beach one day. We didn't consider for a moment the possibility that things might be different in years to come. I would miss everything about Sydney.

However, you will raise your eyebrows to learn that NotNorman and Cindy had no trouble with their goodbyes at all. But before you throw the book on the fire in disbelief, let me reveal all: they did not say goodbye.

As the gangway was swung aboard and the ropes released us from Sydney's loving embrace, Cindy (and a good deal of luggage) had neglected to leave the vessel. She was stowing away in the ship's hospital. The Steward had been handsomely bribed, and the young lovers could see no problems with this course of action. They were together, so the world was as full of blue lovebirds and violins as it was before they'd become Mrs Fugitive and Mr Harbouring-Illegal-Immigrant. Any fool could see that it was all bound to end in tears, but they were in love, and, remarkably enough, as the ship puffed into Melbourne a few days later, she had not been discovered, and was able to rejoin society as the girlfriend who'd flown down from Sydney. The inseparable pair's great love story chuntered on.

For me, Melbourne meant many things. Looming largest, however, was not the city or the trams, the rain or the tennis, but a chap called 'Big Phil'. Big Phil had been synonymous with Melbourne throughout the trip – he was to provide the highlight of our Australian adventure, maybe even of our entire trip – and one of the first items of news to circulate now that we were alongside was that he would indeed be gracing us with his presence. So on the second night we did not go up the road. We were to have a quiet night in with Big Phil and see his amazing show.

The drink flowed freely as the evening built up, and I must admit that the unusually good spirits of my colleagues were a refreshing change. They were obviously looking forward to Big Phil's show, whatever it was.

Eventually the word went out that Big Phil had arrived and a buzz ran through the gathering. The double doors to the bar were opened, and by golly, when BP arrived at the threshold it was just as well both of them were open! P was indeed B. What was more of a shock though, was to find out that P was not a Phillip, but a Phillipa. A strapping, cheerful woman of burlesque style, broad beam and lustful eyes.

Most of the older lads had met her before. She was greeted with unbridled enthusiasm and there was an air of camaraderie and expectation that was unsettling. I started to become conscious of a little alarm bell ringing away at the back of my mind. Now I noticed it, I realised it had been madly trying to get my attention for some time.

Big Phil had a wit and a charm that was quite disarming, and her size became a decidedly secondary issue as her personality shone through. Nobody could call her a classically beautiful woman – and in an ideal world I suppose it wouldn't matter as her character was so special – but as a spectacular presence, and what with boys being boys and an ideal world being unachievable, her physical size mattered a great deal, especially when we found out why she was with us.

Once the formalities of arranging drinks and re-establishing long-lost links were over, Jinx took charge. Heavies were placed on the doors and we first-trippers were invited to sit on a line of barstools carefully prepared centre-stage. I was conscious of a hollow pit in my stomach as I realised we were, once again, to be the night's entertainment. We sat as bidden on the barstools, and my mind was working overtime trying to imagine what horrors awaited us that could so excite a baying mob and involve an industrial-sized woman. Only one possibility entered my mind. It could not be... Surely, surely not... They could not possibly intend...

Jinx stood up and began his speech.

'In the grand traditions of the education and enlightenment of our younger colleagues, it is incumbent upon the elders amongst us to help these boys move from the uncertain deserts of boyish ineptitude to the flourishing gardens of confident manhood. We are gathered here this evening as further evidence that we will do everything in our power to help these young sparrows spread their wings in a turbulent world.

'We will not shrink from the obligations we have to our seafaring traditions, and we will not fail in our duty to these lads, however ungrateful they may become. It is, therefore, my great pleasure to preside over this auspicious occasion, another grand example of the almost literal cementing of Anglo-Australian relationships, featuring, hhhhin the red corner, Biiiiiiig Phil! A tremendous performer with innumerable cherries already popped beneath her impressive undercarriage. Tonight, for your deee-lectation, she will subdue and roger – hhhhhhin the blue corner – these lucky young cherry-boys! Yes indeed! Here tonight, before our very eyes, these lucky lads will make the journey from boy to man. So without further ado, let us go straight over to the selection procedure!'

Can you imagine this? Can you even begin to imagine this? To put yourself in my place? I felt numb, pale, faint, weak, helpless and ill. The boys were like a fully-hyped game show crowd, all screaming and jeering their opinions as to which of us Big Phil should deflower first. In the bar. In front of everybody.

She paced back and forth in front of us rubbing her

chins thoughtfully as the crowd went bananas in the background. She squeezed the odd thigh muscle and touched the odd cheek, like a shopper selecting groceries. I briefly caught her eye and withered under the strength of her worldliness. Like a mouse held firmly beneath the claw, I could see no escape. The fever built higher and higher as the crowd sensed the finger was ready to point. I knew she was going to choose me. It was absolutely inevitable. I rued my good looks, my boyish charm, my muscular forearms and sophisticated aura that... Cookie Short? She chose COOKIE SHORT?

At first I was a little peeved at this. What was wrong with the woman? She must have been bribed. Nobody in their right mind would choose Cookie Short if he was the last biscuit on earth, let alone with me sitting there. Maybe she was saving me for pudding. I decided not to quibble, after all, Cookie Short was better than me at this sort of thing. He lacked my sensitivity and sense of romance and timing. I would let it go this time.

Now call me a party-pooper if you will, but even as Cookie Short of the Full Biscuit was struggling for his jammy dodgers, I was looking for an opportunity to escape, and – eventually – it appeared. In the mêlée and excitement of restraining Cookies there was, for the briefest of moments, a clear path between me and the bar doors.

Now I don't want you to infer from this that I'm the type of chap who would insult a young lady by legging it from her amorous attentions, but without so much as raising my hat I was out of my seat and through the doors before you could say 'meat and two veg'. A few of the boys – anxious that Anglo-Australian relations might become strained if a goodly portion of BP's dinner was allowed to run off – were hot on my heels. I made it to my cabin, slammed the door and turned the lock just as six hefty sailors hit it all at once. I leant back against the door and gasped a sigh of relief, but my problems were far from over. I heard shouts as they organised my retrieval. There was nowhere to run. I had the time it would take them to get the master-key to think of something brilliant. No point in blocking the lock – they would knock the door down if they had to. I was desperate. I unwound the lock on my porthole and peered out into the cool air. Freedom smelt good, but I couldn't get at it. It was a good thirty-foot drop in to the dark water. Besides, I could only just fit my head out and then only by catching my ears on the unyielding brass. I had heard tell that people on sinking ships had been known to escape through portholes. Frightened, panic-stricken people. I felt a curious kinship with them. The scramble outside my cabin was becoming more menacing, and I thought of my last view of Cookie Short, struggling like a desperate, hopeless fly in the web of a Greater Phillipa spider.

I gulped.

Next moment, I was falling through the air, watching the side of the ship flash by me. There was a splash, cold silence under the water, then air and noise again as I returned to the surface. I looked back up at the ship and could hear the distant sounds of the boys trying to find an answer. I turned away and swam – with the unique style you might expect of someone with two dislocated shoulders – across the dock to the steps on the opposite side and walked off into town. There was no way I would return to the ship that night.

Reliable reports from the lads themselves have it that Cookie Short, KiloWatt and NotNorman provided a stage for Big Phil's Burlesque performance, and that a thoroughly enjoyable night was had by all except two (KiloWatt loved every moment), but the fact that will pass down the generations into seafaring folklore was not Big Phil that night – she already has her place in the history books – but that a cadet was so desperately keen to spoil other people's fun that he managed to escape through a porthole. Any sailor will tell you that it is the action of a truly frenzied man. I have stood staring at that porthole many times since, and have hurt my ears trying to squeeze my head through it.

It cannot be done. But there you have it. Necessity is indeed the mother of invention, and as far as I was concerned, it was an extreme necessity to invent a way of escaping that particular mother of a stage performance.

Chapter 17

WALKABOUT

A dart is thrown. Scurrilous remarks on Dunfermline. The train to Nowhere. A long way home. Dunfermline gets a rethink.

IT IS A great idea, leading to excitement and adventure who knows where, to throw a dart into a map and go wherever the Gods of Probability deem, but it can have its pitfalls in the hands of the unwary. Following the embarrassment of Big Phil, the Great Unwashed had an irresistible urge to get away for a day or two, so the dart was fetched, along with a map of Melbourne's hinterland and the state of Victoria, and we rubbed our hands in gleeful anticipation. The trouble was, we let Giewy throw the dart.

When we were on the induction course I'd been introduced to this game and heard many tales of legendary trips to all sorts of outlandish places. Before the dart flies, nobody knows where he is going, and once the destination has been established, nobody knows what adventures are in store when he arrives. It is as close as pioneering adventurers get to 'organising' spontaneity and chaos.

It sounds like the perfect recipe for excitement, but the reason I've neglected to mention this event so far was because the game did not live up to expectations. Some berk carefully avoided the promise of Newcastle, Glasgow, Leeds and Manchester, and threw the dart into Dunfermline for us. Despite the moans and groans, we had to go there. We told ourselves that we would have a far better time than we expected, but it was not to be. Dunfermline was crap. I suppose by rights, among all these stories of world travel and cosmopolitan excess, there ought to be a tedious monologue entitled 'A Definitively Dull Night in Dunfermline.' I cannot say with absolute authority that Dunfermline is the most definitively dull spot on the planet, but it certainly reduced those old rascals Spontaneity and Chaos to a pair of snoring pussycats.

Maybe it's just me. I gather people live long and happy lives in Dunfermline; lives jammed to the rafters with laughter and contentment. Perhaps they do not wish for outsiders to discover their utopian haven, so they implement extravagant charades to convince dart-throwing visitors that Dunfermline is unspeakably pedestrian. They see people arriving over the hill and immediately stop the music, the laughter, the drinking and the making merry, turning it off like a tap. For the duration of our visit the pubs were shut, young girls an extinct species, and elderly locals wandered about in the drizzle yawning like hippos and staring longingly into the cemetery.

I suspect that the moment we had gone, the old folk tore off their masks and started dancing, the gravestones all turned back into juke-boxes, the tired old shop-fronts spun round to reveal casinos, pubs, nightclubs and brothels and the town blazed once more into its twenty-four hour orgy of debauchery and excess.

Maybe.

So I feel sure you will appreciate how, when Giewy threw the dart into the Dandenong Ranges some 80 miles into the Australian outback, memories of my night in Dunfermline came flooding back, as did the recollection of:

> a) a night spent trying to sleep in the Dunfermline rain on a park bench full of sailors;

> b) the subsequent fortnight's sensational and bubbly influenza; and

> c) my recurrent desire to flush Giewy's head down a toilet.

Every time Giewy did something pathetic, I imagined his head flushing down a toilet, and how the shape of his neck would fit exactly round the U-bend. I pray my day will come.

Upon seeing the location he had struck, there were cries of 'Bum deal!', 'No dice!' and 'Flush Giewy's head down the toilet!' but rules are rules, and we knew if we let ourselves off it would be the thin end of the wedge; the top of a slippery slope leading inevitably to anarchy, disorder and the breakdown of civilisation as we knew it. We didn't want that on our conscience, so a visit to one of the state of Victoria's more ticklish extremities was unavoidable.

One hour later, we were on the last train to Nowhere from Melbourne, and it was really quite exciting. The lads were in a buoyant mood and a good time seemed to be on the cards. Mind you, it was the same on the way to Dunfermline.

Soon the city levelled into suburbs with comforting English names like Blackburn, Canterbury, Box Hill and Camberwell, then suddenly civilisation did break down, and there were periods of awesome nothing. Just bush.

After a while we were in the middle of nowhere

when the train hissed, squealed, farted, and stopped. We wondered what was wrong. The guard was passing so we asked him.

'Your stop, lads. Shake a leg!'

'What? Here? But there's no station or anything!'

'We put the steps out for you. Downtown is a couple of miles thataway.'

We looked at each other in disbelief, grabbed our stuff, and climbed down to the parched red sand at ground level. The steps climbed back on to the train, which hissed, squealed, farted and pulled away. NotNorman was looking around and shaking his head.

'How did the driver know this is a station?' he asked. I took his point. There was nothing to indicate the presence of anything at all, let alone a station or a town. No signs, no ticket office, no personnel. Mind you, I suppose all those things were unnecessary in the light of the other factor – no passengers. There were tracks and nothing else.

We looked around in deep, daunted silence. Someone mentioned how neatly we were avoiding the excitement of Melbourne, and tried to recall how it was we came to be here. I remember the same comment outside a closed Indian restaurant in Dunfermline. Had a suitable facility been available, Giewy would most certainly have suffered a cranial indignity.

This was really wild. Our world consisted of the odd bush, a murderous sun directly above us, and a shimmering heat haze in every direction. As my eyes tracked the horizon round, the diminishing train could be made out dimly to the west, and the merest break in the landscape, roughly where the guard had indicated, could be perceived to the north-west. We decided that, although somewhat less imposing than the Manhattan skyline, this must be 'downtown', so we wiped our foreheads, lifted our rucksacks, and began tramping towards it. Soon we fell into a hot, exhausted silence, our heads drooping. We were no longer fun-seekers – we were survivors.

After a while our dying minds were distracted from

the fact that we were voluntarily being fried in the Australian bush by the tiniest hint of a distant hum. I ignored it at first, thinking it was just another of the many symptoms of a slow death. Then Blom stopped, put his head on one side and said, 'Listen.'

We held our breath and listened to the hot silence. Sure enough, the hum was becoming a drone, and it was coming from behind us. We turned to look, and the unmistakable shape of a van became visible through the heat haze. It took a full two minutes for the drone to become a growl to become a din to become a roar, then a Volkswagen campervan zoomed past in a noisy flurry of pink and white coach-work, full of music and cheering youth. Then the roar became a din became a growl became a drone became a hum, and the pink and white shimmer disappeared into the heat haze ahead, leaving us alone in the hot afternoon silence once more.

We shrugged our shoulders and carried on. Shortly, however, the same thing happened again. A hum on the horizon behind us materialised for a second into a large white convertible full of groovy kids and loud music. It roared past, and before that apparition had disappeared to the north-west, another was emerging from the east. There was obviously something happening in the bush that night, and here in the Dandenongs was the place to be!

A couple of vehicles later, a drone had become a growl, but instead of the growl becoming a momentary cacophony of teenagers and music, the growl became pacific, and we looked around to see an open-backed truck pulling up beside us.

'You boys going to the concert?' said the large and friendly looking Aborigine in the driving seat, his silver beard filling the entire cabin.

'Yes!' I said, as Giewy said, 'No!' and Cookie Short said, 'What concert?'

He looked confused by our lack of harmony. 'Well, you gotta be going to the Gulley whatever else you're doin'. There's no other friggin' place to go. Jump on!'

OCEAN BOULEVARD

We leapt gratefully on to the back of the truck. I got the floor space shared with an over-friendly black Labrador sporting a silver beard eerily similar to that of its master, and the truck bumped its way off towards a place called Ferntree Gulley (a place we had already thundered through on the train an hour or two before).

Ferntree Gulley was less of an anticlimax than our railway station, in that it existed in some tangible sense. To us it was like an oasis in the outback. It was lush and green, with new houses and tended gardens, and a proud sign announcing the imposing presence of 'The Ferntree Gulley Hotel'. Below this sign was a poster featuring the legend:

'From England! In Concert! Lomax and Mellish Productions Proudly Presents: SQUEEZE!'

A strip was placed across the poster declaring that the concert was SOLD OUT, and the inside information in the small print revealed that the event was for One Night Only. Now this was absolutely and totally incredible. If you've given me the benefit of the doubt regarding some of the things you've read so far, you need not feel ashamed if you find the presence of Squeeze at the Ferntree Gulley Hotel beyond the realms of possibility. I felt the same way, and I had the black and white evidence in front of me, and hordes of revellers arriving in their droves from all points of the compass. We counted the 'e's in 'Squeeze' (I've been caught out that way before – only 'The Beetles' play Dunfermline. 'The Beatles' play Che Stadium) but there was no Skwheeze or any nonsense like that. There was no doubt about it, this was the genuine article.

What Mr Lomax must have done in order to secure a band like Squeeze – at the peak of their super-stardom – to play the Dandenong Ranges will have to remain one of life's great unsolved mysteries. And what Mr Mellish must have said to Mr Lomax when he did must remain similarly shrouded. Whatever was said or done, I should imagine that their negotiating skills have probably taken them to some elevated positions in the world. They certainly deserve it.

We went to the ticket window and got a shake of the

head from a chalk-white woman with dyed black hair, red lipstick, and house-bricks for earrings. We searched for touts and were moved on by a pair of large policemen who could eat house-bricks along with any incidental black-haired, red-lipped, chalk-white women who might be attached to them. There seemed to be no way for us to get in at the front of the house, so we wandered around to the back of the hotel to try our luck there. Two huge trucks indicated the presence of the band and their entourage, and a large pair of closed double doors, labelled 'Artistes' proclaimed the stage door. Unfortunately, there was nobody around to be badgered, implored and bribed so, because my London accent was deemed to be the closest to that of a loveable Cockney, I was pushed forward to bang on the door.

'Yeah?' came the unwelcoming response to my rappings. The door stayed shut.

'Oh er, lissen, mush, weer from Deptford, init,' I lied in an appalling South London accent. I sounded Pakistani. 'Can you – err – diamond geezers get us in to –'

'Nah! Naff orf!' He'd heard it all before.

'Aw, cam on, cock! We've cam all the way from blinkin' Landin! We've gorn 'arf across the poxy weld to be 'ere, and - cor blimey! - we carn't get no bladdy tickets! We got all yer albims. I gotta big poster of Jules 'olland, honest, and ma mate 'ere, he went an' –'

'You got any beer?' came the gruff reply.

'Er... no.'

'Well, like I said, NAFF ORF, then.'

And that was roughly the size of it. The state laws and hotel policy had it that the gig featured soft drinks only. Cookie Short's excitement at the poster on the front door saying, 'Alcohol Free' was a misunderstanding on his part. The roadies were being denied their lifeblood, so it was hardly surprising that they were somewhat icy, even towards Pakistanis from Deptford.

I turned back to the lads just in time to see

NotNorman heading off round the side of the hotel. I thought he must have been caught short or something, but as we walked around after him we saw what he was up to. Our Aborigine friend was still there. He'd been smoking a little and watching people since he'd dropped us off, and... was drinking a beer. Some swift negotiations from NotNorman brought forth a six-pack, and before you could tie your kangaroo down, sport, the artistes' entrance was banging in the breeze, and half-a-dozen roadies were falling on our necks and blessing us. Some money changed hands, palms were greased, winks and nudges abounded, and within half-an-hour a certain Aborigine had earned a month's money for a short drive and the supply of an unspecified quantity of – to use the local vernacular – the golden throat lubricant.

The term 'male-bonding' is fifty percent reliant upon 'men' to make it male, and fifty percent reliant upon a decent agent for the bonding. Beer is the ideal glue for male-bonding, and to these roadies we were all the world's long-lost brothers rolled into five. We were taken backstage where we began male-bonding ourselves into oblivion with both band and roadies before, during and after the gig. That particular drinking session was made all the sweeter by the knowledge that it was the only booze in town.

I'm not sure how, but I think I may have become somewhat intoxicated, because I don't remember much after the first couple of hours. The gig was terrific, and I can say without doubt that overall, it was a fast-moving evening involving a fair degree of uproar, the details of which conveniently escape me. Suffice to say I opened my eyes to find the sun at twelve o'clock, pounding into my unsteady pupils, a chicken on my chest, my hand in a pile of dung up to the wrist, and an Aborigine woman alongside me who made Big Phil look anorexic. I leapt up and stared at her, ignoring my throbbing head. I couldn't have. Surely there must be... I tried to remember the evening's proceedings.

I had a vague recollection of hanging on to the back of some sort of flat-bed truck for grim death as it thundered through the hot night, my legs flailing behind me like a flag. Then I was dancing in the bush with some extremely friendly Aborigines. I remember swirling stars above me, people leaping around and everybody laughing. I remember the strangeness of larking about hundreds of miles from anywhere. You could shout your heart out and there was nothing to reflect the sound, so there was no echo; the sound just kept going away. It was like having a party in deep space. Then I remembered nothing.

I certainly didn't remember arriving at this roofless chicken hut, or sleeping with this... Where the hell AM I? I stumbled out into the bright sunlight, the horizon shimmering alarmingly in all directions. There was nothing. Certainly no transport. No people. Just one shrub with someone having a crap behind it.

'Mornin'!' said NotNorman. 'Have a good evening did we?' NotNorman was blessed with the inability to suffer hangovers – he didn't get drunk, he just got kind of bigger for a while.

'Jeeezus! Where are we?' I was genuinely worried. 'People die out here, you know.'

'Yeah,' he said reflectively, 'bummer, eh?'

I laughed a mirthless laugh. 'How did we get here? More to the point, how are we going to get back?'

'Well, me old son. See that sand that's a slightly different colour from the rest? That's the road. The sun rose that way, so that must be east, so I suggest we start walking thataway and thumb down a lorry – unless you fancy waiting for a bus. The next one's due in the year 2024.'

I could see no other feasible course of action and I wanted to leave before she woke up, so we slung our shirts over our shoulders and headed off along the road like the heroes of some epic movie strolling off into the sunset.

Come back, Dunfermline, all is forgiven!

As I took up my usual departure position – leaning on the

rail watching a much-loved country receding into the distance – with the customary tear in my eye, I could feel nothing but sadness. I had found paradise in Australia, and kindred spirits in the people. I loved the no-nonsense attitude of the Australians and the classless nature of the society.

One thing I found just brilliant about the Australians was their extremely high 'don't-give-a-shit' factor. Given an opportunity to establish great personal wealth and world super-stardom, your average Australian would happily turn it down in favour of a cold beer if that was the way he felt at the time. Someone told me a story that perfectly exemplifies this Australian humour and attitude. I don't know if it's true or not, but if it isn't it should be.

A couple of Aussies were tracking their way across some uncharted area of Western Australia when they came across a new and undiscovered mountain. It was a very high, very prominent and obviously important landmark. Their discovery would be historic.

Down the centuries, whenever anybody has made a new and exciting discovery, they have naturally named it after themselves, thus ensuring their name is enshrined in the history books, maps and lecture theatres of the world for the rest of time. You or I would do the same, I'm sure. Hence we have Mount Cook, Halley's Comet, Fox Glacier and so on. And these Australians were no different. Their egos would have it no other way. Hence, on today's relief maps of Western Australia you can find a proud and steadfast landmark by the name of 'Me and Harry's Mountain'. Nobody knows who 'Me' or 'Harry' were, but they were 'Australian' enough to thumb their noses at tradition rather than have their names go down into history. Only an Australian could do that and really mean it.

Chapter 18

SOUTH PACIFIC

Surprising discoveries concerning the Solomon Islanders' coiffure, working practices and dancing expertise. The chill breeze of the Second World War.

THE SOUTH PACIFIC contains countless small islands. Many are inhabited, with their own people and culture, many are deserted, but all are beautiful beyond belief, and each has its own distinctive character. Sailing through an idyllic, sparkling sea, with a cloudless sky and a huge orange sun shining on the palm-fringed coral sands is like sailing into some sort of Fairyland, a storybook wonder I am privileged to have witnessed.

We went to around eight of these islands, an experience that will remain with me for the rest of my life. As we weaved through the reefs and lagoons, flying fish skimmed the surface, multicoloured shoals darted and flashed in the clear water, and birds of every size and colour played the breeze with commanding grace. I've never seen such places. Rich and lush with towering coconut palms, flowers of the most vivid reds, yellows, mauves and greens, all set against the backdrop of a turquoise, jewelled sea and white coral sand. A visit to the South Pacific is as much of an experience for the nose as it is for the eyes as each flower competes for air-space. Early Polynesian sailors, lost in the Pacific, would detect the presence of land from the fragrance the islands gave off long before they could see them.

We began with a graceful flit from one rapturous island to the next in the Gilbert Islands and the Solomon Islands, with names like Honiara, Yandina and Tarawa. These were breathtaking, wonderful paradises where we would either anchor in some idyllic lagoon and be serviced by a hundred noisy, chaotic 'bum boats', or we would come alongside a gloriously unsafe wooden jetty and deal with the chaos direct.

We were loading coconut husks - thousands of tons of coconut husks - collectively known as copra. Back in the 'civilised' world (really, to label our culture as in any way more civilised than that of these island people is the work of grossly undernourished brains) this copra would be turned into perfume, soap, cleaning agents and other such items that didn't bear thinking about in this paradise.

The workforce was unconventional to say the least. Hundreds of stocky, chocolate-brown men with huge, broad smiles, wide, flared nostrils, the most laid-back attitudes of anyone on earth, and every last one of them adorned with a shocking mop of curly ginger-blond hair! It was quite alarming at first. The place looked as though the world's best salesman had recently passed through the area with an unbeatable deal on peroxide. Not so, however – no Candid Camera here – every last one of them had his own completely natural orange afro!

They were also extraordinarily agile and athletic, particularly when it came to loading the cargo. Most stevedores are fat, lazy slobs, with about as much athletic ability as a plate of cold noodles, but here it was different. Each net-full of copra, swinging fast and hazardously from the shoreside to the hold, would also contain half-a-dozen black blonds, laughing, shouting and playing the goat. Quite the most dangerous working practice I've ever seen, but they were just enjoying the ride. Each net returning from the hold to the shoreside would be similarly overloaded – I don't think I ever saw a worker use the gangway! They were such lovely people, so full of life and laughter. Every now and then, as boredom with the work began to set in (which it regularly did) a shout would go up, a song would start, and a dance would begin. The infectious rhythm would spread like wildfire and before you knew it, as far as the eye could see and on every surface that could support a man everyone would be dancing and singing their hearts out without a care in the world. The ship would be instantly converted into Carnival Central – alive with joy and happiness – and in the middle somewhere would be the cargo officer. Reduced from a smart, dignified official to a red-faced, rhythmless white bloke, hopping awkwardly from one foot to the other, while the dancers around him fell about laughing and stole his cap. I was so jealous of their ability to immerse themselves completely in a mood and a moment, and to love life so freely. It would take two hours and five pints of ale to get me that relaxed, and even then I would still have the capacity to worry about tomorrow.

Their happiness was all the more poignant after a walk around the island. These people had lived the same way for thousands of years, and as the industrial world developed elsewhere they neither knew nor cared. They certainly had no need of it, and there was precious little they could be taught about values; but inevitably, the cancerous spread of 'civilisation' found its way here, and their fragile utopia became a pivotal spot during World War II.

As the Japanese and the Allies began throwing things at each other, these islands became important. They provided vital refuelling posts for men and aircraft that couldn't make the distance to the battlefield in one jump and meant superior positioning of supplies and equipment. Control of the islands was a huge logistical advantage, so all of a sudden these quiet, peaceful islands learned about 'civilisation' as a desperate scramble for their control ensued.

The people were at best ignored, often abused, and without exception trampled underfoot. The islands were torn apart to make runways and buildings, and were officially adopted as army property, irrespective of what the islanders might think about what represented their best interests. The ripple effect of the war still haunts the islands decades later. These islands are not just a natural wonder of the world, but also an eerie graveyard. Everywhere there are physical epitaphs to the dreadful rape of the islands and their people. Army buildings stand decrepit and empty, hastily-constructed aerodrome runways lie overgrown and silent, stark machine-gun posts stick out like giant malignant pimples – some still equipped with rusted guns and mountings. Along the coral beach the odd truck or personnel carrier sinks chillingly into the sand, gradually being sucked under over the years. You look from these instruments of destruction to the unparalleled beauty of the nature surrounding them and the incongruity is the starkest reminder of what parasites we humans are on this planet. The world would be a better place without us, and Mother Nature would definitely have a much easier time of it without people. The pointlessness of war and the depths of our depravity become an embarrassment. The occupiers' rapes left a legacy of children, some of whom were working our ship now in their middle age. What seems so needless when you look at these places is the war itself, especially a war between distant lands, and one in which these people so patently had no personal interest. They were caught in the global cross-fire.

It is quite an experience to visit these islands and in the tropical sun of an island paradise, to feel the chill breeze of the war years.

Chapter 19

A SEA OF BALLOONS

Policemen in skirts. The captain expresses dissatisfaction. Windy battles valiantly against overwhelming odds. The captain decides enough is enough.

O F THE OTHER islands we visited, it was nice to include a couple of well-known ones. Fiji was fascinating, the capital, Suva, being particularly cynical. Prices quadrupled as soon as the cruise liners and their naïve passengers arrived, and the local 'characters' lined up at the bottom of the gangway with their napkins tucked in, their knives and forks rampant, and slavered through their smiles as their prey descended. Fiji was memorable for two particular events. The second is a sticky subject I would rather put off until later. The first occurred at two in the morning in a Suva nightclub. I was awakened from my deep, hypnotic, personal boogie wonderland by a tap on the shoulder.

'Oi, oi, Windy. Plod's in!'

This was MegaWatt-speak for, 'I say, old boy, it appears the constabulary have arrived.' I looked towards the entrance and sure enough, there was a queue of bobbies lining up behind the counter remonstrating with the ticket girl. And in employing the very British term 'bobby' I do not stray from the straight and narrow. Because apart from being jet-black and seven feet tall, they looked precisely like British policemen. Same helmet, same jacket and shirt, same accessories – no difference at all. That is, from the waist up. But as they stepped out from behind the counter, I nearly pulled an eye muscle trying to comprehend what I saw. The size-twelve black boots were the same, but unlike a British bobby, these coppers were wearing white skirts. Yes, skirts. No trousers at all.

A nervous smile crept across my face and I looked around to see what others were making of it, Candid Camera once more springing to mind. Everyone else was looking uncertainly at one another too, and the nervous smiles were turning into raucous laughter. I looked back at the rozzers. From the waist up they were indisputably mean-and-moody plods, but from the waist down they were Hawaiian dancers in combat boots. Then I saw people dancing around prodding them and laughing, and I cottoned on. The passenger ship! That was it! This was some sort of fancy dress to do with the passenger boat! I relaxed and joined in the laughter at the antics of these fun guys. We asked them to dance, blew their whistles, peeked up their skirts and made lewd jokes about truncheons and shiny helmets. And while the gang roared their approval at every new joke, the funniest thing of all was how the policemen kept stony straight faces. Had I not known they weren't real policemen, I could have got quite concerned at their granite features and mock sternness. It didn't matter how funny we were – poncing about with handbags and mincing around in front of them – they kept straight faces the whole time. The more we knocked their helmets off and pinched their bums when they picked them up, the angrier they appeared to be getting. They were priceless.

The next half-hour was a bit of a whirlwind in my memory. I have a faint recollection of being marched down a street with my feet off the ground, then waking up in a prison cell with my watch and money missing, and a Tom-and-Jerry-style lump on the top of my head that had combined with my alcohol intake to deliver me a previously undiscovered species of headache. One look through the cell door confirmed the minor error that had led me to this predicament. All the policemen running the prison were exactly like normal British bobbies from the waist up, and from the boot-tops down, but with white skirts where the smart black strides should have been. This was their genuine uniform.

The captain was waking me, although so far I hadn't managed to get my head on to the same wavelength as his words. When I did tune in, it didn't sound good.

'Before I bail you out, I have a few matters I wish to make clear to you,' he said pointedly. 'You have been in trouble too often. This trip has about eight more weeks to run, and if you come to my attention once more for ANY reason WHATSOEVER, I will be filing a report to the cadet training officer recommending an extra three months' sea-time on your cadetship. Understand? Right. So let's have less of it. More work, less horseplay.'

I tried to get myself together to explain that I didn't go out looking for trouble – it came bouncing up to me round every corner like an unwanted puppy. Not my fault. I was a victim of circumstances, me. But my voice wouldn't work. My words came out as a series of gurgles and belches, at which the captain shook his head and tutted. He signed a couple of forms for my release and stalked out.

Keeping out of trouble was now a high priority as it carried a three-month extra sea-time penalty, which was to be avoided at all costs. I was determined to start afresh and keep way, way away from anything or anyone smelling remotely of trouble. The problem with this resolve was that ALL the lads on the ship ponged to high heaven, so my avoidance routine began that night.

There was a major drink-up going on in the bar, with a lot of very seedy people from Fiji's substantial low-life invited. I crept out nice and early and steered well clear. I went up the road for a blameless walk, then curled up in my bunk with an educational book at 10:30. I listened for a while to the whooping and hollering, and the cries of ladies of the night, but before long the book was over my face and I was snoring directly on to page four. The ship was on the home stretch now, so thoughts of England were looming large in everyday life, and it was not surprising to find my dreams full of the green and pleasant, the brown and frothy, and the nearest and dearest. The sweet, innocent dreams of a lad who didn't realise how hard people were working on his behalf as he slept...

You probably remember the fate of NotNorman, KiloWatt and Cookie Short in Melbourne when an alleged woman by the name of Phil forcibly introduced them to the delights of public sex in the ship's bar, while I, in stark contrast, squeezed myself through a hole that was too small for me. You may also remember that Big Phil's industry represented the first-trippers' cherry-popping, and that this inauguration, as Sesame Street would have put it, was generously brought to us by bar profits, the bonhomie of the lads, the colour red, and the words 'big', 'Burlesque' and 'all-consuming'. You do? Good. Then those of you who are particularly on the ball will also have thought 'Wait a minute, surely these highly responsible British officers are not going to let Windy get away with an entire and untarnished cherry?' And you would be absolutely right. While the rest of the world slouched around enjoying itself that fine evening, those proud lads were putting in some extra hours with pride and dedication. They put themselves out to whatever extent was necessary to secure the services of six of the largest Fijian women the island had ever produced. They had spared no expense in getting them well tanked up in the bar, and had struck a simple but effective deal with them.

In essence, the deal went like this: any of the aforementioned ladies (hereinafter referred to as the parties of the first part) who could demonstrably extract spermatozoa from the party of the second part (that's me), would receive handsome remuneration for her efforts from the parties of the third part (the boys in the bar).

Once the parties of the first part were clear about the sums involved and the means of accessing these funds, they were keen to get on with the job, and it dawned upon each of the individual members of the party of the first part that the earliest to work over the party of the second part would have the easiest job squeezing out some remuneration. In fact, experienced girls that they were, the parties of the first part were concerned that the party of the second part might not be physically capable of providing enough deliveries for all six members of the party of the first part to get paid, so, working on the reasonable assumption that only the first of them to get busy could be sure of getting paid, the parties of the first part threw their drinks to one side and to roars of approval from the parties of the third part, began a thunderous stampede for the cabin of the party of the second part in order to get first bash at the party of the second part's parts.

Such was their enthusiasm for their work that they came through the door as if it wasn't there. I was actually thinking about my mother when the door was knocked down. After all, I was only seventeen, so a bit of homesickness was inevitable, and thoughts of my mum and crazy family were deep and frequent. So when the door hit the floor, my first thought was that this was mummy, rushing to bring me my early morning cup of tea. I reached out for it with sleep in my eyes. The next thing I knew my entire world consisted exclusively of Fijian womanhood. Folds and folds of it. An all-engulfing sea of blubber and lips was setting about me like the six blubberwomen of the apocalypse (suffocation squad) fighting over a lollipop. Unfortunately, it was my lollipop.

For the sake of decency, I shall not describe the ins and outs, so to speak. A blow by blow account, if you will, would not advance our knowledge of the world, nor indeed would a description of what I looked like or how sore I was several hours later when the last one – after an epic battle – scuttled off to pick up her salary. What I will tell you, however, is that the captain, returning during the height of my ordeal from a highly civilised shippers' dinner party in the town, was distinctly unimpressed. He became curious when he heard crowd scenes echoing round the corridor. As he walked on to my landing, he saw a splintered and damaged door torn from its hinges and cast aside like a used cadet, and as he approached the cabin from which the door had been torn he became anxious at the sounds of a desperate struggle, along with the unearthly squelching noises of a man with wet fingers drowning in a sea of balloons.

He stepped through into the cabin and switched on the light, took one look and switched it back off again. In the two seconds that the light was on I saw – framed between the acres of black flesh around my head – his horrified countenance, quivering like an aspen, turn grey, then blue, then purple.

'I... I WARNED you, Mister Baboulene. This is THE LAST STRAW!' And with that, he stormed off.

Why was it that every time the captain stumbled across me, he got the impression that my life was way more exciting and debauched than I could have ever managed through my own efforts? As it was, I had no choice but to stay where I was, which the captain would surely read as a further example of my putting sinful pleasure before the needs of my career. Disgusting.

As we left Fiji and headed back out to sea, I carefully applied calamine lotion to my raisin-like testicles. I knew a report would soon be winging its way to London Office, and the party of the second part would be as severely dealt with as the party of the second part's parts.

Chapter 20

A STRAIGHT BAT

Windy volunteers for captaincy. Ships don't pass in the night for NotNorman. The battle to make leather meet willow.

THERE IS A word that strikes at the very core of every true Englishman's being. It stirs his blood and inflames his passion. It rouses him to bid farewell to his family, link arms with his fellow countrymen, take up his weapons and fight the good fight to the bitter end for Queen and country. No other word in the English language is quite as powerful. And that word is...

'Cricket,' said Sparky. 'Does anyone here know anything about cricket?'

Now I happen to be rather good at cricket. To me, it is fire and brimstone, hope and glory, love and death all rolled into one. So it was to my utmost astonishment that everyone in the bar turned away from the man as if he'd asked whose round it was. They averted their eyes and tried to hide behind their beer cans. I must have misheard. Surely the mere mention of the great game – one of the very pillars of the British Empire – should bring them out of their seats to a man, champing at the bit to get out there and teach the upstarts a lesson? I can only suppose that my shipmates were suffering a malaise in tune with our national team; despite the fact that only the English truly understand cricket, it seems that nowadays any tinpot country with a population greater than eleven can beat us at it.

Well, I am not one to shrink from matters of national pride, and, being duly inflamed by the use of the 'C' word, I stood up with my eyes aglow and my hand in the air.

'Did you say cricket? Why yes, you know what, I'm really rather good at cricket.'

Sparky's face lit up. He clasped his hands and looked on me as if I was a gift from heaven.

'Windy!' he said with worship in his voice. 'Stand tall, my friend, for thou art at last useful.'

He was obviously pleased with me, but for some reason I didn't feel enriched by his pleasure. He took my beer and placed it on the bar, snaked his arm around my shoulder and, having attached himself firmly, led me to the door. 'The captain would like to see you in his office immediately. And Windy – thank you. The world is indeed a strange place.'

He was a man for whom the clouds had lifted, and I appeared to be the reason. The laughter rising from the bar as I climbed towards the captain did nothing to ease my puzzlement. Besides which, the captain was the last person I wanted to see.

'Baboulene?' He spat as I stood meekly in his doorway. 'I thought I told you you aren't allowed above the boat-deck. There had better be an exceptionally good reason for you to be here, or I will arrange for you to be brutally beaten. Twice. What the hell do you want?'

'Sparky said you wanted to see me, sir.'

'I most certainly do not! Why? Do you think I've gone mad or something? All I want from you is –' He stopped in mid-sentence and his face crumbled like a snowman in the rain. 'Oh, good grief. You're not my cricket man, are you?'

In the time it took him to interpret my 'at-your-service' point and wink combo, he went from an irritated but authoritative captain, to a shattered shadow of a man. I was put out by his reaction. I didn't feel I was getting a fair trial.

'Actually, I'm really rather good at cricket,' I said indignantly.

The captain sighed. 'Didn't anybody else volunteer? Nobody at all?'

As I shook my head he left his desk and went on his habitual circumnavigation of the day room (followed shortly by his clothes), holding a half-dozen of his pendulous chins in his hand while he tut-tutted his course around me. Suddenly, he came to a decision.

'All right, Baboulene. It seems you're my only hope. Let me explain. Global Link has had a presence in Tonga for over one hundred years. We own the land, the businesses and all the trade deals. Everyone works for Global Link. We brought cricket with us when we came, and taught it to the locals. They now have three teams, all fed up with playing each other, so they challenge any Global ship that comes alongside to a game of cricket. And it's deadly serious. You are not a serious person, Baboulene, but cricket is a serious matter, and for a Global Link team to be beaten is unthinkable. They have just Morsed us across the challenge, and we must accept. You will organise a team and you will beat them. Now I realise you may be tempted to drop me in it by throwing the game because you are on a charge at present, so, to give you a little motivation I will do a deal with you. You win this game, and the report is forgotten. You lose, and it goes off to London the same day. Tell any man who refuses to participate that I wish to see him immediately. They might change their minds. Understand?'

I understood, all right. This was a great deal. I could beat these Tongan types standing on my head – knock up a century or two, then bowl them all out single-handed – and I was getting some power over the lads. This would be a cinch. An enjoyable way of showing some islanders how the game should be played, and getting off report! I agreed heartily, gave the captain a broad grin to inspire him with my confidence, and – practising a cover drive every third step – strolled off to do some recruiting.

I was pleased to find that my fellow Englishmen were all properly impassioned by the idea of a game of cricket, (at least, they were after being asked to visit the captain) and pretty soon I had a motley assortment asking me if I minded them taking beer with them to the long boundary, and if they could be excused if they had a note from their mums. I realised that this merry banter was all part of a positive team spirit, and chose not to discourage them. I may be a tough master, but I know when to give the lads their heads. My suggestion that we spend a degree of our spare time practising was met with the same levity, but I decided against forcing them. I didn't want to dampen their confidence. Besides, I only needed them to make up the numbers while I got on with the business of the day. I was as good as home free.

As far as our arrival in Nuku'alofa, the capital of Tonga, goes, I won't bore you with the details regarding how beautiful it is. You can take that as read, but I must impart to you the details of one prominent aspect of the view to the shoreside. I was on fo'c'sle stand-by (again), and as I admired the view, one particularly curvy topographical feature waved at me and smiled. I couldn't believe my eyes, but there was no mistake. As soon as I could get away, I legged it for the cadets' accommodation.

A STRAIGHT BAT

'NotNorman! NotNorman!' I burst into his room and woke him up. 'Guess who's on the quayside awaiting clearance to return to your loving arms?'

'Eh?' said NotNorman. He was never quite up to my pace. 'What are you prattling on about?'

'Cindy!' I said, shaking him. 'It's Cindy. She must have flown all the way here to be with lucky old you! HA!'

'Oh Christ,' he said flopping heavily back into his pillow. 'You are joking, aren't you?'

You may be surprised by this reaction because the last you heard of these two, they were slushing pathetically around the Australian coastline unable to bear being apart for as long as it took to get undressed again. I must apologise for not bringing you up to date on the latest gossip, but the thing is, we were not expecting to see Cindy again. You see, sailors' romances tend to become very intense very quickly. Two people safe in the knowledge that they only have a limited time in which to run the full gamut of love's lifecycle before being torn apart forever, tend to fall more deeply in love more quickly than those who have to face practical realities – such as the prospect of being together till death do they part. So NotNorman had safely fallen as completely in love with Cindy as she had with him, and a deeper love (Available for a Limited Period Only) you could not find anywhere.

The flaw, however, was that Cindy was not a sailor. She didn't realise that the ship's departure was traditionally the end of love's great journey, and she mourned NotNorman's leaving as the end of her life. She moped about, wringing her hands and imploring the moon like a tragic Shakespearian thesp. NotNorman on the other hand, was enjoying a little peace and quiet, and looking forward to another deep and meaningful three-day-forever in the next port. He was relieved to get away. He and Cindy had been together for weeks, which is really quite unnatural when one is a seventeen-year-old sailor, and he often spoke of this romantic experience in the grave tones of a man who has been to the brink and seen over the edge.

So he'd hung in there for the last few days in Australia, safe in the knowledge that circumstances would sort out his problems for him. He'd been pleased to avoid the unpleasant task of splitting up with her, but we reap what we sow in this life, and now here she was, waiting on the quay for chapter three of their great love story in the full belief that her NotNormie would be as chuffed as a train that she had made such strenuous efforts to be with him again.

'So whatcha gonna do?' came the obvious question from Cookie Short as NotNorman paced the bar chewing his bottom lip.

'Well,' said Notters, working the thing through reasonably, 'I shall have to be honest with the poor girl. I must tell her it's all over, that I don't love her, and that she must go back to Australia. No point in any further deceit – it only causes grief and heartache. I shall bite the bullet and let her down gently. Cruel to be kind, and all that.'

'Definitely the right decision,' I said, and I admired his fortitude.

But once the customs procedures had been attended to and NotNorman got close enough to Cindy to see how happy her breasts were to see him, his resolve left him as if it was being physically drained from his feet. He wimped out of his 'cruel-to-be-kind' routine, and acted as if he was exceptionally pleased to see her. Nothing short of a rifle under the left ear could have got him to tell her the truth, so on the first night in Tonga, NotNorman and Cindy sucked each other's faces as if nothing had changed.

The next day I took him to one side.

'I thought you were going to knock her on the head?' I accused. '"Let her down gently" you said. "Cruel to be kind" you said. What you actually meant was you'd shag her for a couple more days, then send her a note from Panama, right?'

'Well, that's not exactly how I'd put it,' he replied sheepishly, 'but there's no point in spoiling her holiday, is there? She's paid good money and come a long way. I'll tell her just before we go.'

I don't know. The youth of today have no moral fibre. You could tell NotNorman had never played cricket. Cricket engenders a more upstanding personality. Maybe the game would do him some good.

On the day of the cricket match we arrived at the ground – a tenderly manicured, pristine baize of grass overlooked by a pavilion that looked as if it had been airlifted from Surrey and dropped untouched into this Pacific island – to find a fairly good crowd had gathered, mostly consisting of respectful Tongans eager to see an exhibition from representatives of a real live empire in full swing. We looked smart in our uniform whites and the pads supplied by our hosts, and once I'd seen the ramshackle bunch we were up against, I felt we were in for a pleasant afternoon. I smelt the air; it tasted of victory.

We won the toss, and I chose to bat first. Cricket is a game of psychology, you see; I was in at number one, so the impact of my knocking up a wholesome score would take the zing out of their best bowlers, frustrate them tactically, and demoralise them before they got into bat. You know, a five-day test match can be fundamentally all over within the first twenty minutes if you get the psychology right. I don't suppose they understood the subtlety of my approach, but we rarely appreciate how we are being manipulated by our superiors.

I strode out to the crease, swinging my bat and acknowledging the reverent ripple of applause from the gathered throng. The sun was high, the light was good, and I was looking forward to a bit of fun. I took up my position at the crease and was surprised that the opposition didn't immediately set about rearranging their field. I am left-handed, and normally, as I line up middle-and-off with the umpire, a certain degree of logistical shuffling takes place in the field. This lot either did not know what to do, or else they were not taking the game at all seriously. From the amount of unseemly merriment abroad, I assumed a bit of both. Either way, they were fielding in couples (presumably to facilitate a cosy chat), another sign that we were going to romp home.

A hush fell over the ground as the umpire indicated the first over. I locked horns with the bowler – a long, chocolate-brown figure – the classic shape of a pace bowler. He held eye-contact and I nodded knowingly at him. They would certainly have pitched their best bowler in against me, and this was he. I knew what to expect here: it was definitely going to be pace. Pure speed. They were making the classic mistake; pace balls run straighter. I would use his pace against him, and was determined to be merciless from the first ball.

He turned at about thirty paces from the wicket, took six little pigeon steps as he curled his fingers about the ball, then dropped his nose to the ground and broke into a run like a bull charging a matador. It was definitely going to be pace. About halfway through his run-up his legs were a blur and his top half began to lean backwards until the back of his head was shaving the grass behind him. It was definitely going to be... the ball whistled past my ear, cleared the wicket-keeper and reached the boundary behind me with one bounce. A stunned silence fell over everyone in the ground. The only noise was a high-pitched whimpering sound (which people later claimed came from me), followed closely by a sickening thud and agonised cries from the spectator who had just taken 200 miles-an-hour off the pace of a cricket ball using only his left kneecap. I couldn't make out words from his howls, but as he rolled around hugging his knee to his chest, the gist of what he was trying to tell us all got across and the group of spectators positioned around him were quick to respond. Working on the basis that future bombshells of this ferocity would be manifesting themselves in the neighbourhood, they gathered up their blankets, picnics, kneecaps and children and hurried off to safer vantage points.

I looked at the bowler, whose run-up had brought him to within a foot of me. He chewed his tongue with a vulgarity I did not care for and snorted through flared nostrils. I had to keep calm. Cricket is a game of psychology; it was imperative at this point that I didn't show any fear to this bowler. It may have been a devilishly fast delivery, but he'd just given us four runs, so to some extent honours were even. I got up, dusted off my trousers, looked around for my bat and retrieved it with a nonchalant air from over near the umpire at square. I eyed the man again. He licked his finger and rubbed it on the ball with lewd deliberation before turning and heading off once more towards his launch pad.

I didn't expect any variation – this man clearly had only one gear – and I didn't get any. He motored into the stumps, leant back and released the pin. I didn't see the ball at all, but the smell of sulphur in the air told me it had been in the vicinity, and the dull thud as the ball found a weak point in the sight screens behind me told me we were a further four runs to the good. It was a scary place to be standing, but at this rate, as long as I could keep my head on my shoulders, we would win without playing a ball.

My memories of cricket at school – where my bat flashed like a scythe in the sunlight, and fielders became exhausted as I distributed them to all points of the compass – were now but a distant fantasy. This guy might only have one delivery, but I wasn't sure that I even wanted to connect with one of these rockets. I needn't have worried. On his third delivery I saw a patch of turf explode about four feet in front of me and then a cloudburst of matchsticks rained about my head. He'd caught a criminally jammy bounce outside the off stump and what should have been another four runs to me cut back viciously and uprooted my stumps. I was out. I had been responsible for eight runs (though I had yet to see the ball) and my bat remained a pure and unsullied virgin.

I walked off in disgust. This wasn't cricket. What is the point in pure pace? Bloody foreigners will never understand cricket. I mean, anyone can just bowl pace, but that's not cricket, is it?

OCEAN BOULEVARD

The home team reorganised their approach for our next three batsmen. They kept the same unsporting bowling technique, but repositioned the fielders. Working on the sad basis that we were highly unlikely ever to make a stroke, and in order to try and prevent the bowler from directly bowling us a winning score, they scattered half-a-dozen secondary wicket-keepers in the area behind the unfortunate guy in the traditional location. So the script took on a new predictability: bowler fires off cannon, batsman hides his face behind raised thigh and forearm. If the stumps don't fly and the keeper with the gloves on misses it, then the line of extra keepers leap for cover too, and we are another four runs to the good.

By the time Giewy came in to bat at number six, we were twenty-eight for four, with all our runs scored by their bowler. None of our team had yet made contact with the ball, and all ten of the opposition fielders were now queued up in a line behind the wickets, leaping vainly at the meteorites passing over their heads on their way to denting the sight screens behind them. I looked at Giewy and felt pangs of guilt and sorrow. The poor goon was grinning inanely, and didn't appear to have any idea what he was letting himself in for. Admittedly, the bowling looked calmer from the sidelines than it did looking down the barrel, but surely he had some idea of the dangers involved?

As the bowler's nose lifted off from the ground once more and he began steaming in I could barely watch. Giewy was standing there as if he was waiting for a bus. I shut my eyes as their loose cannon shot off again. There was a spark like lightning from just outside off stump, a cry of 'GIEW!' and the sound of leather on willow for the first time that day.

Giewy had hit the ball!

I stared in disbelief as the ball rolled off gently across the uninhabited grasslands around mid-off and over the rope for four runs. Giewy looked as shocked as anybody. It must have been a fluke. The law of averages must have stepped in: if you leave a bat hanging around in that general locality for long enough, the ball must hit it sometime. You could hear the buzz ripple through the crowd. This guy could hit the ball!

The bowler prepared again – looking angrier than ever – and Giewy took up his stance. Another delivery cannonballed in... and once again, Giewy did a little fishing movement outside the off stump, and cracked the ball off for another four runs.

To cut a long story short – and I don't wish to dwell on this – Giewy was a revelation. He stood there for half-an-hour scoring heavily as the sweaty paceman worked his way through a steady stream of Giewy's partners. We were all out for sixty. Giewy was undefeated on twenty-four, the rest were scored by their bowler.

As Giewy came off, he was surrounded by admirers from all sides. The lad was hailed as a sporting genius. They wanted to know why he'd never turned professional, how old he was when he started, who his heroes were, how he contrived his unorthodox grip, and how often he practised. He laughed falsely and said he didn't ever practise, he'd never played the game before and that he'd always thought it looked a bit simple. Lying dog. I couldn't explain what I'd seen, but one thing was for sure, it had nothing to do with skill on Giewy's part. Bastard. But now it was MY turn to be the hero. It was our turn to bowl.

Now if there's one thing I can do, it's bowl a cricket ball. Cricket is a game of psychology, you see. A battle of wits. A duel between great minds. It's all well and good to be able to sling the thing at 200 miles-an-hour, but to play at the top level requires strategy and what I call 'complex simplicity'. You see, a truly great bowler takes men out by monkeying with their minds and egos. Sure, a pace-ball is good to have in the armoury, but it is a complete player who can use a combination of several balls to confuse and disorientate before delivering the coup de grâce. That is what real cricket is all about. So as I arranged an attacking field (it's always good to start aggressively) I was more than happy to see that the first batsman up was my talentless,

OCEAN BOULEVARD

flukey adversary – the opposition fast-bowler. Our eyes locked once more, but this time, I was in the driving seat and he was my helpless victim. He tried to look casual, spitting beetle-nut and rubbing his crotch, but I knew he would be worried deep down.

I've always fancied that receiving a delivery from me must be akin to unexpectedly receiving a World War II Spitfire over the garden fence. Descending out of the sun with speed, skill, control and deadly accuracy – one bad decision and you're dead. Nobody has ever told me any different, so I suppose this is probably a fair assessment. I bowl left arm round the wicket off a short run-up that begins from a concealed position. I crouch down entirely behind the umpire before every delivery. This is a brilliant move. It even disorientates the umpire sometimes, who wonders where I've gone. Cricket is a game of psychology, you see, and a batsman always feels less sure if he can't see your grip on the ball. In my case, he couldn't see any of me at all. I then strike quickly. Two paces and I am up to speed. I leap high above the ground, coiling into a power-packed spring hanging ten feet in the air. I then uncurl in a single lightning movement, and unleash a ball that is turning in the air like a jet-propelled butterfly. It is virtually unplayable.

Many batsmen freeze in horror, and even the best can see that this is a fearsome delivery. They know it is fast, but they also know it is spinning furiously. I pitch it short, so they have no chance on the front foot. A stroke player with any knowledge of cricket drops on to the back foot to give himself as much time as possible to adjust to the effects of the spin. I usually deliver two which cut back, and occasionally get lucky with an LBW, then I bowl the third out of the back of my hand so it whips through dead ahead off the bounce. It's a certainty for an off stump or a thick edge and a catch in the slips.

From my first delivery it was immediately apparent that my adversary was not worthy of the contest. I was playing on a totally different plane to him, and he stood

228

there as naive and innocent as a newborn babe. He didn't know how good my delivery was. He didn't know that the most effective response was to drop on to the back foot and play a defensive shot as best he could. Out of sheer lack of knowledge he came galloping down the wicket, caught my ball on the full toss and walloped it for six over mid-on. He had no clue whatsoever.

He came running down the wicket on the second ball too, and got four through extra cover. The man was unbearable. He obviously hadn't the first idea how to play cricket. I had to drop to his level and rethink. I pitched the third one even shorter, in order to trap him on his ridiculous gallop up the wicket, but he must have run out of puff, because this time, he stayed back. This gave him an age to watch my delivery sit up nicely before cracking it off for another six. It was pathetic. The crowd were applauding warmly, but anyone with any knowledge would have known that were he playing properly, he would have been out by now.

I outsmarted him with the fourth ball. My class shone through. I hid behind the umpire, danced out, coiled and sprang. He ran down the wicket, caught the ball on the full toss and gave it 500 miles-an-hour towards square leg. I looked towards square leg hopefully – and there was Giewy, staring gormlessly off into space as the fireball flew into his midriff. His cheeks ballooned and he doubled up as the ball carried him bodily backwards for around thirty feet, ploughing a deep furrow arse-first across the pitch towards deep square. When the smoke cleared and the fizzing stopped, Giewy was lying motionless with his head between his feet, ten yards back from where he'd been standing. A worried crowd rushed over to him. They rolled him over and were horrified at the appalling sight that met their eyes. They gasped and turned away, unable to look at the carnage before them. But he was fine. He looked like that all the time. Soon enough he was up again, posing around like a tit and saying how he was happy to play on. He plucked the ball from his belly-button and the penny dropped. It was a clean catch! Using only his belly, Giewy had caught the man out!

The next few overs featured me from one end and Blom (displaying a laughable style) from the other. They reached forty for the loss of only the one wicket. The crowd was beginning to get behind them, a carnival atmosphere developing around the ground, and things were looking bleak. I decided a change was in order and thought it best to swap Blom for someone fresh. I pointed past Giewy to Cranners who was from Surrey – surely he had picked up something from growing up in the spiritual home of cricket. But Giewy thought I had pointed to him, and trotted across, wagging his tail. He picked up the ball and gangled off to bowl. I tried to call him off, but he couldn't hear me over the frenzied crowd cheering his name. Blom stopped me from running after him. 'Aw, let the guy have a bowl. He looks pretty stylish!'

It was too late anyway. Giewy was scuffing his feet like an impatient bull (whose mother was a vulture). He was already into his preparations, and 'stylish' was not the word that immediately sprang to mind. He rubbed the ball against his crotch for a while – with a crooked look on his face and no idea of the purpose of this technique – then gave a snorting laugh like a dastardly villain. If cricket was a game of psychology, Giewy was the patient. He didn't commence his delivery with the mandatory half-dozen pigeon steps, in the style of Botham, Snow and Lilley. He commenced with half-a-dozen steps reminiscent of a woman in labour running for a bus. Then he was off. His knees wracked sideways with every frantic footfall, his fists pumped and his eyes and cheeks bulged. His face, pointing skyward, puffed and grimaced with the effort of it all and before long the entire Giewy contraption was up to its hectic maximum speed of around two miles per hour – markedly slower than the pace at which a pregnant woman could have walked it.

As Giewy jerked and puffed and jolted and grunted his way feverishly towards the crease the batsman couldn't believe his eyes. He rose from his preparation and looked around for support, but all eyes were on Giewy's inexorable advance. The sound of children crying reached my ears as Giewy's shirt buttons gave up the unequal struggle and his belly broke free to express itself. And he was still only halfway there. As Giewy entered his final approach he began to spin both his arms in great windmill circles. Faster and faster they spun, like propeller engines starting up. And as his arms swung, his head wobbled from side to side to prevent his ears getting caught.

His arms were a whirling blur, his head was an oscillating haze, his legs pumped and jolted and his face was contorted with effort. Women covered their eyes and strong men comforted the elderly as he approached the line. From somewhere in the stroboscopic mass of Giewy the ball emerged and flew directly upwards. All heads turned skyward as it shot one-hundred feet in the air. The batsman would have to contrive something like a tennis player's overhead smash to sort this one out, but he was finding it hard to take his eyes off Giewy, who remained out of control and was heading his way, so he was not concentrating when the ball bounced two feet in front of him, beat his feeble defensive stroke, and sailed through to take out his centre stump. Giewy had clean bowled him!

Now I don't wish to bore you with the details of the next thirty minutes, and I hesitate to dwell on the fact, but Giewy was a revelation. Every delivery was different – although they all featured the same alarmingly bizarre twin-armed, windmill-wobble run-up – and by the time he got the last man out they had only reached 54. Incredibly, we had WON! We left the opposition crying and complaining and consulting the rule books, but it was fair and square, and we headed back victoriously to the ship to celebrate another foe vanquished in the name of Great Britain.

Well, well, well,' said the captain, 'so we won, did we?'

What was he talking about, "we"? He didn't even turn

up to watch.

'Yes, sir. A tough tactical battle, but my team and I won through in the end.'

'Indeed? I'm sorry I couldn't make it. I hear young Giewy was our star man. Is that right?'

I curled my lip.

'I can't take anything away from the lad, sir. He did exactly as I told him, and it paid off. For a time I think he got a little uncertain, but I stood firm and he believed in me, and between us we carried it off, sir.'

'Indeed. So, Giewy's a cricketer, is he?'

I gritted my teeth.

'He, er, he had a good day, sir, but no man is an island. There's more than one link in a chain and all that. Teamwork did it, sir. It's what I always say: an army is only as good as its general, sir.'

He stopped and looked at me.

'Do you really think so, Baboulene? Do you really think that?'

Now we were getting somewhere. I puffed my chest out proudly.

'Indeed I do, sir. A group of the finest individuals are as useless as tripe unless a strong man is at the helm. A team has to be guided from the front by a man they believe in, and I firmly believe that is the case here, sir.'

He looked kind of weird and sat down again, looking at me all the while.

'Well, that's awfully kind of you to say so, Baboulene. I'm really touched. I thought we had a real problem with you, but this is marvellous. I'm pleased this game of cricket has caused you to see the sense in a rigid adherence to rank and discipline. I never thought I would see the day when a game of cricket could get through to the soul of an ignoramus such as yourself. Cricket's all about psychology, you see, and now you've seen the light, you'll find tremendous depths in such things. Cricket engenders a more upstanding personality, Baboulene, and I hope this little episode has gone some way towards maturing you. I'll put this report of yours in the bin, and I hope to see you flower into officer material in what remains of this trip. Go and talk to Giewy about the lessons you've learned today. I feel sure he'll be able to help you up on to the new moral plane you've discovered.'

Good grief. The people I had to work with. I didn't know whether to laugh or cry, but with the report in the bin, at least there was one monkey off my back.

Now, after such cheering events, I would like to be able to tell you that we all lived happily ever after. But it is my unpleasant duty to tell you that this was not the case. As we left Tonga some four days later, we still had the sticky matter of Cindy's unrequited love and the heavy weight of deceit upon NotNorman's droopy shoulders. He had not found it too hard playing the loving partner, and they were having such a lovely time that he couldn't bring himself to drop the bomb. I had to admit that it would take a tough man to top off a few days like those with the summary dismissal of a beautiful, loving, smiling, humorous young lady with bosoms 'n' that, so as the ship pulled out, nothing had changed.

'You promised,' I said, rebuking the deceitful chap. 'That poor girl is going to hold a candle for you until the day you get back to Australia, and did you shake the head and wag the finger? You did not! You said you'd tattoo her name on your forehead and request another ship to Oz as soon as we get home!'

'I just couldn't do it! We'll go straight to my cabin now and compose a letter and send a telegram and some flowers or something. I've got to get this sorted. I know it's cowardly, but there's no other way now.'

So as our mighty vessel headed for Samoa, NotNorman and I sat down and composed a letter and a telegram to send to Australia for poor Cindy to receive upon her return. The telegram and flowers were dispatched immediately, and the letter was sealed up, ready to send from Samoa. Then the dirty deed would be done and NotNorman would be free to continue his rotten, cowardly existence once more.

Chapter 21

WESTERN SAMOA

The Motorbike Murders. Windy behaves illegally and finds a beautiful girl. Windy, Criminal Mastermind, is caught in the act. Phillips crosshead jungle biking.

WESTERN SAMOA WAS a new style of island. It was large with a sizeable population, a beautiful capital called Apia, a mountainous central region, large areas of impenetrable jungle, and a motorbike rental agency – called 'Apia Bike Higher' – containing a cheerful, round-faced man who was smiley, helpful and genuine, and whom we instantly liked very much indeed. The price was very reasonable, although we each had to put down a five-hundred-dollar deposit, but we would get that back at the end, wouldn't we?

In no time at all we were a chapter of Hell's Angels. We were untamed and free. A pack of wild kids living close to the edge (on 50cc Hondas). We were rebels without a cause. Well, nearly. A couple of the lads had some shopping to do, and two needed to get back to the ship, so like children who would leave home if only they were allowed to cross the road, we put off our rebellion until later. We agreed to meet in a couple of hours for a beast-machine cruise hog-jam that would seriously wake this island up.

A couple of hours suited me fine because I had a little personal business to attend to myself before I could put on my leathers and Peter Fonda sneer. In Melbourne we had loaded a large and interesting wooden crate into one of the now-empty deep-tanks. The tank was then bolted back down, so whatever was inside was clearly top-security. A conspicuously rich sleaze wearing a broad-rimmed black hat, sunglasses and a black trench-coat worn as a cloak had overseen the loading while sucking a large cigar. During the latter stages of securing the special consignment, he sleazed up to me. He spoke in a conspiratorial undertone and a fake Italian accent.

'You wanna get yourself a liddle Christmas money, my friend?' he asked, re-lighting his cigar.

I narrowed my eyes. I knew the game.

'Maybe I do – and maybe I don't,' I looked to the left and right for earwigs. 'What's the blag, then, John?'

He stared straight ahead and spoke out of the corner of his mouth. He looked like one of the Ant Hill Mob.

'I'd like you to make a leedle delivery for me when you arrive in Western Samoa.' He handed me a piece of paper with a hand-drawn map, a convoluted address and the name 'Roly' on it. 'I want you to take ten bottles of whisky from that cargo we just loaded, and deliver them to Roly. He'll be expecting you.'

He slipped me a hundred dollars – a hundred dollars! – and said Roly would do the same upon successful delivery. I looked at the readies and decided that I was more than delighted to help this fellow out, and as he slunk off the ship like syrup down the side of the pot, I had the spring in my step of a man who is up on the day.

Now that I was in Western Samoa with a motorbike and an attitude, it was a simple matter. I visited the cargo in deep-tank three with a spanner for the manhole cover – yes that manhole cover – but this time there were only four bolts as there was no need for a watertight seal. I disappeared down through the manhole and some minor implements of destruction made short work of the wooden crate. I slipped the booty into a haversack, and walked blithely from the ship, whistling a cheery tune and smiling at everyone as if I'd be giving a sermon later that day. Soon enough I was riding high and fast into the outskirts of Apia with the haversack on my back, the warm wind in my hair and thoughts of a career as a criminal mastermind filling my mind.

The tarmac of Apia soon gave way to an unsealed track, and I climbed steeply for some time. Then I found the correct turning and eventually a sign indicating that the residence I was looking for was down a long driveway hacked out of the jungle to my right. When I say 'residence' I may be misleading you slightly. The address I was given by the Mafia man was:

'Seventh window along on the right-hand side of Temperance House. If there is a cross in the window, knock three times. If not, come back later.'

The unusual directions to the window had distracted me from the name of the place, but now as I approached it, I could see it was some sort of institution. If I had any idea what 'temperance' was, I might have understood entirely. It was not big and imposing as an English residential institution might be, it was modern and spread out like a giant bungalow, with carefully tended lawns fighting back the surrounding jungle.

I decided not to park the bike, but to ride directly round the side to facilitate a quick getaway, but as I rounded the side of the building I had to swerve suddenly to miss someone, or to be more accurate, to miss an angelic vision of feminine excellence directly in my path. She had her hand to her mouth and was frozen in horror at the dangerous approach of a James Dean look-alike on a speeding motorbike. As I ploughed my bike into a bush and somersaulted over the handlebars I didn't take my eyes off her for a second. I was utterly in love, and the somersaults and airborne nature of my physical demeanour merely served to match my emotions. Her big eyes and open mouth – registering surprise and fear for my well-being in equal measure – and her long blonde hair flowed into every corner of my consciousness.

Fear not, my love, I thought as I flew through the air, once I have landed, I will be by your side forever to soothe the dread that hath seized thy troubled mind. I shalt mop thy brow and pat thy hand. I shalt – Ooof!

I landed on my back – on a haversack full of bottles. I was winded like never before, and although physically unable to move, I was determined that the angel would meet a serious guy, on a secret mission, on a motorbike – not a chicken on a moped whining about how his bum hurt. I wanted to tell her I was Mr 'X' from British Intelligence – in Apia only for a few hours, but that I had just enough time to fit her in for one fiery lifetime of unceasing passion. The trouble was, I couldn't breathe.

She came running over and looked into my eyes. Good grief, she was beautiful. My first thought was to try to get a kiss-of-life out of her by feigning unconsciousness. It would have been worth stopping my heart with a spanner for resuscitation from her. One kiss would jump start the oldest corpse on the planet, but my image as a rugged international spy would be shot so I thought I'd go for, 'Hi, my name's Bond. James Bond. You must be Heavenly Boobies.' I don't know why, but these words emerged into the open air as, 'Eeeaargh! Oh, bollocks!'

'Are you OK?' she purred, running her hand over my brow. Her touch fizzed on my forehead and shimmered through my entire body.

I was cured.

'Oh, er, yes, yes. Nothing really. Happens all the time. Ha, ha!' I tried to get up but just wobbled about on the floor.

'What are all those bottles doing?' she asked. Her huge, enquiring eyes were full of innocence. She looked like a lamb asking the wolf what the shiny knife was for. I looked around me. The treacherous haversack had forsaken its load and the lawn of Temperance House was strewn with whisky bottles.

'Ah,' I said, 'special delivery. A kind of international deal. This kind of thing goes on all the time in the Secret Service. All very hush-hush, you know.'

I gave her a wink and nodded slowly. I was amazed to see that she was genuinely impressed. Her child-like expression gave away her age as about the same as mine rather than the early twenties that she looked.

'Wow!' she said. 'You were on a secret mission, and now I've ruined everything for you! Whatever can I do to put things right?'

My mind flooded with good ideas, but I kept my dignity.

'Well, I'm here for a couple of nights. You could let me take you out somewhere?'

Her eyes lit up. I could not believe her reaction.

'Oh yes! That would be exciting. We could go to Jazzies on your motorbike. Let's do your mission, then we can go to the beach on your hog!'

I wanted to tell her that I didn't give a fig for the mission and that the trip to the beach should begin immediately, but for the sake of continuity, I simply stammered out some sort of agreement and began picking up bottles.

'What do we do now?' she said. 'You're the spy.'

I looked at her. Beauty with innocence. I was, to say the least, distracted.

'Oh, yes. We er... we knock on the window. Yes. That's it. Knock. Seventh window along, and there should be a cleavage in the... CROSS! I meant cross. There should be a CROSS in the window. Yip, this is the one, I'll give the secret knockers. KNOCK! Yes. That's it. Knock.'

I gave the knock then stood staring at her like a rabbit in the headlights. Her eyes were mesmerising. I hadn't seen such a fascinatingly beautiful girl since...

'Yes? Hello? Can I help you?'

The window had opened and a gentleman with round spectacles the size of portholes was disturbing our perfect relationship. I snapped back to international spy.

'Oh! Are you the man they call Kissy? ROLY! I mean Roly!'

He looked puzzled for a moment, but recovered fast.

'Yes, yes. Have you got the stuff?'

'Sure have – ten bottles! You got the money?'

'Too right I have! Pass that stuff in here quick-smart my beauty! I have got to get a snifter down me or I will die! And listen here, mate. There's forty bucks a bottle for each one on top of this you can get us. Here, love, cop this.' As I passed the bottles through the window (and calculated that I could retire on the proceeds if I could get the entire hold-full up here) he passed the money to my fiancée. I could see the excitement on her face as she joined in with our illegal activity, and I felt a definite bonding as she moved from being an incidental girl to an accomplice. Things were going extremely well.

'You've got a deal,' I said through the window. 'I'll try to get back up here with some more lovely big bottoms – BOTTLES – in the next day or two. I've only –'

'What in the blue BLAZES is going on round here?'

A new voice roared into the arena, and not one I particularly liked the sound of. The girl spun on her heel, then burst into fits of giggles with her hand in front of her mouth. She was not put off by this blot on the landscape, so I assumed he was one of the inmates. I thought it would be most impressive if I came down hard on him.

'Quiet!' I said. 'If you want some too, join the queue

and get your money out. Place your order with the girl, here, and I'll see what I can do.'

He turned purple and shook like a space rocket just before take off.

'I don't know who you are, my lad, but let me tell you: many others have tried to gain financially through smuggling alcohol into my sanatorium, and all have ended up in the prison, but none of them went so far as to try and embroil my grand-daughter in their sordid affairs! I shall track you to the ends of the earth, my boy, and shall mete out the fiercest punishment the name of God will allow!' As he said these words, he picked up a stick and started towards me. 'And for starters, I shall flay you to within an inch of your life!' He was shaking all over and screaming his head off.

Despite this unnerving outburst, it was still vitally important for me to look cool in front of this girl. He was not a young man, so I felt confident that I could keep out of his reach. I leapt on the bike and set off down the drive with the old buzzard in stick-waving pursuit. Once I had led him about twenty yards, I doubled back past him and headed for his grand-daughter. I circled round her three or four times.

'I'll be in touch,' I said, with mystery and intrigue in my words, 'as soon as I can. I don't know where and I don't know when, but I'll be back.' I picked a flower from a passing bush and delivered it to her as a romantic touch. She clutched the flower to her bosom and swooned as I blew her a kiss, narrowly dodged the wheezing stick-waver, and with a dismissive, 'Up yours, Grandad!' I disappeared up the drive.

I had never been so callous to anybody in my entire life, but he was old enough for it not to require an act of great bravery and I didn't care what I had to do to impress this girl. And she had been so impressed! That was probably why I liked her so much. No girl knows from where her prince will come, but when he turns up on a motorbike with a sack of goodies for the needy like some sort of latter-day Robin Hood, she knows she's got a good 'un. It was this thought that made me realise just what a great guy I was, and I could see that now I had a slightly mean streak, I was going to have even more problems with girls swooning around me than I had ever had before. I vowed to put up with it.

This said, I hadn't laid a finger on her and didn't even know her name, or how to contact her. How could I get back to her? There was no way I was going to knock on the door of Temperance House – something told me I'd get a frostier reception than a pair of boxer shorts in a nudist colony. I thought about the impression the stick-waver must have of me. I'd propositioned his grand-daughter, corrupted her into illegal dealings and sold illicit whisky to the inmates of his health farm. I liked the image, and made a mental note to buy a studded leather jacket at the next possible opportunity.

I agonised over what to do about my blonde bombshell for over an hour, and rode back up to the entrance of Temperance House four times. The demonic threats of the stick-waver had obviously hit home to some extent – even now I was such a tough guy – because I couldn't bring myself to ride in. I resigned myself to a strategic retreat. It was almost one o'clock, and we were supposed to be meeting back at the ship to go off on our motorbike tour of the island, so I headed for home trying to ride a bike in the pose of The Thinker.

I have no idea how many lives I was dealt when Saint Peter put me in to bat, but I knocked a good half-dozen off the tally during the afternoon's biking. There were nine of us, on six extremely unsafe mopeds, and none of the six – or the nine – was roadworthy. The competitive spirit began on the very first gravel road, and we lost two bikes at the first corner. They went through a hedge into a field and we spent twenty minutes trying to drag them back through. At thirty miles-an-hour the bikes and their incumbents had ghosted through the hedge like it wasn't there and – except for a few leaves floating serenely to the road – there was no evidence of the visitation in the composition of the hedge, but now, without the benefit of momentum, neither bikes nor personnel could find their way back again.

Sparky, NotNorman and Benny the Dog decided in the end that they did not need to come back through the hedge, and that the rest of us – having the road at our disposal in order to get up the necessary speed – should imitate their actions and pass through to their side. We told them not to be so ridiculous, and they told us that it was fun; a bit like a fairground ride. We couldn't see each other because of the foliage, so an argument developed with Sparky, NotNorman and Benny the Dog jumping up and down in order to harangue us over the hedge, and the rest of us standing on our bikes, peering back over the hedge shaking our fists and ranting back at them.

Eventually a coin was tossed, and despite the inverted logic, we were honour-bound to attain the appropriate velocity and ride our bikes through the hedge to their side. As I approached the barrier at thirty miles-an-hour, I remember trying to figure out how we'd arrived at the belief that this was a sensible course of action, but we all piled our bikes into the hedge nevertheless, and reappeared on the far side.

So we were half-an-hour into our motorbike tour, still in sight of the ship, standing around like sheep in a field and unable to get out. Only half the bikes would start, and we all looked as if we'd been dragged through a hedge forwards. Eventually, we got all the bikes going again, and bumped off unsteadily round the field looking for a gate. It transpired that there was a bumpy jungle track leading up into the mountains, and we took to it at ill-advised speed.

During the passage along the lumpy track it became obligatory, if one came close enough to one of the other runners and riders (usually during suicidal overtaking expeditions) to attempt to knock ones colleague into the thick bushes on either side, so after a further ten minutes of quite ludicrously dangerous malarkey we stopped once more by the side of the track. We'd each come off once or twice, and now we'd lost Giewy. He'd last been seen doing a handstand. On the handlebars of his bike. At thirty miles-an-hour. On a machine that was already eight feet off the ground and heading off at right-angles to the track.

'Giiiieeeeeeeeeeeeeeeewwwhhhhhaaaaaaaaaa!'

BOOF! He disappeared through the thick foliage into the jungle and all went eerily quiet. Search as we might, we couldn't find him. I was in pain with a mixture of injuries and laughter at the antics of the ride thus far, and when the bedraggled Giewy emerged wobbly-kneed from the undergrowth clutching nothing but a set of handlebars I just about keeled over. His motorbike was a complete write-off, partly because it had wrapped itself round a tree like a frightened child clinging to its father's leg, and partly because it could not be extricated from the tangle of plant-life that had adopted it forever. That was Giewy's five hundred dollars down the drain.

All was not lost for him, however, because NotNorman – who had sustained impressive injuries during a piked, double-back-somersault with three-and-a-half twists earlier on the track – no longer had the stomach for the ride and was going to walk back to the ship. He was more than happy to hand over his death-trap to Giewy.

Soon the eight of us were bouncing along through thick jungle on narrow, uneven paths. Bushes swiped at my steering arm and overhanging branches thumped me in the chest as we flew through the air after hitting stumps and roots on the jungle floor. It was lethal.

Before long the novelty of multiple injuries began to wear a little thin, and the bikes, as we steered them from one crushing disaster to the next, were beginning to wise up and think twice about doing their masters' bidding. But spirits were still high because it was principally Giewy who continued to suffer above all others. He was a nutter, although a grudging part of me couldn't help but be impressed by his apparent fearlessness. In his latest bid for the front runner's spot, the bike had flung him skyward, waited patiently for him to return to earth, then jumped on his head. Giewy got up, cut to ribbons but unbowed as ever by his umpteenth injury. The bike, however, had more sense than Giewy and, having failed to murder him, no longer had the strength to carry on.

We tried kind words and we tried shaking it ferociously. Then we tried wiggling wires around and switching switches on and off, but all to no avail. This would need some real engineering. Benny the Dog, as the senior engineer present, took charge. He was a man from a long line of engineers, with a degree in mechanical engineering and eight years' shipboard engine-room experience. He took a good run-up and kicked it in the vitals. The bike immediately leapt into life and promised never to fail us again. Unfortunately, as we turned to congratulate Benny on his engineering prowess, the engine noise didn't level off and calm to idling speed, but built and built until it was roaring at the absolute top of its range, and it would surely have committed suicide by revolution if Cookie Short of the Full Biscuit hadn't had enough chocolate chips to cut off the petrol.

'Ahaaa!' said Benny the Dog. 'You remember that brave and impressive bid for first position Giewy made just now? Now we know why – the throttle was stuck open!' Benny the Dog tinkered around for a while before announcing, 'Well, the good news is, I know how to fix it. The bad news is, I need a Phillips crosshead screwdriver.'

'Good grief,' said Blom, 'I thought your toolbox contained nothing but different-sized hammers!'

'Aye, well. If I had a hammer I might easily find a use for it, but the thing we need to fix this bike is a Phillips crosshead screwdriver, and we've as much chance of finding one here as we have of finding Giewy's brain.'

This analogy allowed us to fully appreciate the gravity of the situation. We stood around the toppled charger proposing and rejecting creative but unworkable plans. We were, in the eloquent words of the Mancunian Benny, 'boggered'.

The best plan put forward was to tear further bits

from the bike and try to cobble together some sort of tool from these amputations that might do the job of a Phillips crosshead screwdriver. Cookie Short and Benny the Dog set about this task, and the rest of us stood around pointing and giving them advice, until all of a sudden, a distraction was discovered.

'Giew!' cried Giew, pointing up the jungle track. 'Gie-ew-ew!'

And there, about thirty yards away up the path, crouching behind suspicious eyes in the jungle undergrowth was some sort of pygmy. He was short and brown, carried a stick and was completely naked but for some kind of loincloth. A pucker, genuine, 24-carat pygmy, of just the specification Doctor Livingstone mixed with. I was amazed, but the others thought he was hilarious.

'HOW!' boomed Blom in his best Red Indian voice, saluting like an Indian chief. 'We come in peace!' Everybody laughed and I could see the pygmy tense up.

'Shut up, you lot,' I said firmly, 'or he'll bugger off.'

We quietened down and made smiling, friendly-type gestures. I was utterly fascinated, so I have to admit I was less than chuffed when Benny the Dog screwed the whole thing up just for the sake of a cheap joke. He stomped off up the path towards the little chap, waddling like a chimpanzee, and in a deep, patronising, Tonto-like voice called, 'Kemosabe, YOU HAVE PHILLIPS CROSSHEAD SCREWDRIVER?'

The laughter from the lads and the preposterous figure of Benny bearing down on him proved too much, and he disappeared instantly into the deep undergrowth, leaving not a speck of evidence that he'd ever been there at all. The fun was all over, so we returned to watching Cookie Short and the Bad Dog and their ritual humiliation of the motorbike.

I was really angry with Benny for what he'd done – he was indeed a Dog, but, being the kind of international spy who had others do his fighting for him, I just laughed vigorously at his superb sense of humour and boiled up inside instead.

Eventually, the bike was in even more pieces, and Benny the Dog had managed to fashion a sort of Phillips crosshead daffodil from the torn metal. He held it up proudly, then set about trying to fix the throttle cable with it. His Phillips crosshead daffodil was all very pretty, and seemed to be highly efficient when it came to slicing fourth engineers' fingers, but didn't seem to be of any help at all when it came to undoing screws. Benny was sweating profusely and becoming steadily more brutal with both the tool he'd crafted and the patient. Suddenly he rose from his task, held his daffodil high in the air like a pilgrim imploring a sacred object, gnashed his teeth and questioned its parenthood, then drop-kicked it deep into the undergrowth. This caused a good deal of unrest both amongst those present and apparently amongst his toes. It had taken some time to create this daffodil, and great hopes were resting on its utilisation. Now, in a moment of Dogged impetuosity, it was gone forever. Then, over the noise of the ensuing row, Giewy's whining voice could be heard once more.

'Giew!' he said. 'Giew-ew-ew-ieww!'

We followed his pointing finger back up the trail.

Sure enough, back in his place up the path, was the pygmy. This time, however, he strode confidently down the path towards us. I thought he was going to produce a blowpipe and kill us all for being so obnoxious, but as he drew closer, we could see he was proffering... a Phillips crosshead screwdriver.

During the minute it took Benny to fix the bike, the pygmy didn't talk to us. We knew he could speak English because he'd understood Benny the Dog's request for a screwdriver, but he stood inscrutably quiet, ignoring our attempts at small talk, and simply waited. We felt fairly embarrassed because we'd been rude and patronising, and he'd still lent us the tool. As he walked back up the path, I called after him.

'Why – why won't you talk to us?'

'Because,' he said, turning and staring back down the path at us, 'we didn't coincide in this world.'

Then he disappeared forever.

Chapter 22

A WATERY GRAVE

Notes on picking up girls in church. How to drown rather than be called names. Adventures underground. The Ascension: Windy rises from the dead. A new career as a mantelpiece ornament?

THAT EVENING WE were counting the cost. Major surgery was going on in both the ship's hospital (to rescue survivors from the *Global Wanderer*'s motorbike display team) and in the engine-room (to rescue five-hundred-dollar deposits).

I was working the evening, which disturbed me immensely. Apart from the fact that it was Christmas Eve, I wanted to get out there and retrieve my fair maiden from the clutches of her evil grandfather. It would probably be difficult to prize her out on Christmas Day, so time was running short. I could only hope she would see my non-appearance as supreme coolness and fancy me all the more by Boxing Day.

Even for the lads who didn't have to work Christmas Eve, it didn't feel very seasonal. Not so much as a steady drizzle or a massive credit-card bill for true festive atmosphere, and with temperatures soaring in blistering summer sunshine, the bookies were offering long odds on a white Christmas. Even so, the lads were becoming hyped up like five-year-olds at the prospect of Santa delivering a few beers, but were all agreed that the resource distinctly noticeable by its absence was – women.

Jinx was summoned and a strategy for integration with the local concubinary was demanded. A wry smile emerged, and the ends of his twirly moustache twitched promisingly. The signs were all there that a plan would shortly emerge.

'OK, lads!' he cheered rubbing his hands. We leant forwards expectantly. 'It's Christmas Day tomorrow, so we're all going to church!'

A stunned silence fell over us. This was not what we wanted to hear at all. Jinx could usually be relied upon to come up with unbeatable schemes for meeting young ladies, but this time he had definitely failed to cut the mustard. Church did not equate to romance to my way of thinking, and besides, it was Christmas, the traditional time for excess and debauchery.

NotNorman put the thing in a nutshell. 'Who the hell goes to church on Christmas Day?' he asked, puzzled, and we all nodded our agreement. The scheme was a loser. It had no redeeming features whatsoever for anyone who was not a lover of cassocks, choirboys or abstinence.

Jinx must be losing his touch, we thought, and he confirmed it by adding, 'And full uniforms, lads. Full uniforms,' as he left the bar.

A discussion ensued during which Jinx was accused of being (among other things) a fink, a charlatan and a miserable impostor. I agreed heartily. The last place I wanted to go was church. We were generally agreed that a new plan would have to be thrashed out. But then Benny the Dog piped up. He was a devotee of Jinx, having recently benefited to the tune of one legal secretary on the Australian coast, and what he referred to as a 'deep and meaningful bath' in a nurses' home in Louisiana, all as a direct result of Jinx's activities. Benny stood alone but defiant in Jinx's defence. He reminded us of the great man's performance to date. He spoke enthusiastically of the Australian parties, the strip-poker night with those girls on holiday in Barbados, of the fifteen-girl dance troupe he'd managed to coax back to the ship in Houston. All around the room, resolute hearts began to weaken as each man remembered the fantasies that Jinx's enterprise had transformed into full-breasted reality. All those extremely fit dancers running, giggling and half-naked, around the ship; drunk, screaming girls losing heavily at cards in Barbados as they turned up yet another ace from a totally rigged pack – they were a memory for life. Australian nurses partying the night away as only Australian nurses can – I would never forget them.

People rarely saw Jinx in action. He generally disappeared up the road and returned like the Pied Piper with a bevy of lovely ladies. And they were always 'nice' girls, such as nurses or British workers overseas. This led to a greatly improved demeanour on the part of the lads. Shavers were employed, clean shirts found and swearing was – at least initially – kept to a minimum. Jinx's parties always went extremely well for all concerned. Deeper, longer-lasting relationships were established (relatively speaking) and the compliment was often returned as invitations to private parties and family homes came back to us. Jinx always found it quite touching when there was a small group of broken hearts waving white hankies from the dockside as we left a port, and he must have heard more promises to write than you could shake a stick at.

Now, however, I had to be firm. I dismissed the curvy, pouting images from my mind and took stock of the cold hard facts.

'Let's face it,' I said, 'firstly, I do not wish to waste a pressed uniform on a visit to a blooming church, and secondly, I think there's a trick here. I'm dead suspicious of this one. There's definitely a practical joke behind this somewhere. I mean, who goes to church to meet girls? I recommend we beat him at his own game and nip off swimming, eating, sunbathing and drinking somewhere as ungodly as we can find.'

Despite my logic, most of the lads didn't have the strength of character that I'd shown in shaking off the images of dancers, drunk bikini-clad strippers, and Australian nurses partying the night away as only Australian nurses can. There was a degree of dispute and eventually all but two wandered off to apply their weak minds to sorting out their uniforms and stumbling haplessly into Jinx's trap. I was convinced there was a hidden agenda to the plan, and stood firm. NotNorman and Cookie Short – the other two main sufferers on the trip to date – also showing a healthy degree of suspicion about a plan that involved uniforms and a church. Which is how I came to find myself swimming in a tropical lagoon on Christmas Day, and how I nearly managed to kill myself in the water without the aid of a single shark.

It's rather strange to put on your trunks on Christmas Day and go swimming in a tropical lagoon. At least, I think it was a lagoon; it may have been a fresh-water spring, but whatever it was, it was idyllic. Fresh water emanated from a huge cave at the base of a cliff to the landward end. The lagoon therefore comprised clear, cold, fresh water. Then the tide would come in and flush out the lagoon with warm seawater. Above the cave entrance were steep cliffs rising high and out of sight, and all sorts of wildlife trotted and flew about the place enjoying the festive day off. NotNorman, Cookie Short of the F.B. and I peacefully wished the world a happy Christmas.

The cave fascinated us. It was possible to swim deep inside until it became too dark for our nerves. We decided to return with torches and head into the dark inner sanctum to explore on another day. Our exploration, however, was to come sooner than we expected, because as we swam into the cave for another chicken-hearted sortie, we were given the fright of our lives by a huge Lock Ness monster, emerging from the half-light and looking for cadet pie. I nearly ruptured myself trying to get away from what turned out to be two divers.

'Sorry, mate,' said one of them looking at my face. 'Did we give you a fright there, mate?' They were New Zealanders. We were pretty sure they hadn't entered the cave from our end, so the obvious conclusion was that it must lead somewhere.

'Oh, wow!' I said. 'We were just talking about getting some gear down here and checking out these caves! Must be magic in there.' I neglected to tell him that my 'gear' consisted of a bucket, a spade and a rubber duck.

'Sure is!' said the first one, adjusting some important-looking valves and straps. 'But you don't need all this gear to check out the best bit. It's just here.' He indicated the water under his feet. 'There's a hole about eight feet down, goes along about eight feet, then you pop up in this massive grotto. They used to hide in it during the war, so there's loads of old stuff they've left in there, and there's a big long ladder to the roof with a hatchway.'

My mouth was open. Underwater tunnel? Grotto? Ladder and hatchway? The other diver picked up the story.

'We guess it must come out in the town somewhere. During the war, the locals would open the hatch in town, climb down the ladder, then dive out through the hole here and into this cave. They'd have boats hidden out there in the lagoon and escape anything. How cool is that?'

It would have been pretty obvious that I thought it was waaaay cool. I love things like this, and my jaw had dropped so much that they must have thought I was dredging for plankton. 'You are joking,' I gabbled eventually. 'You have got to be joking. The town must be about five miles away from here!'

'Maybe it is if you go round the road, but you go straight up, and the town's just there. We're gonna go through now and climb the ladder. We want to find out where the hatch opens up. Nobody's used it since the war. You can swim it dead easy and come with us if you like. There's nothing to it. Just follow us!' And with that, they duck-dived and disappeared into the dark rock about eight feet down.

Instead of asking them why, if you don't need any gear to get through to the grotto, they had enough life-support equipment to start a human colony on the sea-bed, I strained my eyes underwater and watched their flippers disappear into the hole. NotNorman, Cookie Short and I were fascinated, curious... and cowards.

We spent a good ten minutes diving down the eight feet and staring into the deep, forbidding hole. None of us had the guts to commit ourselves to swimming in. I wanted desperately to see inside the grotto, but didn't want to take the risks involved in getting there. I was frustrated by my own lack of bravery. Each of us in turn dived down, took one look and returned to the surface.

'It's pitch black in there. It's got to be more than eight feet to the grotto once you're in. You can't see any sort of light at all,' said NotNorman, shaking his head in despair.

'That's 'cos it's dark in there, Spanner-brain! The exit's in sight, you just can't see it,' replied Cookie Short logically.

I was at the end of my tether. I was spellbound by the prospect of this grotto and the secret passage from the town, I was determined to find a way of getting in. 'We've got to do it, lads,' I said. 'This is a once in a lifetime opportunity! After the first time through, it'll be a piece of cake. We'll wonder why we were so soppy about it!'

But after another half-dozen cheek-expanding, goggle-eyed dives, neither of them had fallen for my master-plan and gone first.

'Tell you what,' suggested Cookie Short, 'why don't we go into town and climb down through the hatch?'

A WATERY GRAVE

That sealed it for me. I realised that we had no idea where in town the hatch might be found, and that we might never see the Kiwis again. The only way into this adventure was through the tunnel and I, Windy Baboulene, was man enough for the task.

'Right. I've had it with this! I can't float around here with you carpets any longer. Am I the only one with any balls around here? You two have a nice day – I'm going through.'

I took a deep breath and disappeared beneath the waves. I sunk down to the hole, gripped the sides and stared into the darkness. It was inky-black and noticeably colder. My head shouted at me to swim in – 'Eight feet, for God's sake. It's only eight feet!' – but my arms stayed rigid and my hands gripped the sides more firmly than ever. I looked up at the legs of my scorned shipmates at the surface and imagined the ridicule I would receive if I wimped out after what I'd said. I was far too egotistical to go through that, so my head told my arms that we were not allowed to go back to the surface, and I was amazed to find the rest of my body agreeing that drowning was better than humiliation. My grip on the sides relented, my whole self worked as one for once, and I began to swim into the hole. I was BRAVE! 'OK body, let's go for it!' I shouted, and in we went.

As soon as I entered the hole I regretted it. Humiliation suddenly seemed a massively preferable option. The passage was shaped like a teardrop; as I floated higher, it became increasingly narrow and restrictive. I couldn't move my arms properly to swim or even to 'climb' along the walls. I considered going back, but found that reversing was even harder than going forwards. I didn't wish to die of indecision, so I scolded myself to keep calm and keep going. 'Just keep a grip,' I told myself, 'it's only eight feet.'

I felt my way ahead with my arms outstretched in front and kicked as hard as I could with my legs, but things quickly went from bad to worse. Not only could I not use my arms, but I was now scraping my back and head painfully against the sharp, abrasive coral roof of the tunnel. The roof also served to greatly restrict my legwork as the backs of my feet and calves suffered similar agonies against the brittle, unforgiving coral. 'KEEP CALM!' I insisted to myself. 'PANIC AND ALL IS LOST. It's only eight feet, KEEP CALM!'

'But we must have swum twenty feet already!' screamed my nerve-endings, 'And we need oxygen to survive, and there isn't any down here! And the blood we are losing from scraping along the coral will attract sharks and piranha! And we need to see light to know which way is up. And we're running out of air, and its dark and we're going to die! PANIC! PANIIIIIIIIC!'

With a massive effort I held on to my breath, dribbling the remaining air from my mouth as calmly and slowly as I could. Meanwhile my legs flailed painfully against the rock, my arms groped desperately into the black void ahead, and my head and back scraped agonisingly against the cheese-grater coral. I continued, getting steadily less and less effective for what seemed like an age, while my bodily panic and my mental calm were both reducing as hope of survival slipped into the fog of my oxygen-starved brain. The passage ahead promised nothing but more of the same, and there seemed no prospect of any change in the texture of the ceiling. There was no point in turning back (impossible anyway) and the last of my air was dribbling from my blue lips. I remember very clearly thinking about what the next twenty seconds held for me; my last twenty seconds of consciousness. My lungs were empty and every reflex in my respiratory system was triggering frantically, trying to get me to breathe in. I knew I couldn't resist the urge for much longer, but that my next intake would not be life-giving, fresh cool air, but a thick, choking, soupy ingestion of cold, dark water. The water would rush in, pushing down my throat and filling my lungs, but my brain would continue to function long enough for me to experience all the horror, and I would beg for death to take me from this nightmare. As my head knocked feebly against the coral roof, and the water pressed coldly against my tongue, I found myself recalling a distant memory.

I'd nearly drowned once before, back when I was about seven. I was diving for coins in a swimming bath and, while I was upside-down and underwater, I got my foot caught in the ladder. I became aware of this as I floated towards the surface. I simply bent my knee so that I could float upwards, but about six inches from the surface, I found I couldn't get any higher without breaking my leg. This I would gladly have done had I the physical strength or leverage, but underwater, I was simply stuck. I flailed wildly trying to make it the few inches to the air, but getting nowhere because of the ladder, and I was in too much of a panic to go back down and release my leg. A lifeguard rescued me that day, and now my life passed before me from that moment onwards. It was as if everyone I'd ever known had made a slideshow of all the significant events in my childhood and presented all five thousand snapshots to me in a split second. The house where I was born, primary school teachers – Miss White, Mrs Foreguard – playing football on the recreation ground, old Doctor Beeston with his stethoscope, my first bicycle (I'd forgotten it had white tyres – it suddenly seemed very important), climbing trees in Wolf's Wood, playing with a hose in the back garden, my happy face at the far end of a birthday cake shaped like a football pitch, building a snowman with my sisters and sledging into it, Mum's Morris Minor, riding on Dad's shoulders, getting chased for pinching golf balls, Grandma cooking, our Collie dog jumping for a stick, the day I cut my own hair – thousands and thousands of snapshot images; absolutely vivid, and quite incredible. I know it sounds clichéd, but it's true what they say: your life passes before you as you drown.

My family and friends were just saying goodbye and powering down the slide-projector to go home, and I was about to sleep forever when I became aware of a jolt. I coughed and spluttered and the world whirled around me as I tried to focus on the face of Saint Peter leaning over me.

Saint Peter was wearing a wet suit, and was pushing hard on my chest. It was one of the New Zealanders. I finished coughing and my entire body gasped, tearing at the precious oxygen, sucking like a black hole until all the rocks in the grotto began to move towards me. I then began a record-breaking exhale.

'OOOH, MY GOD!' I rasped, putting all the rocks back in place again.

'You made it, then,' said the Kiwi glibly.

Once I had recovered a little, we inspected my wounds. Apparently they were fairly serious, but because they were behind me I was able once more to give the impression of admirable bravery. Had I been able to see the state of my back and head, I may well have passed out, but the injuries and the blood were out of sight and merely smarted at the time. To the Kiwis, I was impressively brave. And I was about to impress them again.

'Right, let's explore the old grotto then,' I enthused from the prostrate position, dismissing concerns for my mental condition and the state of my back and lungs.

'Are you kidding, mate? We should be getting you to the doc's.'

'Sure I'm sure! And I want to climb the ladder and emerge in the town. I didn't suffer all this just to go back. Let's rock and roll!'

The Kiwis looked at each other in amazement. I had now been brave twice in succession, something noticeably without precedent in the slide show that had just passed before me. They must have thought I was quite a guy. However, following my harrowing experience they decided it would be best to nip back through the hole and collect NotNorman and Cookie Short before they too injured themselves horribly trying to follow me. The Kiwis left me to stare at the black void above my head and drop gradually into a state of shock as they went for the others. NotNorman and Cookie Short were led through like girlies by the Kiwis, and I made as much out of the fact as I could.

While the others were thus engaged, I reflected on

the look on the Kiwis' faces. They were genuinely impressed with me. What I had omitted to tell them was that the only reason I was looking so brave now was because of simple and abject terror I was feeling at the prospect of getting into the water and going back through the dreaded tunnel. There was no way I could manage that.

The guys ooh'd and aah'd around the grotto while I pretended I was absolutely fine. Were I in a calmer frame of mind, I think the grotto would easily have lived up to expectation. As it was, I needed urgent medical assistance and there was no easy way out. It felt like a prison.

Soon we decided to climb the ladder. Heights don't usually bother me up to about four feet, and I had grudgingly got used to the thirty-foot ladders in the holds on the ship, but this was a whole new ball game. This was an extremely old and unsafe ladder, towering up into the blackness. We shone the torches up into the void and still couldn't see the top. The ladder just disappeared into the darkness.

When we were about halfway up, I couldn't see either the top or the bottom. I felt as if I was suspended in space on a totally disconnected ladder. This was a weird and disarming experience. I began to feel hypnotised by the height and had a tremendous urge to jump off. I wisely managed to resist the temptation as a conversation began on the subject of the reactions of the townsfolk as a hatch lifted up and five lads appeared as if by magic from the middle of the road. It would be something, particularly as all our clothes and shoes were on the beach back outside the cave.

Eventually we reached the top of the ladder. We were immersed in an eerie blackness that the torches cut through like lasers. The bottomless void beneath us was overwhelming. One of the Kiwis pushed at the hatch. Nothing happened. He pushed again. Not a sausage. Here we were, five little dots in the top corner of an underground cavern, with every prospect of having to return to the real world via a murderous underwater tunnel. I channelled my panic into assertiveness.

'Come ON!' I said, as a return down the ladder was mooted. 'Great adventurers do not turn back simply because of a sticky hatch. Put your backs into it!'

The Kiwis obviously thought that bravery such as mine must also be accompanied by a fearsome temper, so they jumped to it. They contrived to get next to each other at the top of the ladder and brought their combined strength to bear on the recalcitrant hatch. Still no luck, so they gave up with their arms, stood two rungs further up the ladder, braced their backs against the hatchway and bent their knees.

'One, two, three – HEEEEAAAAVE!'

In the church on the edge of town the Christmas service was in full swing. Jinx and his flock, putting heart and soul into 'Good King Wenceslas', were looking very smart in their uniform whites and despite the sobriety of the church, they were in thoroughly cheerful spirits and were contributing heartily to the proceedings. A look around the congregation revealed the reason for their good mood, because as the congregation had arrived for the service, it became clear that they were predominantly British and that there was no shortage of what employers of the vernacular might refer to as 'crumpet' amongst their number. For their part, the resident folk were impressed by the attendance of smart, religious British officers, and introductions to daughters and invitations to homespun Christmas celebrations had been readily forthcoming. Jinx had done it again. His plan was showing its substance, and although it meant sitting through a church service before it bore fruit, the lads were salivating at the peaches and pairs that were ripening before their very eyes.

So you will understand that it was something of a distraction for all present when, as they split into descant and congregation for the line 'When a poor man came in sight', a large floorstone in the middle of the church began to join in the chorus. It scraped a bit, then it roared like two scuba divers contracting a hernia each before finally throwing itself up in the air and plonking itself down to one side. And as if this wasn't enough, a pair of Kiwi heads popped up through the resulting hole like nervous chipmunks checking to see if the wolf had gone. The resounding carol tailed off into silence.

'Good heavens!' said the vicar, never one to mince his words, 'I shat m'cassocks!' (Well, that's what he should have said.) He had been at the church for twenty years and had no knowledge of the hatch. For all he knew this was Beelzebub himself, coming up from Hell to question the validity of his theological standpoint personally. The assembled gathering was now sharing a stunned silence.

I was stuck ten rungs down the ladder behind the other lads. I couldn't see past them, and could feel panic welling up. The exit was finally in sight and I wanted it badly. I decided that the silence and the lack of activity above could benefit from a little more of my new-found authority.

'Come on, you wankers! Get a wiggle on up there! Jesus H. Christ, we'll be here all day if you don't shift your arses!'

My shouts filled the church as roundly as if God himself had spoken and the poor congregation, assembled choir and clergy were offended not just the once, but every second for the next minute or two as the church's superb acoustics echoed my profanity a thousand times into each sensitive ear. 'WANKERS, wankers, wanke... JESUS H. CHRIST, Jesus H. Christ Jesus.. ARSES, arses, arses...'

Despite my encouragement there was still no motion above me on the ladder. It was as if they'd seen a ghost, so I batted on with more of the same as one by one, the lads above me slowly trickled out and stood sheepishly by the hole. I continued to rant as I followed them out, swearing vigorously the whole time. The lads smiled wanly at the masses as my words filled the church.

When I emerged and saw where we were, I was completely lost for words – although some of my old ones were more than happy to fill in for a while in the absence of anything new. I gulped, shut myself up, and stood half-dressed and bleeding with my latest profanity reverberating like Christmas bells around the throng; every echo another kick in the shins of decency for these highly principled churchgoers.

The five of us stood in a line and stared bashfully at the floor like naughty schoolboys in the headmaster's office, shifting awkwardly from one foot to the other. Had we pockets, we would undoubtedly have thrust our hands deep to the bottom, and had cans been available we would certainly have kicked them coyly.

And as if things weren't tough enough, a new horror was about to befall me. As I caught the vicar's eye, the slow light of recognition dawned on his greying countenance – he knew me from somewhere. I recognised him too, and the presence of his beautiful blonde grand-daughter in the front row confirmed my worst fear… and his.

'Y-Y-YOU!' he cried, pointing a shaking finger at me and searching his congregation for support. 'This – this - this man is a criminal! Grab him! Call the police!'

A great gasp went up from the congregation and the ladies pulled their jackets protectively over their peaches and pairs in horror while the men jumped up and rounded on us. Never one to miss an opportunity, Jinx leapt from his pew and raised his clenched fist high in the air.

'Stand back, everyone! Let us handle this! You lads, get the ruffians!'

And like a well-oiled crack troop of SAS, our own shipmates leapt on us from all sides and began pummelling us impressively.

'It's for your own good,' whispered Jinx and as if I wasn't suffering enough physical pain, he knocked me to the floor, and set about me with all the vigour one would expect from someone who wants to make it look realistic. 'They'll hand you over to the police if we don't make it look good,' he whispered as he kneeded my head. He held me prostrate on the floor and squeezed my throat through a half-inch gap in his hands and began banging my head on the unforgiving flagstones, telling me all the while how I would thank him later. Then he turned to catch the eye of his intended in the congregation and posed, smiling for a photograph as I turned purple from the neck up. For some reason, I found it hard to feel grateful as they practised their best wrestling moves on us. I guess I just wasn't in the mood. On the other hand, the lads loved every minute and you could sense the entire female population swooning with admiration at the swift actions of those smart British officers. They were well in.

We picked ourselves up from the dusty road outside and brushed ourselves off. I was still choking from the impressive throttling Jinx had so generously given, still dazed from the drowning and still losing blood at a dangerous pace from my back, head and legs. And no, that wasn't all. We had no money, no clothes, no shoes, and a nice long walk ahead of us.

It took several hours of trudging and complaining to get back to the ship, but only a minute or two for the second mate – in his capacity as medical officer – to take one look at the state of my aft, turn me round and rush me off to hospital.

I awoke on Boxing Day to a spinning head and vague dreams involving my spine being worked over by a combine harvester. Apparently, if coral gets into a person's blood stream, for instance mine, it can grow and spread through the veins and arteries, turning the victim into a brittle blue and red mantelpiece ornament within a month. Death may also figure in the process. Not that I cared, really. The chances of my ever running into my loved one were now as remote as winning the Best Kept Spine Award for 1977. I was in hospital for the rest of the day for sure, and the ship was due to leave the next day. I had also lost a five-hundred-dollar deposit on my moped, despite Cookie Short's best efforts at emergency surgery. I supposed I should look on the bright side, at least it was the moped that had passed on, and not me.

The burning issue was the girl. I was seriously considering jumping ship for this girl. I had planned a small wedding and a long and happy life spent staring into the oceans of her wide blue eyes, but apart from the practical stuff – such as finding her and guessing her name right – she had not, so far, received a good an impression of my net worth. She had seen me impersonate an MI6 agent, handle stolen goods, exploit alcoholics, damage hired goods and private property, appear half-naked and bleeding through a church floor, marched off and thrown out of said sacred premises, take the Lord's name in vain, shout 'wankers' and 'arse' during a religious ceremony, and lie blatantly to her and her grandfather. Her tall mysterious spy, sweeping her off her feet on a white charger had turned out to be a skinny vulgar cadet on a moped.

I pictured her standing next to me at the altar, and when asked, 'Do you take this man?' instead of saying, 'I do,' she laughs a hollow laugh and – to roars of approval from the congregation – grolleys up something unspeakable from the back of her throat and spits roundly on my shoes. It was becoming a definite possibility that the marriage might be off. If my life couldn't include this girl, then passing it as a rather sad mantelpiece ornament somehow seemed a fitting finale.

So, having had the doctors save my broken-hearted life against my will, the last thing I felt like doing was socialising. Have you ever noticed that whenever you are in pain, everybody and everything conspires to aggravate your injury? If you have a sore throat, it's salty, overcooked chips for dinner. If you have a headache, it's on the night you have front-row tickets to see Motorhead. If you have coral growing in the wounds in every part of behind you, everyone wants to pat you on the back for emerging so entertainingly through a church floor. It's always the same. Then they want to tell you how successful they were in impressing parents and granddaughters alike with the swift and clinical suppression and ejection of bleeding swimmers from places of worship, and they insist on boring you with the vital statistics of the girl they have coming to the ship's barbecue that night and what they intend to do to them. Disgusting, depraved, immoral, unprincipled and shallow in the extreme. These dogs had no idea of true love, and not so much as an ounce of sensitivity between them. Most of them had barely emerged from the primordial soup. They should have been strangled at birth for the benefit of womankind and the planet. I was damned if I was going to go to any poxy barbecue with a bunch of bottom feeders. They could stuff it.

I lay on my bunk for an hour and listened to the sounds of the party getting underway on the boat-deck. The distinctive barbecue aroma floated to my nostrils, and the sounds of glasses chinking and laughter jangling regaled my ears. I could hear Benny the Dog holding forth on the story of the Phillips crosshead screwdriver – he even did the Tonto voice – and the happy sound of awestruck ladies' laughter rang out. I put my pillow over my ears and harrumphed miserably. I couldn't even lie on my back. I was starving and uncomfortable – and I could tell that story WAY better than Benny the blooming Dog. A ring-pull fizzed. I imagined a cold beer washing its way around my dry mouth and I cracked. I decided to throw on some shorts and sit in a corner of the barbecue getting hideously drunk.

I limped onto the boat-deck and grabbed a beer from the Esky, then turned to look for a quiet corner in which I could fester, but a splash of a very distinctive colour took me flashing back in time to the one moment in my life I had seen that particular colour before. Now as then, my mind was swamped with blonde hair and the sensation of falling through space in slow motion. She was leaning over me at Temperance House. I felt her hand on my brow and a tingle rushed through my entire body just as it had then. I blinked and shook my head back to the present. There she was – walking towards me – here on the boat-deck of the *Global Wanderer* – with smiling eyes and laughing lips.

'Hiii!' she sang, 'I thought I'd never see you again!' Was she pleased to see me? I couldn't believe it. Why wasn't she bombarding me with unprintable adjectives? Why wasn't I wearing her drink? 'When they said you weren't coming tonight, I thought I'd never get the chance to thank you.'

I didn't understand. Not at all.

'So... you know who I really am, then?' I hazarded.

'Oh, yes. One of the other lads here was trying to chat me up after church and he told me. He got pretty mad when all I wanted to talk about was you, but what you did was so funny! Grandad absolutely wet himself when you came up through the floor! I've never laughed so much in all my life! He's been banging on since the beginning of time about religion and his abstinence. Then you come along and break every one of his top ten rules in thirty-seconds! He's shut himself away in his own temperance home for a week to contemplate the state of humanity, and I AM FREE! So where are you taking me, then? Bearing in mind that I owe you!'

I didn't need asking twice. The poet in me sprang to the fore.

'What would you say if I were to sweep you away from all this, to a wooden villa nestling under the palm trees of a South Pacific island,' I grabbed a bottle of wine and a six-pack, 'where we could slide away to a warm moonlit beach and...'

She interrupted doubtfully. 'Can you guarantee that this beach will be completely clear of grandfathers?'

'Now there's a piece of luck – I happen to know just the place. May I escort you to a perfect sunrise?'

'But the sun won't be up for hours! Whatever will we do all night?'

'Well now, I'm sure we'll think of something, won't we?'

And we strolled off hand in hand.

Chapter 23

COPRA BUGS

Homeward bound. Setting up home with several million others.

AS WE LEFT Western Samoa it struck us like a frying-pan in the face that the next port was effectively Liverpool. Apart from the briefest kiss with Panama, and a whistle-stop in the Azores, we were nearly home.

As the islands disappeared over the horizon behind us and the sun set behind them, I was sad to see the retreating silhouette of a wonderful place, and once more I vowed to return. My advice is to do whatever you must in life to visit the South Pacific islands. They are a magical part of the world. Skip Clacton this year and go to Rarotonga.

OCEAN BOULEVARD

The outstanding feature of the crossing to Panama was the population of copra bugs that had booked up to make the journey with us. Copra bugs live on, in and because of coconut husks. They are oily-black beetleish chappies that can fly. They are also incalculably numerous. For each coconut piece there must have been eight copra bugs. That's roughly 32 to each complete coconut shell. We had thousands of tons of coconut husks. That's MILLIONS of copra bugs, and they got everywhere. Absolutely everywhere. They appeared from the shower head instead of water, they got behind the screen and featured strongly in every television show. Clouds of them accompanied me to bed, they crunched underfoot with every step taken (both inside and outside my boots), families of them swam happily in our beers, they broke every mechanical entity on board through mass suicides in the workings, they shared our tea and rendered every meal, snack and lick of toothpaste crunchy with copra bug. One is never alone with copra bugs.

Jinx had a nest of them set up home in his left ear (he eventually had to be hospitalised) and Crate – who discovered an unfortunate phobia for them – went seriously barmy trying to escape their omnipresence.

They were also incredibly resistant to attempts at murdering them either individually or en masse. It was nigh on impossible to kill them without endangering the lives of any humans in the vicinity, and their massacre quickly became the principal source of entertainment on board. They had the most astounding ability to accept a total flattening as if it was a dinner invitation, then bounce back into shape and continue about their business as if nothing had happened. If you stamped on a copra bug or smashed it on a tabletop with a clenched fist, it squashed flat and round as if it was a butter bean. You looked on, taking pride in a job well done as it remained squashed flat for a few satisfying seconds. Then, just when you were shaping up to squish the next one, ping! Up it pops, back into fit and healthy mode once more and beetles off as good as new! I think it actually did them good to get bashed about in this way – they queued up and begged to be next. It seemed to invigorate them and set them up for the day.

Numerous experiments were set up in the bar to subject copra bugs to all sorts of torture, and bets were placed on how they would fare. The ones left to swim in vodka didn't drown or sink. They adapted to the conditions, had a family and grew old gracefully. The ones placed next to the diesel generator exhaust-outlet grew bigger, bent the bars and escaped. They all lived long and happy lives irrespective of our actions and we just had to learn to live with it. When copra bugs take over the planet, remember, you heard it here first! The only clue I can provide for a future generation vainly fighting back on The Day of the Copra Bug, is that we put one in a jamjar with one of MegaWatt's famous farts. It died horribly in three toe-curlingly painful minutes.

The return through Panama was a very routine transit. Everybody was too tied up with thoughts of England to bother with practical jokes, and there was no cargo to deal with, so we shot through in next to no time. The Atlantic looked, smelled and felt different. It was summer in the southern hemisphere, and the change in the weather was noticeable, to say the least, but it was not the cold that occupied us. We were getting close to Europe, and the focus of my attention – and everybody else's – swung like the ship to face north-east: home. Nobody could talk of anything else. Every effort was made to get the ship aquaplaning towards payoff, and everyone on board was preoccupied with plans for the ensuing leave which would begin the moment we hit Liverpool. But first, we had one final port of call. A swift cargo stop in Ponta Delgada in the Azores. Nothing of any import could possibly happen in this windswept corner of the Atlantic, now could it?

Chapter 24

A CLASS ACT

A lady of great repute is taken to a restaurant. Everybody is ready for her. Windy takes her home. Everybody is ready for him.

I SWAGGERED INTO the bar. All eyes were on me, as I knew they would be.

'Baboulene! There you are at last. Well? Did you give her one?'

I shut my eyes and turned my face away, shunning the uncouth questioner. I then gave one of those smiles that turns down at one side – the side opposite the raised eyebrow – for the fans, and sauntered towards the bar. I removed a beer from the fridge, signed for it and turned back to my adoring and expectant public.

'Well, come on, Windy! There's a lot of money riding

on this! Did you give her one or not?'

I looked down on the poor fools – all wide-eyed and drooling like seals awaiting fish – and took a long, slow slug on the beer. It was going to be pleasant enough taking all that lovely money from them, but I would have gladly forgone the cash just for the pleasure of telling them all about it. In fact, just to prolong their agony, let me tell you all about it, starting two days previously.

The Azores are a beautiful, if exposed, group of islands belonging to Portugal and stuck way out in the middle of nowhere. This was much nearer home, and although the weather was all right, the wind was up and the general flavour was definitely Northern Hemisphere once more.

Shortly after the ship came alongside, we gathered in the bar to discuss the forthcoming evening, when the shipping agent entered.

He said something along the lines of, 'Hi guys! I'm Bob Rumsby from Barrion's Shipping Agency. I know you're only here for a couple of days, but if you need anything I'm your man...'

Good old Bob petered out to nothing as he realised that nobody had heard a word he'd said. Not a syllable. Because behind him was the most astoundingly beautiful woman I had ever laid eyes on. And 'woman' was the operative word. A curvaceous thirty-something in a very expensive, very full suit. Bob was sharp. He noticed a room full of tongues and eyes-on-stalks and turned his sentence round to make it worth bothering with. 'And this is Michelle. She works for Turbo TV in the UK. They're filming here in the Azores and they need some shipboard stuff. Michelle is the assistant director so you'll be seeing her around the ship a fair bit. I'm sure you'll all make her feel at home.'

'Good afternoon, boys,' she purred, her voice licking the inside of my ears and rummaging in my underwear. Very business-like and upper class, she was clearly the kind of woman who could hold her own in the television industry, but simply oozing sex whether she wanted to or not. I noticed people around me were breathing again. She was gone. There was a fair amount of collar-loosening and brow-wiping before Sparky – who was in charge of such things – announced, 'Bar profits are proud to announce SIX cases of beer to any man who can assist the assistant director out of her panties! NO! Make that TEN! Bar profits are safe as houses with a class-act like her and a bar-full of prime-time tossers like you! Any takers?'

It's at times like these, a wise man keeps his mouth shut, has a drink and looks around for the idiots, but then I noticed myself jumping up and down with my hand in the air, shouting, 'I'll take your profits off you, Sparks!'

Sparks looked at me in disbelief and a general buzz ran round the bar. Not laughter as such, more a murmur. OK, giggling. Sparky did some sums in his head and never took his eye off me as he chanted:

'Bar profits are proud to announce a book on the chances of Windy shagging the director! Starting at fifty-to-one against!'

Silence.

'OK, SIXTY-to-one! Who can resist odds like that? Come along now gentlemen!'

Nothing.

I held my head up high. 'I will offer ten-to-one against me failing – that should finance your book for you,' I said. And with that, Sparks was besieged by frantic crowds waving money at him. It looked like the dealer floor of the Bombay Stock Exchange. Nobody wanted to put money on my being successful. Then, amidst phenomenal derisive laughter, I put a tenner on myself. It occurred to me that I was not a wise man.

Gambling was taken very seriously on board, and the perceived likely outcome made this particular wager more extreme than the usual couple of quid. As the odds settled, the people who eventually placed money on me would be extremely miffed were I to come away empty-handed. Those who'd placed money against me would be equally miffed were I successful. Either way, I would be unpopular with most people for a long time. And I'd be skint myself if I didn't manage to seduce the lovely Michelle.

I got up and headed for the door, a man with a mission.

I left in a storm of heckling and laughter, but I wasn't interested. I was regretting my actions already, but I knew I had to get to this woman at all costs or my life wouldn't be worth living. I ran up to my cabin and threw on my uniform whites. Then I dashed out on to the foredeck. Michelle and a small entourage were surveying the scene, planning angles, lights and backgrounds for filming to come. I swanned up to her all business-like, set my cap at a jaunty angle, and offered her my hand.

'Hi, Michelle. My name is Windy Baboulene. I'm the officer in charge of, er... (Seduction? Orgasms? Filming? Good grief! Why didn't I think before I opened my mouth?) in charge of... well, I'm in charge, and I've been asked by the captain to look after you while you're on board. Your wish is my command!'

I bowed with a musketeer's flourish and beamed at her. She looked me up and down. She was old enough to be my mother, and here I stood, feeling like a ridiculous child. Then she smiled back.

'Well, thanks very much, Windy. I appreciate that. Do we have to open a hatch to get into the cargo holds?'

Great! I knew the answer!

I leapt into action, tripping over a stray foot that was hanging around the bottom of my other leg and banging my nose horrifically on the corner of the hatch. I bounced back up as if nothing had happened.

'Doe, doe, dot ad all. Dare is a dadder dowd into de 'tween-deck from dat masd-house over dare.'

I was carrying a clipboard in order to enhance my (admittedly excellent) look of authority, but as I swung it out to indicate the masthouse, it left my hand and flew gracefully over the side of the ship into the sea. I looked at

Michelle and could see she was having trouble suppressing her laughter at this, at my nose – which was now throbbing like a distant lighthouse – and at my voice squeakily trying to force its way out through the right-angle halfway along my poor old hooter. I composed myself and went to speak just as my clipboard splashed rudely in the water. Michelle was close to bursting. She put a handkerchief to her nose to cover her laughter. I straightened my own nose with a loud CRACK, and tried to keep the mood up.

'Come on! Let's do it now,' I enthused. 'We'll need some lights in the 'tween-deck anyway. I'll take them down for you.' She honked with laughter in a way I found disappointing in a lady of such class. Then I realised my double entendre. 'NO! No! What I meant was... the lights. I'll take THEM down for you. I wasn't talking about anything else. For taking down, I mean. I wouldn't want to take anything else down for you... I don't mean to be rude by that. I mean, don't get me wrong, it's not that I don't find you attractive or anything, I mean, I don't mean that if you wanted me to take something down for you – even it is was rude – that I wouldn't because of course I would – if you wanted me to, that is – just not now, of course, because we are talking about lights. Not pants. Or anything...'

Michelle was laughing so loud people thought another ship was passing. But the damage was already done. I was a plonker and had walked up and proven it to her in under a minute. What a genius. I picked up a cluster lamp, dropped it into the 'tween-deck, plugged it in, climbed down the ladder and set it up. Fortunately there were a couple more lights down there already, so I nipped back up to get Michelle. When I got back out on deck she was nowhere to be seen.

I trudged off sadly towards the accommodation to get something for my pulsating nose and bruised ego.

The next day I was on cargo watch. Cargo was being loaded at hatches one and two, and Michelle and her team were filming at hatch three. I didn't intend to look for her again. I felt that a lifetime's worth of uselessness had already been imparted to her the like of which I couldn't match if I spent all day trying. I didn't care if I never saw the silly cow again. She obviously wasn't my type of woman if she laughed at people's misfortune. Obviously bossy, too. That's how she got to be an assistant director. I realised now why I'd put my hand up for Sparky's bet. It was because I wanted to get close to Michelle. I wanted to bring a total fantasy to life, and must have thought putting myself in the smelly stuff like this would somehow make it happen. Now I just wanted to go to the lads and try and back the whole thing out.

Then one of her lackeys came up to me and said, 'Michelle was wondering if you could help us at all?'

'What? Me? Of course! I'd be delighted!' and like a white knight recently released from a dungeon, I sprang – carefully – across to hatch three.

'Hi, Windy!' she cooed, smiling broadly. 'We need a shot of all these winchy wires moving. Can you arrange that for us?'

She gave the international hand gesture to indicate wires moving, and the couple standing next to her – apparently quite well off city types from the 1940s – nodded their approval for the wire moving activities. I gave her my reassuring 'leave-everything-to-me' smile – the one that so excited the captain – and swaggered across to the controls. It wasn't a winch, it was a derrick, and getting the wires to roll was simply a matter of pulling out the safety switch and turning the lever. I knew I wasn't supposed to be doing this alone and unsupervised, but there was no way I was going to let Michelle know that, and besides, what could go wrong? I wasn't even lifting anything.

'What, like this?' I said triumphantly, and whacked the lever over. I then stood proudly awaiting my applause. Instead, there was a creak. Then a LOUD creak. Then a whip-crack. I opened my eyes to see tripods, cameras and lights being knocked over as the 1940s toffs did a fine show of being motivated by fear and dived for cover. The cargo hook on the end of the wire was still stowed – hooked over the topmost railing at the ship's side. I was now applying a steadily-increasing tension to the wire, hook and railing, and the noises we could hear were nature's way of indicating that something was about to give. The creaking was the railing bending upwards, and the whip-crack was the wire straining before it reached breaking point. I whacked the lever the other way and released the tension – just in time. Thank God nothing went – although I had a rather obvious problem with the upper railing on the port side, which was now eight feet long instead of three, and pointing towards the sky. People began to emerge from their shelters and mop the sweat from their brows.

'Jesus! If that wire had gone, someone could have been killed!' pointed out the cameraman, quite unnecessarily I thought.

'Sorry? Oh. Didn't you want any tension on it? My fault. Let's try it again.'

Half of them dived for cover once more, the other half gave the international sign for 'Please for Christ's sakes leave that thing alone', but I insisted with chivalry. I nipped down, unshipped the hook and reeled the wire in and out as required. Anything to help.

Much to everyone's relief, the shot of the running wires went smoothly this time, and they moved on to some long shots at the next hatch whilst the 1940s couple leant on the bulwarks smoking cigarettes, then threw themselves into each others arms and kissed as if their lives depended on it. I had no idea what was going on with those two. They'd been fighting like cat and dog just a moment before. I replaced the cargo hook on the bent railing and hoped no one would notice it.

Having succeeded in my mission, I felt rejuvenated. I was once again confident that Michelle would be swooning with desire, so I trotted across to her with the loping self-assurance of a victorious tennis star about to jump the net. Fortunately, she was on her own, looking down into the hatches, mapping out some future scene in her mind while the others set up the next shot. I was also mapping out a future scene, but I doubt it was the same one as her.

'Was that OK? Did you get your shot?'

'Yes, Windy. Er... Thank you.'

'Not at all, not at all,' I said, sweeping her gratitude away with a magnanimous gesture.

'Sorry about your railing.'

'Oh. You noticed that did you?'

'Couldn't really miss it! Another second and that railing would have been on the moon! Are you always this accident prone?'

'Not at all! It's just that I am so nervous when I'm... when I'm around you. I can't seem to do a thing right!'

She took this in her stride.

'Really? Well I'd better leave you in peace while you still have a ship that can float.'

'No, no, no. That's the last thing I want. In fact, I want to see more of you. Any chance I could take you out for dinner?'

She gave me that maternal look again and shook her head.

'Windy, I'm very flattered, but really I don't think it's on, is it?'

'Why not? You've gotta eat, haven't you?'

'Well, yes, of course, but –'

'And you must like a good French restaurant?'

'Well, yes, of course, but –'

'So what's the problem then?'

She laughed and I could see she was going to give in.

'OK, OK. I'll risk it! But only if you promise me you won't touch any railings or wires.'

'I promise.'

'OK. Pick me up at the Hotel Flores at eight.' And she walked off. I was so blown away, I dropped the spanner I was carrying, and spent a constructive minute hopping around holding my foot.

Two hours later I had tracked down the most expensive French restaurant in the Azores. La Restaurant D'Amore was absolutely perfect, with intimate, romantic tables amongst plants and water sculptures. It was just right. I called the waiters, the manager, the wine waiter, the maître d', the chef, old Uncle Tom Cobbly and all into a huddle, handed them a handsome bribe, and outlined the importance of the situation. They all grasped the thing readily – as Frenchmen are apt to do in affairs of the heart – and we agreed our strategy. We pulled out of our huddle, slapped our high fives and looked forward to the evening's teamwork. I might have struggled to seduce Michelle on my own, but having secured the services of half-a-dozen Frenchmen, she wouldn't stand a chance. I looked at my watch. It was two o'clock. I had to get back to the ship. I only had six hours to prepare my body.

As it was such a special evening I even found my toothbrush and employed it in the traditional fashion. This may not seem like much to you, but when a toothbrush has been down behind a toilet for a couple of months it takes quite a man to use it for the first few minutes, I can tell you. Mind you, it didn't seem to do my teeth a whole lot of good. Anyway, I borrowed some soap and got someone to show me how it worked. I used one of those girly, lavender-scented ones – didn't half pong! – and a shampoo that allegedly brought to me 'The Fresh Austrian Atmosphere of Old Pine'. I then used a pre-shave cologne, a lemon-scented shaving foam, and a traditional 'manly musk' aftershave. I was definitely going to knock her dead. However, looking at the range of aromas I had employed, I began to doubt that the whole effect was masculine enough, so not wishing to give Michelle any chance of escaping me, I added an aerosol can full of Sea Spray deodorant to the mushrooms under my arms, half a bottle of Old Spice to my chest (including a good splash of it on my shirt and jacket – a trick I learned from one of the lads) a light splash of Brut all over my neck and a subtle dab of Men's 'eau de' behind each ear. I felt a little woozy for some reason – for a place set in mid-ocean, the Azores had pretty poor air quality – but I felt good. However, I didn't seem able to smell too much considering the work I'd put in, so I added a four-year-old bottle of Denim – with an octane rating along the lines of rocket fuel – to my crotch, feet and trousers, and hoped nobody was going to put a match too near me. By 7:30p.m. I was all ready, so I set off for the hotel.

It was a most peculiar journey marked by that problem with air quality I mentioned earlier. At one point I had to stop before crossing the road, and was completely enveloped in a fuggy cloud. It was good to get moving again. It was also on the journey to the hotel that I noticed another problem peculiar to the Azores. Apart from the air quality, it seemed the dog population was inexhaustible. Every time I looked around, a motley gang of mongrels lolloping along behind me was growing in size. I don't know how the locals put up with it. Between the dogs and the smell, a walk was almost unbearable. Funny I hadn't noticed it earlier in the day. It was good to escape through the revolving doors into the hotel.

The receptionist called up to Michelle and shortly she emerged from the lift like a blooming flower. Her image shimmered a little through the cloud, so I kept moving from side to side to keep my vision clear. She tacked her way across to me, a little confused by my side-stepping, but we joined hands in the end and I reached up to kiss her. She held up a wagging finger.

'Ah, ah. None of that. I agreed to go for dinner with you, but really, Windy, no more than that. I'm old enough to be – ahem! – to be – aHEM!' she went into a small coughing fit. 'Goodness me!' she said, screwing up her nose. 'They've overdone it a bit with the cleaning fluids in this reception, haven't they? I can hardly breathe!'

I helped her to a seat where she had another coughing fit, produced a handkerchief and made a noise into it like an engine with no oil. She nipped back upstairs and took a couple of hits of Ventolin, and returned looking better. She said she would be all right and that she needed some air, so I helped her to the door where the doorman was struggling with a couple of dozen dogs that had gathered outside. Really, I was amazed that the authorities didn't do something.

The air outside was only marginally better than that in the foyer of the hotel, but once we got moving, the dogs took her mind off the whiff, and she began to pick up. I said I supposed the smell might be the processing plant in the middle of town, but I was only being polite: for all Michelle's obvious class, she had definitely overdone it with the old eau de Cologne this evening. A lesser gentleman might have made an issue of it, even a joke, but I knew women and decided to let it go. I was probably making her feel all young and girlish again by asking her out, and she had overdone it out of nervousness. All rather cute really. And she was certainly turning heads! As I walked along with my head held high and this wonderful woman on my arm, everybody was looking, and even making way for us. It was as if we were royalty, the space we were being given. You could see the jealousy in their faces, too.

About nine of the Frenchmen in my pay met us at the door and beamed dutifully as we arrived.

'Bonsoir, Madam. Welcome to D'Amore,' drawled the maitre de, as his colleagues clasped their hands together with reverence, half-bowing to the lovely Michelle. With a good deal of surreptitious nudging and winking from my Gallic collaborators, we were led through the water features to our table where the onslaught began that was to part Michelle from her sensibilities. Alcoholic cocktails arrived instantly, and the wine waiter and I decided on a good fruity red in seconds. Michelle was taken aback.

'Wow! They don't mess about in here, do they?'

'Cheers!' I said, raising my glass. 'To your very good health!' and we both disappeared into the foliage and umbrellas of our extravagant cocktails (one of which was highly intoxicating).

Soon the conversation was flowing as quickly as the

aperitifs, and the team was attacking Michelle along two main avenues. The obvious one was the alcohol. There is nothing like a few drinks to lower the inhibitions of a lady who is on her guard, and Michelle had such a terrific sparkle in her eye I couldn't believe she was anything but a nymphomaniac once tanked up. The second – and less obvious – line of attack was the food. Men often ignore this important source of success. Lots of food. Piles and piles of heavy, rich food. It makes girls feel lethargic and easygoing. It means they can't be bothered to fight you off if it comes down to a bit of a struggle. I'm a great believer in packing them to the gills with big dinners.

So within a mere twenty minutes Michelle had succumbed to two cocktails, a Dubonnet, and was well into her second glass of wine (each wine containing an extra shot of something a little lively to fortify it). She'd lowered a good big starter (some red-meaty thing in a rich, brandy sauce) and the maître d' was just explaining to us how it had happened that we now had coq au vin for four instead of for two, and that we could eat as much as we wanted for the same price. I thanked him warmly, invited him to serve it up and raised my glass to Michelle once more. She was looking very happy. She seemed to have forgotten what an inept young boy her suitor was, and was chatting about her childhood and laughing at her inability to say 'Welwyn Garden City' – the place where she'd grown up – and when it came out as 'Willy Garden City' the image of a Willy garden got her laughing like a drain. I winked at the wine waiter as he brought her another 'vodka Côte du Rhône' and she grasped at it like it was a life-preserver.

And she proved no slacker when it came to putting the food away. I lowered a biggish single portion of the coq au vin, and felt I was doing well, but she worked her way through two of the other three portions like some sort of earth-mover, and was licking her lips at the prospect of the third. This also meant she'd taken aboard a fair bit more vin with the coq, and I watched her jaws and oily red lips working with great satisfaction.

When she wasn't eating, she was now talking in a very, very loud voice, and her accent had taken a surprising journey from the posh suburbs of Welwyn Garden City, down the A1 to somewhere out behind Arsenal Football Club. I was amazed. She cackled like a gossip, swore like a fishwife and laughed like a hyena at anything I said. She reached across and touched me during her conversation, and I felt the time was getting ripe for my organised highlight.

Michelle was still talking away nineteen-to-the-dozen, her words fighting their way past her full mouth, when I signalled to the waiter. The strolling musician sauntered over and launched into action with his violin. Dulcet Mozart tones filled the air and the moment was perfect for me to strike to her heart. The violin had sounded to her more like an air-raid warning than a young Amadeus, but she looked at me, a stray giblet hanging from the corner of her mouth. I looked longingly back into the one of her eyes that was looking at me (the other finding an involuntary interest in the ceiling fittings).

'Michelle,' I said, reaching across for her hand. 'I just wanted you to know,' she belched roundly, holding the air in her cheeks and releasing it under pressure, 'that meeting you has been the most incredible experience for me,' I moved closer, holding her other hand too. 'I can't bear the thought that we may be parted in the next day or two,' she was still blowing a bit, but I decided to go for the biggie, 'and, well, I think I love you.'

The violin swelled dramatically in time with my declaration. As did Michelle's cheeks. She threw her chair away and ran to the toilet with her hand over her mouth.

To give her her due, she was a tough one. When she came back, I thought she'd want to go home to her sick bed, but she was apologetic and didn't wish to spoil the evening, so she sat down, and after only one Perrier, set about not only the coq as if she hadn't eaten in a month, but also the vin once more with a vengeance. Within half-an-hour the party was up to speed again. Her stamina in the food and drink department was unparalleled. Our meal for four was reduced to a large, empty pot containing only the least digestible bones and the bouquet garni (which was only there because Michelle, at the height of her energies, had spat it back out with a screech of uncontrollable laughter).

She topped herself up with a family selection of cheese and biscuits (tastefully accompanied by a Napoleon liqueur), followed by an industrial caterer's delivery of tiramisu (tastefully accompanied by a bottle of dessert wine) and a plate of chocolates.

With no space left for so much as an espresso, I suggested we adjourn to her hotel room for coffee and 'afters', and we left amidst much curious gesturing from the French contingent. Despite now having the limpest Visa card in the North Atlantic, I felt things were definitely going my way, so I got a taxi to speed the prey to the lair, and within a trice we were shutting her penthouse door on the outside world and I was rubbing my hands for the ensuing festivities.

And that has brought you up to date with my awestruck audience in the bar. Michelle and I had been spotted entering the hotel, so they knew I'd got as far as her room, and as outlined, they were now keen to know how their investment got on in the bedroom.

'Well, come on, Windy! Stop standing there like a prize prat! Did you give her one or not?'

'Lads, lads, lads. Calm yourselves and I shall tell all,' I took another long swig on my beer. 'I didn't "give her one", as you so crudely put it,' I waited for the furore following this statement to die down. 'Easy lads, easy. I haven't finished yet. I didn't "give her one" – but we did make wild and passionate love ALL night!' Another furore, then they wanted to know the details. I eventually gave in to their clamourings. 'All right, all right. I am not usually one to kiss and tell, but as this is a business matter – she was like a tiger! All over me, all night long. I didn't get a moment's rest! And so skilled was she, so insatiable, curvaceous and passionate, that each time I thought I could give no more, she got me going again. It was unbelievable! That woman was a sex goddess! She nearly killed me with sheer, undiluted, continuous SEX!'

This was all going over very well. I was playing my audience like a master. All that is, but Sparky, who, having organised a book on the basis that I couldn't possibly get my hands on Michelle, stood to lose out big time. He stood up and calmed the madding crowd.

'Wait a minute lads, wait a minute. We all know Windy and how full of shit he is. We bookies can't possibly be expected to payout purely on his word. We need proof!'

'Hang on!' I interjected. 'You can't go moving the goalposts around now just 'cos you lost. I give you my word as an officer and a gentleman, and I'm afraid that will have to suffice! The only witness was Michelle, and I don't think you can go and ask her to tell you all about her earth-shattering multiple orgasms. You have no witnesses, and that's just your tough luck!'

I know how to put someone in his place when the time is ripe. I may run for government one day.

Sparky held up a videotape.

'I don't think you're quite right, there, Windy.' There were big, alarming smiles on the faces of all the lads. 'You remember she's doing some filming here, right?'

I didn't like this direction.

'Well they were filming some panoramic views across the bay. From her hotel balcony.'

Not one little bit.

'We thought it might make the bet a bit fairer if we persuaded the cameraman to turn the camera round a tiny bit, so instead of looking out across the town, we might all get a look at Michelle's bedroom!'

My bowels turned to water. They could NOT have filmed last night. THEY COULD NOT!

'So when you arrived back in reception, the cameraman started the camera and left the bedroom. He then nipped into Michelle's room this morning, retrieved the footage and made a tape. I think it's now time for your finest moment to have its world premiere! Mr BlimBlom! The television, please!' And Sparky set off across the room towards the video player with the dreaded tape in his hand.

My mind was sand, my legs jelly, and my bowels had turned to ice. I rushed over to intercept Sparky in a flat panic. I grabbed him – and the tape - and we wrestled for a while. Eventually Sparky, giving in to my desperation, shouted, 'All right! All right, Windy. We have plenty of other copies. Gentlemen, I believe Windy wants to make a short introductory speech before the performance!'

I stood there. There was no way out. I'd lied my way into the lads' admiration, and now I was about to be shown up in the most embarrassing way possible. All I was doing was playing for time. But what could I say? What really happened was terrible. This was the worst – the very, very worst – moment of my entire life.

But I had no choice. I hung my head in shame and explained to the lads what had really happened. I figured it would soften the impact of the video if I provided a context. This is what actually took place in the hotel room.

I made some coffee, found an old movie on the television, and sat down beside Michelle on the sofa. I snaked an arm round behind her, leant over and kissed her softly.

'No, Windy. I said no!' she said weakly. I sensed her resistance was low so I pushed on, hoping to raise her excitement level enough to dispel any reluctance. She didn't object too strongly, so I leant across and kissed her on the lips. It was like kissing an ashtray into which someone had thrown up, but I wasn't going to let this one go. I moved on, employing my tongue, gentle words and hot breath expertly in her ear. I then moved down and began snarling away at her neck – always a winner. I looked for signs of arousal and was disappointed to find them few and far between even though she looked every inch the sexpot. Finding her less responsive than the promise in her eyes would be a dreadful disappointment. I increased the tempo and bit hard at her neck. Ah! There was more response! A low moan. She was coming round to my way of thinking! I bit her again – the idea of Michelle sporting a love-bite on deck the following day was appealing. Another long moan. No, no. Not a moan. More of a... oh.

A snore.

I pulled away and looked at her. Her mouth was open, her tongue halfway out, and a highly unattractive grinding noise emanated from the back of her throat.

To my credit, I ended up doing nothing to the poor girl. Whether the seediness of it all got to me, or the pointlessness, or simply the flatulence, I cannot tell, but having circled her a few times, squeezing her here and there like a shopper checking fruit and veg for freshness and trying to decide just how depraved I could be, I gave it up as a washout and went to sleep in her bed. When I awoke she was gone. My embarrassment in the bar was much more due to my having lied so extravagantly than due to Michelle going to sleep during my amorous advances, but knowing the boys as I did, the video would be unimpressive stuff.

The lads took my story with a childish lack of dignity and absolutely no self-control. I'd decided to tell them the tale so that the video could remain unseen, but that was short-sighted of me. They were laughing and shouting – it was like a chimps' tea-party – and they wanted to see the video more than ever.

And I feel sure you can appreciate that I felt that the video must not be played at any cost.

I gulped.

'Listen lads, give me a break. I've come clean. I... I didn't sleep with Michelle last night, and I –'

'Ahaaaa!' laughed Sparky. 'So what's all this sex-mad tiger stuff?'

'Well, that's what I was about to explain, you see –'

'Shut up, Windy, and stick the video on!'

'Hold on, let me explain, you see the thing was –'

A CLASS ACT

'You've got three seconds to put it on Windy, or else we're going to do it for you!'

I looked up and noticed they were not actually guarding the door, and although they could get further copies, it would at least give me some time. Escape was my only chance. I tucked the video under my arm, dropped my shoulder and headed for the door like a wing three-quarter.

But there was no escape this time. Eleven men jumped on top of me. The Windy lungs became winded and the video was removed from my possession.

'OK, lads! Take your seats for the show! Windy, you sit there in the middle where we can watch your face.'

'But lads, what I –'

'And SHUT UP! Good griefo, you do go on, don't you? Welcome everyone to the world premiere of "Windy Lust: One Man and his Sex Tigress"!'

He fumbled with the video player, and I freely admit that I was praying for a war, an earthquake, everyone to be gassed, anything at all to head off what these bastards were about to see. I would never, NEVER live it down. Even my explanation was a complementary version of the truth, and now they were going to get the full unexpurgated, technicolor version. Truly and definitely the very worst moment of my entire life was about to get worse.

The picture came on with an intro screen. More eyes were on me than were on the video. I wanted the world to swallow me up. Then the music started. The piss-taking sods had even edited on a film score – it was the music to Match of the Day. Good grief, Michelle's entire post-production team must have seen it. Then the music ended and Des Lynham came on the screen introducing football league action from the previous week. I looked around at the faces grinning back at me. I couldn't bear it.

'What's going on? This... this is football!'

'Well, you like football don't you, Windy?'

'Er... yes, but, what about the film of me and Michelle?'

'Eh? Sorry? Film of you and Michelle? Oh. There is no film of you and Michelle. I'm afraid we made the whole thing up as a sort of joke. Good of you to tell us the truth though. A lot of people might have lied about last night!'

And the laughter rang out all over the Azores as I tramped off to kill myself.

About an hour later I was lying in my bunk. I was actually worrying about my financial situation because on top of everything else, I'd been warned that my bar bill was too high, and that I had to have a quiet month running into Liverpool or I'd be in debt to the ship. This latest episode had put paid to any quiet bar bill for this month. The number of beers I'd have to buy for failing with Michelle, getting tricked by the lads and the gambling side of things all added up to something astronomical.

There was a knock on my door. I ignored it. Another knock. I ignored it again, but the door opened anyway. I waited for one of the mob to enter with some new joke they'd come up with, but it wasn't one of the boys. It was Michelle.

'Windy? Are you there? Sorry did I wake you?'

I sat up in bed. 'No, not at all. Er, how are you?'

'Bit of a hangover this morning, but I'm fine now. Listen, I just wanted to thank you for last night. You were so generous and kind, and then you put me to sleep when another man might have taken advantage of me. And I wanted to apologise for my behaviour. I thought I could hold my drink, but it seemed to get to me in a big way last night! I was a dreadful embarrassment to you.'

I laughed. 'Not at all, Michelle. Being with you made it worth every moment.'

'You're too kind. And it must have cost you a few bob, too. How about I make it up to you. How about I take you out for dinner this evening, and I'll keep my intake down?'

I gave a hollow laugh. This sounded like a fantastic turn-around, leaving the episode ending happily in my favour if I could take her out and get another chance. That would have been nice, wouldn't it? But the cup was to be dashed from my lips once more.

'Oh, Michelle, I'd love to, but we're due to sail at ten this evening. I'll be working from around eight. There's no way.'

'What a shame. I am sorry.'

'How about in England? Can I see you in England?'

'Windy, I don't think my husband would like that too much. I'm sorry, looks like it just isn't meant to be.' She turned to go, then looked back at me and winked. 'And I would have slept with you tonight as well.'

I'm sure she meant that as a comfort to me, but it had just the opposite effect. She looked at her watch.

'Oh well, better get back. We only stopped for a break. We'll be finished in around an hour, so I'd best say goodbye now.'

She came over and kissed me on the cheek, then we grabbed each other and she kissed me long and hard on the mouth. She pulled away and that perfect behind left my room forever. So near and yet so far. I sighed deeply and went back to calculating my financial ruin.

A little while later I was contemplating how cruel life can be when the door opened again. This time it was NotNorman.

'Hi, Windy!' he said, cheerfully. 'Great gag, wasn't it? You should have seen your face! You are going to go down in history as the greatest tosser ever to sail the seven seas!'

I groaned. 'What a life, NotNorman. What a goddam life! Just when you think everything's going to work out your way, the pendulum swings back and you're shot away to nothing again! If only I'd given her one while she was unconscious, all this would have been unnecessary and I'd be solvent again.'

'Yeah, well, you're right. The boys would definitely have admired you for that! And my news won't cheer you up. There's been a hold-up with the cargo. New departure time, noon tomorrow. Isn't that crap?'

I flopped back on my bed. Liverpool and home were but a few days away from the Azores, and now we had another night in this hole. Especially the way I felt, I just wanted to get on with –

'WHAT? Wait a minute! Another night here? A WHOLE NIGHT?'

I leapt out of bed and barely touched the deck on my way out to the foredeck.

Twenty-four hours later, I stood in my boiler suit, staring down into the grey Atlantic waters as they scudded beneath the ship. I finished counting the money and tucked it away safely. Quite a windfall. I placed my chin on the rails and a smile on my lips. What a life. I'd found matters a little difficult to bear at one point, but now I looked at things squarely, I couldn't quite remember why. I'd be home within a week, I was a romantic and gambling success, and was not just financially solvent, I'd made a small fortune into the bargain. Perhaps life wasn't really so bad after all.

Chapter 25

THE RETURN OF THE NATIVE

Liverpool is overcrowded to the tune of One. A customs man makes an exciting find. Swell the finale music for the homecoming reunion.

WE CORNERED THE Porta Delgada lighthouse on two wheels, burned rubber across the East Atlantic, and if anyone in County Cork blinked as we flew past they would have missed us. We gave an impressive handbrake-turn into the Irish Sea and before we knew it, we were at anchor in the cold February air at the mouth of the Mersey, requesting a pilot over the radio. A calm, reassuringly English voice came back to us, welcomed us home, told us the pilot would be with us in no time and that everything would be fine. I felt as safe and secure as I did in the womb. After six months, two weeks and three days of tough campaigning we were back in good old

OCEAN BOULEVARD

England. We were home at last!

Well nearly. They left us at anchor until four in the morning, then we had a two-hour passage to get up to the docks at dawn. The sun did its best to welcome us home, but the impression that England is protected from the sun by a huge Tupperware lid was as strong as ever. I didn't mind. English drizzle was exactly what I wanted. It was proof that we were home.

I smiled affectionately at the Liverpudlian wharfie who gave me a mouthful of Scouse abuse as I threw the line ashore without warning. I loved him. I felt like Sir Francis Drake returning from a pioneering voyage, and the King George IV docks in Liverpool felt like my true home. Yes, that's how bad my sentiment had got. I happily breathed in the crisp morning smog and took in the Englishness of the scene around me. The docks, the grey Liverpool skyline, the sun failing to break through. Even the pretty girl waving her handkerchief had a certain familiar... girl? What girl? I looked more carefully and sure enough one of the dockside workmen was not a man. He was a girl. And the smiling face and hanky-waving antics told me exactly who he was. He was Cindy. I couldn't believe my eyes. NotNorman would not believe my eyes either. He was sleeping after his earlier bridge watch, so as soon as the gangway was in position, I nipped down to see what she was doing here.

'Hiya!' she said, throwing herself round my neck. She was brimful of happiness and expectation. 'Are you surprised?'

'Er, not half as surprised as NotNorman will be,' I ventured, not knowing quite how much to say.

'I know, isn't it great? I didn't even go back to Oz. I flew straight here from Tonga. Aren't his folks great? They let me stay with them the last few weeks, and me and his mum, we've prepared EVERYTHING! There's a big surprise party for us tomorrow night, and the wedding will have to be in about three weeks because we want to get a honeymoon in before NotNorman and I have to go off on his next ship. Oooo, I'm so excited!'

'Er, did NotNorman agree to all this?'

'Oh, didn't he tell you? He proposed to me on our last night in Tonga together! It was sooooo romantic!'

'Er, I guess you didn't get any letters or flowers or anything from NotNorman?'

'Yes – well – no. That is, they got to my house in Sydney – my mum told me that loads of flowers and a letter had arrived from NotNorman, but I didn't get to read them or anything because I came straight here. He's such a cutie-pie for sending them, though. I just love him to bits!'

I excused myself on the pretext of duty and promised to nip off and fetch cutie-pie from his bunk. Cindy was not allowed aboard as yet because Customs hadn't cleared us. I galloped up the gangway and along to NotNorman's cabin.

'NotNorman! NotNorman! Wake UP! You've got a visitor!'

'Wha...? Eh? Wassammarra? Are we alongside yet?'

'We are alongside – but you are sunk, Mush. You have a visitor.'

'Aw, shucks,' he said, 'I told mum not to come all this way to get me. I can catch a train straight to –'

'No, no, Notters. It's not NotMum. It's... a rather less-expected visitor.'

'Well who is it then?' he began to sense the atmosphere. 'Must be one of my family.'

'Er, well. I suppose she thinks she is, so, in a way, yes.'

'Stop talking in riddles Windy, and get to the point or I shall, in the words of good old Rip, fillet your spine for you. Who is it? The police?'

'OK, calm down. It's not the police. It's worse than that. Stay lying down, 'cos you're not going to like this.'

Isn't it great when you're in command of some really powerful, dead juicy gossip? I could have messed him around for hours if I wasn't such a nice guy. Besides, I like my spine the way it is.

'Since we left Tonga,' I said slowly and quietly, 'England has increased its population of Cindys to the tune of one.'

NotNorman's eyes came out on stalks. His hair stood on end, his jaw flapped up and down like an epileptic bread-bin, his tongue popped in and out and a siren sounded from the back of his head. It was like watching an episode of Tom and Jerry. While he animated thus, I filled him in on the state of things re: his mother's love for his fiancée, her failure to get the message in Sydney, the surprise party, oh – did I say fiancée? Yes, there was his wedding to prepare for and he only had three weeks. I expressed annoyance at not yet having received an invite, and suggested yellow as a good theme colour for an early spring wedding. I also suggested that, as a eighteen-year-old boy, he should maybe think twice about whether he was rushing into it a little, but shucks, what the hell, I gave him my blessing.

None of this man-to-man, old-friend stuff seemed to help. NotNorman was definitely NotHimself. He looked as Tom does when Jerry has just jammed his tail in the mains socket.

'I'll go and make sure she can't get on board for as long as I can. You think about what you're gonna do. I'll be back as soon as I can.'

We had a stroke of luck in that the Customs men had become suspicious and wouldn't be allowing outsiders aboard for some time yet. My family was in a hotel in town, and they were waiting for a call from the shipping agent before coming down to pick me up. They probably didn't know we were even alongside yet, so the magic moment when we would be reunited was once more delayed. Still, it was a reprieve for NotNorman.

Apparently a keen young Customs man – searching in a forward masthouse – had discovered a rather splendid, brand new and boxed stereo system hidden behind some ropes. He pulled the box out and turned to run proudly to his superiors with it, when, much to his surprise, another one dropped down to replace it. With promotion glittering in his eyes, he pulled that box out too, only to have it replaced once more! Soon he had an impressive display of hi-fi equipment stacked up behind him, with further units appearing each time he removed one. The forward masthouse looked more like a Comet warehouse. It appeared some enterprising but foolhardy sailor had completely filled the hollow metal mast with cassette-radios, and was about to make a heavy loss on his investment. This meant that Cindy was not allowed on board, and that we all had the additional hassle of an interview with Her Majesty's Customs and Excise. It was 11:30 before we were given clearance.

The new crew arrived on a coach and began trundling their gear up the gangway. They looked depressed. Now I understood what it meant to receive a letter while on leave, telling you to join the *Global Wanderer*, and I saw it in their faces. They looked like a funeral procession. I saw a spotty nervous-looking lad who stood out like a skyscraper as a first-tripper. Had I been as obvious as that all those months ago? I guessed so. I looked at his colleagues and pondered what must be ahead for him. Could they possibly consist of another NotNorman? Another Jinx? Another Famous Dick Wrigley? Another Benny, Cookie Short, Crate, SmallParcel, MegaWatt, KiloWatt and the rest? Surely, not another Giewy? I felt a sudden affection for my gang, and a sudden warm realisation that I'd just had the adventure of a lifetime.

I helped the first-tripper carry his gear round to the cabin and listened to his tirade of jumbled, jumpy questions. There is a fine line between excited and scared, and this guy was springing from one to the other like a mountain goat with an itchy bottom. I gave him the 'don't-let-the-bastards-grind-you-down' routine, but for some reason I neglected to tell him anything about cranking competitions, mules, crossing the line, electric hammers and the rest of it. He'd find out soon enough about all this character-building stuff. He shook my hand and I shook my head. I knew what was ahead of him, and that he'd have the time of his life in the six months ahead of him just as I had done. No doubt about it, he was lucky – even privileged – to be here. I wasn't going to tell him that, though. I bit my lip, put on a nervous tick as I slugged hungrily at a whisky bottle (full of apple-juice) and told him to run away while he had the chance.

Next came a long round of hand-shaking and number-swapping. The lads who had made my life such a living hell for the last six months were all very sincere in their goodbyes, and were generous in praise of how very enjoyable my gullibility had been for them.

I had to see the captain in order to officially pay off and get my passbook stamped. He was pleasant and wished me well for the future. Everybody was just so offhand over a moment that to me was momentous. I suppose in the Merchant Navy one just gets used to life becoming a series of goodbyes.

I went to say cheerio to the mate. He was handing over to the new mate who looked even more of an animal than our one. The two of them standing together looked like competitors in an illegal boxing match. I shook hands with Harry Tate, and he turned to the new mate and, indicating my hand said, 'Do you know what? That's the first bit of shit I've had in my hand all day!' And they laughed long and heartily. Must be Chief Officer Humour. Goes straight over my head every time.

I put my head round NotNorman's door and was met by two glaring faces and the message, 'Shove off, we're busy.'

I said, 'I'll call you next week,' and shoved off as bidden, although I was dying to know how he'd handle it. Knowing NotNorman, he'd probably marry her rather than upset her, but I think, from the atmosphere in the room, he had already dropped the bombshell. He'd have some explaining to do over the next few weeks.

I made three trips up and down the gangway, saying fresh goodbyes on every pass. Soon there was a pile of luggage and souvenirs plus one Me, waiting on the quay for my leave to begin with the arrival of my mum, dad and sisters to pick me up.

I was going home.

Six months is a long time to be away from home, and for most sailors it becomes more and more difficult to reintegrate into 'normal' life as the years go by. The joys of another ship and the geographical jewels of the world pale behind the upset of family upheaval and instability. For me, however, the whole thing had been a long, hard adventure. Too long really – I'd been wishing the days away since Samoa, and was more than ready to go home. Telling all my friends and family of my adventures would be a pleasure in itself (for me, if not for them) as well as spending all the money I'd won and saved. But seeing my family again after all this time was the big one. They were on their way – my three sisters, my mum and dad – and I could hardly contain myself. Absence truly makes the heart grow fonder, and I couldn't wait to see them.

Giewy came trotting down the gangway to say goodbye, and he gave me a nasty shock – and I don't just mean because he crept up unexpectedly from behind.

'Prob'ly see you next trip,' he smarmed, and it hit me. Next trip! I hadn't even thought about any next trip! All I could see were acres and acres of leave! As a cadet I'd earned six weeks' leave, and couldn't see beyond that. I was like a schoolboy, seeing the summer holidays as lasting forever with no concept of anything beyond that. I saw my leave as an everlasting orgy with no work to do and money to burn, but there would of course be another ship; this was my life now. And the chances were that because we cadets had all earned precisely the same amount of leave, we would share the ups and downs of the next trip, too.

As Giewy waddled back up the gangway, I was even able to look fondly on him. I called up the gangway to him: 'Oi! Giewy!' I shouted. He stopped and turned back to me. 'Take care.'

He laughed stupidly, then there was a pause as he

adjusted his trousers and considered his answer. He lifted his eyes, pointed and winked at me. 'Giew!' he said nodding, then turned and carried on up the gangway. My main worry was that I was beginning to understand what he meant.

I looked up at the great metal flank of the *Global Wanderer*. My relationship with her had been hard graft for the most part, but now I was leaving, I felt a sentimental glow and realised I would miss her. I walked across and stroked my hand against her like a vet checking a beloved old horse. We'd come a long way together since I had stared up in trepidation at those great flanks in New Orleans six months earlier. Then I'd only seen fear. Now I saw a magnificent ship. A thing of great beauty and depth in which I had invested a lot of time and effort. There was hardly an inch of that ship I didn't know intimately, and not a square inch of wood, brass, rope or wire to which I had not given of myself.

Throughout all my scrapes, all around the world, she was always there waiting patiently for my return. We'd seen good times and bad, laughter and tears, pain and joy. She had been my home. I felt a great affinity for her, and a pang of sadness that she would be leaving Liverpool for her next adventure without me. I found myself picking at the plimsoll mark and criticising the workmanship. It needed repainting. I had half a mind to nip up and report it to the mate. I knew how important it was for stability and cargo. I laughed at myself. When I'd first seen those marks in New Orleans I'd thought they were graffiti.

Suddenly, the sounds of skidding tyres and the heaving roar of a clutch slipping filled the air. Up at the gate my mum's car came bouncing on to the quayside, tooting the horn and flashing the lights. I saw five happy, smiling faces. Faces I loved. My crazy family. I felt tears of happiness welling up, and a lump in the back of my throat. There was a sister hanging out of each of the rear side windows, and another clinging on as she hung out of the sunroof. I saw them waving and heard their shouts as the car bumped over the crane-tracks towards me. I caught sight of my reflection in a van window nearby. I'd been through so much since they saw me last. They had said goodbye to a schoolboy six months earlier. Now they were welcoming home a hairy-arsed, confident man who knew his way around the world.

They all piled out of the car and ran screaming round me. They jumped on me all at once, and the whole family gelled as one, hugging and hugging longer and harder than any hug I've ever known. As we hugged, I made my first decision since coming home with my new-found worldliness.

I cried my damn eyes out.

PACIFIC HIGHWAY
ALSO BY DAVID BABOULENE

PACIFIC HIGHWAY

Further adventures on the high seas

David Baboulene

"A seriously funny man with a great gift for storytelling." Spirit FM

The publishers hope you enjoyed *Ocean Boulevard*, and invite you to sample Windy's adventures in East Africa taken from his second book – *Pacific Highway*.

EXTRACT FROM PACIFIC HIGHWAY

MOONING THE BONGO

Nature's wonders fail to grip. The big game hunters' search for a Big Chicken. 70's Nite at the fever tree. The name's Bond... Jumbo Bond. Windy survives alone on the Serengeti plains.

WE ARRIVED IN Mombasa to two pieces of unexpected news. Firstly, the ship hadn't arrived yet. In fact, it was days away. We would be put up in a hotel to wait. Secondly, I found out that Mombasa is in Kenya, Kenya is in East Africa, and the whole region is extraordinary from the very moment you touch down. The adventure was beginning, and it was doing so in fine style.

So what do you do when you find yourself with time to fill in some far flung place in the world? You summon the Jinx. Simple as that. I remembered how Jinx had convinced an entire troupe of dancing girls to come back to the ship with him in Baton Rouge. How he had emptied a training hospital of its nurses, and coaxed them all out with us in Melbourne. It was said of Jinx that if NASA wanted to find life on Mars, they simply needed to send him up there. With his sheepskin coat, spivvy moustache and his purring Leslie Phillips tones, Life would emerge from every nook and cranny of Mars, probably in the form of pole dancers, wanting to make up for lost time having been deprived of male company as they devoted themselves to their studies. Jinx was just kinda gifted like that – he had The Knack – and, here in Mombasa, he came through in typical fashion. Word went around the table after breakfast on our first day that he had a rather special contact here in Mombasa (he always had a rather special contact), apparently going by the name of 'Precious', and between them they had cobbled together some sort of safari. We were to drive for five days up to Mount Kenya and back, stopping at a couple of lodges, riding the steam trains and enjoying the wild and unparalleled glory of Tsavo National Park in Kenya. Was this really my job? Was this *work*?! I couldn't believe my luck.

The next morning we all convened in the hot Kenya sunshine outside our hotel. Jinx introduced us to Precious. He was a long, black gentleman, built along the lines of a huge rotary washing line, but with huge hands and feet at the end of long limbs. This was the man who was was to guide us through the wonders of East Africa. He had a gun (which wasn't his) and a safari truck (which wasn't his), but if his height was anything to go by he was on personal whispering terms with the giraffe population, so it wasn't all bad. NotNorman's guess was that he must have eaten too many leaves as a child. There was great excitement as we loaded up. We were off on an adventure of the type generally associated with the rich and Royal. A safari in East Africa.

The participants leapt aboard: Ffugg, Payphone, NotNorman, Giewy, Jinx, The Famous Dick Wrigley, MegaWatt, KiloWatt and me. Precious folded himself up like a collapsible chair into the driver's seat of the car, and adopted his very own driving position: one knee either side of his ears, arms running down outside his legs and under his knees to hold the wheel in-between his calves, with the back of his neck flat against the cab roof. He looked very uncomfortable; all curled over like a grown-up on a child's tricycle. I looked at him doubtfully. If that guy ever got cramp, it could turn the truck over. Once or twice on the journey he attempted to drive and simultaneously unwrap sweets and place them in his mouth. He was fortunate to be amongst sailors who knew how to untie him.

The first day of the safari passed pleasurably and with no unseemly events to report. Spirits were high, the case of beer had not yet run out, and the novelty of a wild horizon, the bound of a Thompson's Gazelle and the classic silhouette of a fever tree at sunset had not yet withered. The first night was spent at a spectacular lodge where we oooh'd and aaah'd over fine food, spotted big game from a balcony terrace overlooking the watering hole, and enjoyed a great night's sleep in the cradle of humanity. It was nothing short of magic.

But on day two, as we bounced off in the truck for another day's wild riding, the cracks began to show through. These were young men. All but Jinx were under twenty-eight, and the best of them was acting no more than fifteen. It is, alas, the nature of man – and particularly that of sailors – that they should find nature's bounty short on what they would call Essential Facilities. The kind of things that talk to a man's fundamental instincts and makes him feel life is worth living, such as bars, clubs and that special type of local friend with whom a young sailor, in the prime of his life, can have a fight.

The lads were getting bored.

'Oi, Precious!' shouted MegaWatt, tapping the Long One on the shoulder. 'Where's The Business, then?'

'Yeaaah!' agreed KiloWatt in a slovenly drawl, stoutly supporting his boss. 'Wot he says. Yeaaaah!'

Precious looked puzzled. 'Business? What do you mean, business?'

MegaWatt explained with exaggerated patience. 'Precious, this is *Africa*. We want to see some Business.'

'Yeeeeaah, wot he says! Yeaaah!'

Precious pulled a face. He already knew it was Africa. MegaWatt took a deep breath and spelled it out for him. 'We wanna see like, a spider leopard beastie mother drop out of a tree onto a pig!'

'Yeeeeeah!'

'Eh?'

'And we wanna see some lions killing some

villagers.'

'Ooooo, yeeeah!'

'What?!'

The others were getting the hang of it now, and the call for blood grew stronger.

'Yeah! We wanna see tigers and – and –'

'...and – and bears, and and – '

'Yeaaaah'

'..and... and sharks!'

'Yeaaah! And... and.. and we wanna see a snake eat a whole cow, yeaaah!'

'Yeah, and we wanna see a cheetah leggit after one of them Bambi jobbies!'

'Yeaaah!'

'Yeeeahhh!'

'Yeeeah, wot he says, yeeeah!'

There appeared to be a general thirst for blood that no number of grazing wildebeest could satisfy unless they were being torn apart by something.

Precious stopped the truck and turned around to address us in deep, golden-black tones from beneath his right knee. 'You mustn't expect to see any big cats. It's very unusual that we even *see* any big cats, and they certainly won't be hunting in the daytime. You have to expect that we won't see any at all.'

Well, it's no exaggeration to say the lads were deflated. There is only so much merciless plains of Kenya that a chap can take without a kill before he begins looking for alternative forms of entertainment. There didn't appear to be any change coming over the horizon, so a plan of action was required.

'Jinx,' said the Famous Dick Wrigley placing a hand on the great man's shoulder with a certain solemnity in his voice. 'It is now perhaps more important than at any time in your illustrious career that you come up with something brilliant.'

Now here was a challenge even for the notorious Jinx. He had proven himself in this way on many

MOONING THE BONGO

previous occasions, but this, surely was a bridge too far even for the Pied Piper himself.

We looked on with apprehension as the Jinxed brain churned and the moustache twitched like a divining fork above his ever smirking lips. There were definite signs of activity. I, personally, was not confident that Jinx could create a party under these circumstances. I had a brain, just like he did, and could see no potential for a happy ending. There was no raw material here. Nothing to work with. I looked in the trees for the beautiful girls he might summon out of nowhere. There were none. The lads would simply have to wait until Mombasa's Kilindini Road rolled over the horizon again; a place where they could definitely give themselves diseases.

A smile began to rise at the edge of Jinx's lips. His eyes flitted furtively from one breath-holding onlooker to the next. Precious looked back in wonder as the sense that something was about to be delivered overtook us all. Suddenly, Jinx clapped.

'OK!' he said. 'If there's no sizeable pussy around, we'll have to see if we can't hunt down a different species...' he opened his arms wide to emphasise his point, '...we are gonna bag ourselves...' he milked the moment as we all waited with bated breath, '...a Biiiiig Chicken!'

We all cheered. We didn't understand why, but the build up meant that cheering still felt like the right thing to do. I could see through him at last! He just buzzed people up and came out with nothing! Africa had exposed him. I was about to ask why it was that anyone ever rated Jinx so highly, when he continued.

'And Windy. You are the first-tripper, so you get to go first. Let's see if YOU are the Biiiiig Chicken!'

I shut my eyes and counted to ten before delivering my withering retort.

'I am NOT a first-tripper. As you all well know, Jinx, I am on my SECOND trip, and I refuse to be treated in any way unbefitting of my status.' Sometimes a chap has to stand up for himself. I wasn't going to be the butt of everyone's jokes for the next six months as well as the last. 'Ffugg,' I said, using both hands to indicate the six-foot embryo sitting next to me, 'is the first-tripper.'

'Chic-ken! Chic-ken! Chic-ken!' chorused everybody towards me. Even Ffugg joined in with *them*; he placed me in a chummy sort of half-nelson and noggied me on the head with his knuckles, and The Famous Dick Wrigley attempted to strut about doing a chicken impersonation (a tough trick in a safari truck, but his commitment to the programme was there to be admired).

Jinx leaned forwards and looked me in the eye. He appeared to be surprisingly angry.

'Listen, to me. When we are all in our old age and we have grandchildren on our knees and we are telling them of the time we went on safari, we want to be able to show them some special photographs. Now, if I can't show a picture of myself with one foot victoriously atop a fallen lion, then I want the next best thing: a picture of me with a Big Chicken. One of us, in this truck, will go down in history as that poultry figure, and will be derided by generations to come. Is it you, Baboulene? Are you the Big Chicken, and proven to be so before we have even begun our search?'

Now, I didn't particularly want to patronise his childish game (or at least, I didn't want to go first) but as he spoke, the Baboulene brain was working. The others may not have realised it yet, but I could understand the coded message Jinx was imparting to me. He was letting me know that there wasn't a *real* Big Chicken at all. There quite possibly wasn't even such an animal in Kenya. This was going to be a test of bravery. Jinx and I were now in tune. I looked from the enigmatic expression on Jinx's face to the gormless one on Ffugg's and I instantly knew what he was getting at. Jinx and I were communicating on a higher level of conscience – and it was Ffugg who was to suffer.

'OK!' I cried, slapping my thigh in the manner of

MOONING THE BONGO

Hercules approaching the first of his tasks. 'Tell me what I have to do.'

'Good man!' said Jinx, the anger evaporating as rapidly as it had arrived. 'Did you ever play 'Dares' when you were a kid? Knocking a policeman's helmet off, that kind of stuff?'

'Ooooh, yes,' I said. 'Only last week we put a hose pipe through next door's letterbox. Ha, ha! And whilst they were trying to stop the water, we went round the side, rang the bell and ran away. Yes, and then we got a roll of cling film, right, and we stretched it across the toilet, you see, and when my dad came home –'

'Yes, yes. OK. I forgot – you're *still* a kid, aren't you. Well, we're going to play dares now. AFRICA style…'

A chill ran down my spine as the words emerged from his mouth. These supposed grown-ups were planning to play childish games, but not risking an irate neighbour, the wrath of a village bobby or even a little parental splash-back. These guys wanted to go and take childish risks… on the savage, uncompromising plains of Africa.

Now, I'm sure you realise that it is not actually very difficult to take childish risks on the S.U.P. of A. Indeed, it's very easy to find dangerous things to do. Having said that, it turns out that there is fundamentally only one obviously dangerous thing to do, and that is to leave the safety of the safari truck and the reassuring presence of the long bloke with the gun, and wander off by yourself. The *variety* in the dares will only ever come in the *manner* in which you risk being pounced upon and eaten.

'OK,' drawled Jinx. 'Your first round test, young Windy, is to re-enact for us a scene from a James Bond movie. Your co-star will be – Jumbo, over there.'

I followed his pointing finger. There in the bushes, lazily tearing shoots from a camel hair tree, was a large bull elephant.

'What?! You want me to –?'

OCEAN BOULEVARD

'Get on with it, then! Nothing more to discuss!'

And they bundled me out of the truck. As I headed away from the truck the earth felt strange under my feet. Was this real? I was walking on Masai earth. Wild earth. The reality of what this meant made me feel instantly insecure. This was dangerous terrain. I had read only the day before of the notorious man eaters of this area – the Tsavo lions. People who didn't stay in the truck got themselves killed, it was as simple as that. It didn't seem to matter to my sniggering shipmates whilst it was Me roaming the plains – they had yet to feel the reality of walking on this earth – but the sense of vulnerability was instant and alarming from the moment I stood outside the truck.

The elephants are tame in Tsavo National Park. Well, no, that's not the right word. They are not exactly tame, but they are not scared of us – why should they be? You can wander amongst them quite safely, provided someone is there who can recognise when it is best to leap back in the truck and hide under the seat.

I tiptoed gently up to the large bull. He stopped his ruminations and looked down on me with a profound, reproachful eye. His head was huge and wrinkled. Had he been wearing a judge's wig, I would have begun a full confession immediately. I looked back to the truck, some thirty metres away, and was met by hand-signals from Jinx telling me to get on with it.

I looked the elephant in the eye, took a deep breath and adopted a thespian pose.

'Sshoo, Mr Bond...' I said, in a Sean Connery drawl. 'We meet again.' I changed my pose to place my gun-finger across my chest. 'But this time, you... are an elephant.'

We stared at each other for a few moments as my point hit home. The elephant raised his eyebrows. No doubt about it, he was surprised to be mistaken for James Bond. He was about to make the point that, given that I had called *him* Mr Bond, it should surely be *he* who was allowed the Sean Connery accent and that

MOONING THE BONGO

I had therefore just turned myself into Miss Moneypenny, when his co-star suddenly cut the scene short, turned and galloped back to the safety of the truck. I was sweating heavily by the time I got back to my seat. I counted my limbs and it became evident that I had not been eaten. I had done it!! I wasn't the Big Chicken, and I could hardly contain myself.

'Wow, man, what a BUZZ! You guys have just GOT to get out there! This is a great game! Whose turn next?!"

For the first round of dares, we were only going twenty or thirty metres away from the safari truck – hardly a trek into the heart of Africa – and yet it was ridiculously scary. Each of us in turn was obliged to creep nervously off, perform some pointless charade, then scramble back to the truck in a blind panic, being pursued by a thousand imagined beasties with teeth. Payphone, for his first round dare, had to score a goal for England. He had shown a little more of his character since London office, and he was more than just an anxious telephonist. He had been born within the sound of Bow Bells, and was a cockney through and through. He had a pork-pie hat to fend off the sun ('a titfer wot set me back a nugget up Whitechapel,' apparently), a permanent roll-up (known fondly as his 'oily rag') in the corner of his mouth, and he spoke with such an extraordinary cockney accent that I could barely understand him, even though I had grown up not ten miles south of him. He was excited by his task (it was, to be precise, 'aaandsome'), as it had always been an ambition of his to 'stick one in the old onion bag' for England. He hopped out of the truck, ran over to a patch of open land, took off his left 'ow-do-ya-do, and placed it carefully and centrally in line with two acacias which were to act as goalposts. He took a few paces back and took a long, dramatic drag on his oily rag as he psyched himself up for the penalty that would put Germany out of the World Cup. He eyed the keeper (a small bush, well out of position to the right hand end of the goal line), stretched his neck, flexed his elbows and his knees, took his short run up and, with his right boot, booted his left boot high up into top of a baobab tree.

'Geddin, you beauteeeee!!' he yelled, wheeling away victoriously with fists clenched. He pulled the front of his T-shirt over his head in the classic style of an Italian striker, and ran in a circle with his arms out to the sides as if pretending to be a plane. Luckily, when he ran headlong into the baobab, it gave it such a jolt that it caused his boot to drop back down to earth again. He picked it up and jogged triumphantly back to the truck looking pleased with himself.

'You missed,' said MegaWatt, dryly. 'Go do it again.'

Giewy's first-round task popped up when we stumbled across an apparent rarity. A large, striped antelope known as a Bongo. We all laughed at the name, but Precious stopped the truck some distance from the beast and told us in an excited whisper that it was very unusual to find Bongos in this part of Kenya. They were very rare, very timid and we should feel honoured to see one. Once we heard this news, Giewy was charged with performing a scientific experiment to test Bongo timidity. The research process required Giewy to adopt the professional standards of a nuclear scientist... and go moon the Bongo. Or for those of you who don't understand all these scientific terms, showing it his arse. If the beast was as timid as Precious said it was, Giewy's bum could surely make it burst into tears.

Giewy prowled, cat-like, up past the bushes to get near to the creature. He then leapt up, dropped his trousers, and with a sing-song 'Nurr-nurr-ne-nurrrrr-nurrrrr!' waved his bottom at the poor defenceless creature. The animal twitched palpably as he tried to get his head round what was, one assumed, a new experience for him. But he did not react as we predicted. There were no tears. It didn't even run away. He merely sneezed heavily – perhaps some sort of allergy to tit-heads – then returned to his ruminations as if this sort of thing happened on a daily basis. So much for timid. I guess if you live with the nightly opportunity of being mauled by lions, it takes more than the contents of even Giewy's trousers to make you jump. Mind you, from what I'd seen, I'd take the lions any day. As Giewy climbed back into the truck, KiloWatt cruelly suggested that he should wave his face at it next time, but was immediately told to calm down. We wanted to have a bit of fun, not eradicate a species.

Ffugg got a childishly simple exercise, having to go and pretend to take some money out of a cash machine. He acted it out as if there was one in the trunk of a tree, and his acting was rewarded with laughter from the boys. It wasn't funny, but they laughed. It was pathetic. Were these guys actually *protecting* him?! How come they were so brutal towards me on the previous trip, and so easy on him this time?

By the end of the first round of tests, we had not definitively established a Big Chicken. There had been some shaky moments in which a couple of eggs had been laid, but each of us had successfully completed our tasks. We would have to turn up the heat for round two.

So off we went again, but this time moving further from the truck to perform our pointless charades. A lot further. We were moving up to around one hundred metres away from the truck. Off into inner Africa the length of a football pitch distant from basic safety. This was properly scary, with additional tension in the atmosphere coming from Precious. Even he was getting anxious about the risks we were taking. He was responsible for our welfare and was not happy to see us larking about in this way. His agitation gave a certain additional bite to the second round, not only because it let us all know that what we were doing was now confirmed as genuinely dangerous, but also because he was now refusing to stop the truck. His theory was that if he kept moving, nobody could get out and risk their lives. This was a complication, but, as the saying goes, the show must go on, so the charades now absorbed this additional component: before you could commence your task, you had to trick Precious into stopping the truck. This was achieved in a safe and controlled fashion, of course, for example, placing your hands firmly over his eyes (and fighting hard to keep them there in the ensuing flail of spinning washing line).

The charades themselves didn't get any more grown-up in the second round. NotNorman, for instance, was given instructions to travel up to the top of a hill, put a pretend handbag on to the grass and then perform a little seventies disco dancing around it. We got hold of Precious' gun, pulled it into the back and began larking about with it. Precious knew us well enough by now to see the lethal potential of letting us loose with a high-powered rifle, so he stopped the truck and leaned into the back to fight over it with us. Before you could say 'Earnest Hemmingway', NotNorman was out of the truck and off to the top of the hill, mincing outrageously all the way up with his pretend Dolce and Gabbana swinging casually on the end of outstretched fingertips.

At the brow of the hill, NotNorman placed his handbag carefully on the ground, then – as the strains of his singing 'Stayin' Alive' by the Bee Gees wafted across Africa – he began gyrating away, pushing his bottom out from side-to-side, like some hideous cross between the Pink Panther and a slow death in Erasure.

The animals of Tsavo stopped their grazing and looked at NotNorman silhouetted perfectly against the African sky. It was as if they'd never seen or heard anything like it in their lives.

'*Well you can tell by the way I use my walk I'm a woman's man, no time to talk...*' NotNorman's grating falsetto rang out horribly across the Serengeti.

Precious couldn't take any more. He roared the engine and spun the wheels. The truck ripped round and bounced off-road in exactly the way they do on those wildlife documentaries in which they chase a rhinoceros to shoot a sleeping-draught into it, but this wasn't one of those occasions. Precious was barrelling across the plains not in pursuit of Big Game, but to stop an errant sailor from poncing about on the African plains.

I honestly do not think Precious can possibly have been worried about NotNorman's chances of survival. Personally, as I watched him – now deep in the groove and thrusting his pelvis outrageously – I couldn't even begin to think about eating him. Any self-respecting carnivore would surely feel the same way. I think Precious was more concerned firstly, about the damage to the environment caused by hundreds of different species all throwing up at the same time, and secondly to the wider image of Africa. I mean, can you imagine being in another safari party, driving along on the other side of the hill? You are enraptured by the sights: to the left – the impala, the giraffe! To the right – the elephants, the wildebeest! Above us – the monkeys, the weaver birds and, oh! Look there! Dappled in the sunlight, a sailor, disco dancing around a pretend handbag as he murders a Bee Gees' song... You see? It spoils the savage imagery of the place. People will stop taking Africa seriously. Perhaps Precious was worried that the animals might start picking up the behaviour. Then where would we be? Whichever way you looked at it, NotNorman – now acting out the letters 'Y, M, C, A' with a chorus line of Botticelli's Gazelle – was not good for the environment.

Soon enough, it was my turn again, and I was not looking forward to it. The sun was going down and I was hoping that the game might be wrapped up for the night and get itself forgotten. No chance. We browed the top of a hill and central to the view that greeted us was a lake.

'There you go, Windy,' said The Famous Dick Wrigley, indicating the lake with a wave of his hand. 'You have to run round that lake. On your way!'

There was general agreement amongst the lads that this was a good task. But this was because most of them couldn't have made it around that lake without a cardiac support team pushing them in wheelchairs. I was young and fit. I could run round a little pond like that in no time – I mean, you could hardly call it a lake –

and I'd still have enough puff left to tell everyone how easy it was afterwards. I was well chuffed with getting such an easy task, and set about it right away before they had time to change their minds. I reached forwards, picked up Precious' wallet, and lobbed it out of the truck. He screeched to a halt, and I was off over the side and swiftly up to an easy cruising speed down towards the pondy lake thing. It would be nice to stretch my legs and get a little trot. This would be a breeze. Windy's Breeze.

What I hadn't bargained for was that this was Africa. It seems I had forgotten.

You see, the thing about Africa is that it is really, really big. Unless you have grown up here, the sheer scale of the place monkeys with your head. For instance, we had been motoring towards Mount Kenya for two days; we could see it, but it didn't seem to be getting any nearer. The sky meets the land on a horizon so distant that the sky seems low. So low it's almost claustrophobic. At night, the canopy of stars we are used to isn't a canopy in Africa. It's a three-dimensional myriad of stars; you can see *past* the near stars to more distant stars, and more beyond them. Africa is beyond the understanding we gain from growing up elsewhere on the planet. My point is that this pondy sort of lake was, well, much, much bigger than it had first appeared. I hadn't been running three minutes when it hit me, quite hard, that it was a darned sight further to run round it than I first imagined. Of course, this also meant it was going to take me proportionally longer than my initial estimates. A lot longer. So long, in fact, that it would get dark in the time it was going to take me, and when it gets dark in Africa, it gets seriously dark and it does it quickly. As my mind filled with grim reality, it also hit me, quite hard, that this was NOT a lake, was it? Nor was it a pond. I suddenly knew exactly what it was. It was a *watering hole*.

At sunset.

In Africa.

And here I was, trotting round it looking like a

giant sandwich on legs. All I needed was a big, neon sign with a pointy finger over my head, flashing the words 'Eat Me' to complete the mistake I was making.

There was a varied mix of wildlife around the watering hole already, chatting of their day, and, one could safely assume, a good deal of other wildlife lying in wait for it in the long grass nearby. I realised that perhaps running round a watering-hole at sunset wasn't such a clever idea after all. In fact, it was life-threateningly dangerous and, for a Baboulene so renowned as an intellectual force, a notably stoopid thing to do.

I felt the spring go out of my stride and a wave of doubt wash over me. I also experienced a major and involuntary adjustment in my priorities. I no longer cared if my ship-mates called me names. I could be a Big Chicken if that was what pleased their juvenile minds. I had to rise above their childish games and make a grown-up, responsible decision for everyone's sakes. They would lose their ebullience pretty quickly if I was to get eaten alive, wouldn't they? It wouldn't be so funny then, and it was best for everyone if I simply let them have their fun and resigned myself to the status of Big Chicken. I had to choose between losing a childish game and losing life and limb. It wasn't a difficult decision.

Despite all these thoughts I was still running forwards, albeit without enthusiasm, when suddenly the decision seemed to be made for me. In the middle of the watering hole a large hippopotamus surfaced and set about his evening yawn. It gave me a shake which stopped my legs turning. I stopped and stood frozen to the spot, looking around at some of the other local gang members sent to spoil my day, and for some reason, the clincher was a large bird, waiting for me about half way round. It was one of those big crane-like jobbies – almost as tall as me – on long, spindly legs. It had hunched shoulders, no neck, and a huge heavy beak like a wind-sock full of sand. The Godfather of Africa. It had the angry deportment of a bird who has just been informed that Windy Baboulene has been going about the town calling his mum a sparrow.

'Jeeez, I'm going to have to give him a wide berth, too,' I thought. He looked all shifty, like he was packing heat. And that was it. All the evidence suggested that a return to base was the only sensible course of action. It was nearly dark, I was nearly knackered and there were miles to go – particularly with the extra ten minutes it would take to get round the mafia hit-bird. I knew what had to be done. It would take possibly more bravery to go back than it would to continue my run around the watering hole, but I had decided. I would rise above their childish games and go back.

I stopped. I turned round. I looked back the way I had come and...

and...

and...

...there was nothing there.

The truck had disappeared.

They had gone.

I rubbed my eyes and stared through the shimmering heat haze again. There was nothing in the direction from which I had come except more Africa.

THEY HAD GONE.

I felt my knees go weak and an enormous adrenalin rush remove my stomach. My blood froze in my veins.

THEY HAD GONE.

I span round through three-sixty to check I had my bearings right. There was nothing but a heat haze, wildlife, fever trees, acacias and more Africa in every direction. No safari truck. No shelter. No Precious with a gun. No safety.

The world stood still. I had nothing with me; no protection. No weapons. Nothing. I was bereft of the basics for supporting life, and closer to nature, red in tooth and claw, than humans can advisably get. I felt a kind of static, sickening panic and an indescribable

MOONING THE BONGO

hollowness in my stomach as all the blood rushed away to serve my muscles. My muscles! How laughable! My speed, my youth, my agility, my brain! All were worthless in this merciless, savage terrain. I felt as though someone had removed all the flesh from my midriff – all the organs and fat and meat – and was blowing a chill wind through the exposed skeleton that remained. It was the feeling of death's arrival. A kind of priming one's body does when it thinks it's going to die. A horrible feeling I hope never to experience again.

As I stood in the enormous silence and stifling African heat, the details of my local area began to come to life. It wasn't just lions and leopards one had to fear in this part of the world. There were insects that could kill you! Plants that could maim! Spiders, snakes, crocodiles! Who knows what might drop out of a tree?! Even the dogs would tear you limb from limb – none of that 'nice-doggy-fetch-the-stickie-have-a-bonio' stuff around here. Just Death. This was nature with the roof off. In the West we live in ivory towers, insulated from the workings of nature. Here I was now, a tiny cog being turned remorselessly in the wheel of life, and would be unlikely to survive a single night on my own.

And night was upon me. It was getting dark. In Africa, the sunsets are short but spectacular. The sky goes from slanting warm daylight through a laser show of brilliant yellows and oranges, through vivid scarlets and violets, through blood reds and portentous purples until pitch darkness comes down like a cold blanket, and the hunters and hunted change shifts. You can feel the creatures of the night stirring to life. You can sense the foreboding amongst the prey. In the morning some of their number will be gone.

I don't honestly know how long I stood there. A sunset takes around twenty minutes, and I guess I was alone for around half that, but let me tell you now, it felt like a lifetime. I can still remember the feeling as if it was happening to me now, and I can bring myself goose pimples just telling you about it. It was mortal terror.

OCEAN BOULEVARD

When the lads finally returned, I climbed shakily back into the truck, a significantly older man than the one who had hopped out a few short minutes earlier. They didn't understand what I had been through. They thought it was hilarious, but I was too traumatised to hear their taunts. What I did divine was that they had chipped Precious about a year's money, in his terms, to drive off. Precious, our guide and protector. Precious, the faithful man who had been so concerned for our safety. Yeah, right. As soon as he was offered enough cash he was into gear and off over the hill, steering with his knees and counting notes with his fingers before you could say 'Daktari'. To them, it was just a laugh, and I hid my feelings as best I could, but I had suffered a trauma that would last me a lifetime. I would never forget the day I survived alone on the plains of East Africa.

But, you know, there was some good news too. You see, the boys *didn't know* I hadn't run round the watering hole. So I was NOT the Big Chicken! Ha! I was officially brave, despite being more scared than ever in my life before or since. Strange old world, isn't it?

The Big Chicken was later revealed to be none other than Ffugg. Ha, haaaaa!! The new boy was exposed for the lily-livered spineless child he truly was when he refused to run off a mere forty or fifty paces into the Serengeti. I mean, how weak is that?! Admittedly, it was pitch black out there, and there were some blood-curdling roars from quite close by, but really. I mean, what sort of animal would want to eat a giant baby? Yeesh. He would have got through it all right, wouldn't he? Some blokes just don't understand a bit of fun.

No guts, kids nowadays. No guts at all.

Pacific Highway will be released into the wild in March 2008. Signed and personally inscribed copies of all Mr Baboulene's output are available from

www.baboulene.com

ACKNOWLEDGEMENTS

So there I was, turning circles aimlessly in the street, when I was picked up, taken in, fed and washed, and then propelled to authordom by three good Samaritans, without whom I doubt you would be reading this now.

Special thanks must go therefore to those rascals, Julie Urquhart and Sara Brown at Verbatim Communications. I dearly love these people and highly recommend them for your PR requirements:

www.verbatimcommunications.com

And to Stewart Ferris at Summersdale for his unswerving friendship and support through, firstly, the long and arduous publishing process, and secondly, the long and arduous process of getting me to understand what was going on and what was required of me next. You are a truly patient man...

Thank you.

David Baboulene

Get wind of what's happening next as well as some **free** stuff including (if you can stand it) some more of my writing and some, well, odd stuff at:

www.baboulene.com